Group Theories of Politics

G. David Garson

Volume 61
SAGE LIBRARY OF
SOCIAL RESEARCH

SAGE PUBLICATIONS   Beverly Hills   London

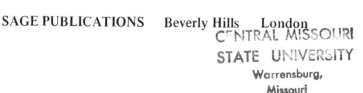

For information address:

SAGE PUBLICATIONS, INC.
275 South Beverly Drive
Beverly Hills, California 90212

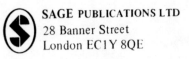

SAGE PUBLICATIONS LTD
28 Banner Street
London EC1Y 8QE

Printed in the United States of America

Library of Congress Cataloging in Publication Data

Garson, G. David.
　　Group theories of politics.

　　(Sage library of social research ; v. 61)
　　1. Pressure groups. I. Title.
JF529.G37　　　　　322.4'3　　　　　78-134
ISBN 0-8039-0518-1
ISBN 0-8039-0519-X pbk.

FIRST PRINTING

GROUP THEORIES OF POLITICS

Volume 61, Sage Library of Social Research

Sage Library of Social Research

CONTENTS

To Margaret F. Rea
with affection

Chapter 1

On the Origins of Interest-Group Theory: A Critique of a Process

The history of political science is one of gradual encroachment of ideas rather than the sequential building of scientific study upon scientific study. Yet the general idea of a science of politics, or at least of an accepted general framework of political analysis, is as old as the discipline and promises to remain an enduring part of its professional ethos. Of the many general frameworks that have been advanced in recent decades, few can claim the prominence of the body of ideas associated under the label of "interest-group theory."

In the early years of the postwar wave of interest in group theory, Avery Leiserson (1951: 45) reviewed David Truman's modern classic, *The Governmental Process* (1951), predicting that political scientists would receive the work enthusiastically because of its utility as a framework for presenting "the great mass of empirical, historical, and descriptive materials that political science has accumulated about the 'realities' of political organization." This prediction proved accurate and Truman's work, along with the interest-group approach to politics that it advocated, rapidly became established as a central part of what was perceived as a hopeful new period of growth within the discipline.

AUTHOR'S NOTE: *An earlier draft of this paper was presented at the 69th Annual Meeting of the American Political Science Association, New Orleans, September 4-8, 1973.*

A decade later Robert Golembiewski (1960: 971) still could write, "only small further innovations in method (if they imply much effort) are required to achieve a major research breakthrough in 'the group theory,' to push beyond what Bentley cannot be expected to have known and beyond his incomplete break with the restraints of the leading ideas of his time."

New excitement was attached to the development of interest-group studies on a comparative basis. Yet, as Graham Wootton (1972: 1) noted recently, "the excitement engendered at Rome, Pittsburgh, and Geneva from the mid-fifties to the mid-sixties has long since evaporated." This decline, Wootton noted, was associated in part "with the discovery that, in certain contexts, neither pressure groups nor lobbyists enjoyed the importance popularly or even academically attributed to them."

With this ebbing of intellectual interest, group theory finds its domain intruded upon by a legion of "newer" frameworks: systems theory, role theory, communications theory, symbolic interactionism, phenomenology, and many others. As with other great conceptions of political process, the decline of group theory has not been due to "scientific" refutation in the ordinary sense. Rather, it has subsided amid the accretion of other ideas, other issues, and other terminologies.

In many ways the "scientific" appraisal of interest-group theory is less important than seeking to understand this process of encroachment of ideas itself, as illustrated in group theory. The present essay focuses on this process, using as "data" a survey of all articles and book reviews pertaining to the group theory of politics appearing in the *American Political Science Review (APSR)* since its inception in 1906. Articles and reviews were considered to fall into the purview of this essay if they (1) discussed the role of groups *qua* groups in political science; (2) treated specific organizations in the nongovernmental sector; or (3) treated classes of such organizations (e.g., labor groups, church groups, farm groups). In addition, the works of twenty frequently cited group theorists were included. The study was limited to consideration of nongovernmental groups except where a governmental body was analyzed in group-theoretic terms.

Reading of the *American Political Science Review* since its beginning gives one a unique and interesting account of American political science thinking about groups. In spite of its pervasive effect on our discipline, this history today is remembered little if at all. This tendency to neglect the history of thought within our discipline reinforces the "growth" of political science through a process of accretion in which the shifting of basic premises, questions, and terms occurs largely without explicit or even conscious consideration.

The very purpose of theory is to simplify all-too-complex reality by discarding less important information until what is left can be utilized to understand and to predict. As the evolution of group theory illustrates, what is dangerous for a discipline is not selection *per se,* but rather the making of that selection without sufficient explicit consideration of the criteria for shifting premises, questions, and terms. All too often, the intellectual modes and ideological needs of the times sweep over the discipline, followed by a "scientific" reaction seeking to insulate political science from such forces. Rather than seek a wedding of theory and practice, necessarily requiring a base in normative theory, the discipline vacillates between these poles. In this process the hopes for "scientific" advance are surrendered to the gradual encroachment of ideas, each of which in turn is treated as if it were better than the last, and the fittest theories are equated with those that have survived. The history of that process with respect to group theory is the focus of the remainder of this essay.

Pluralism and the Critique of Formal Jurisprudence

I believe it is commonly accepted among contemporary political scientists that the turn away from "nineteenth-century jurisprudence" was an unmitigated good. Illustrative is the following excerpt from a contemporary text on interest-group theory (Zeigler and Peak, 1972: 5).

The fundamental characteristic of political science at this (Bentley's)
time was its preoccupation with law. This meant that the legal aspects
. . . embodied in formal constitutions served as an adequate guide to
the realities of politics. . . . As David Easton rightly declares, "Most
tended to act as though the study of the distribution of power as delin-
eated in the constitution constituted the core of political research."

The authors of this text emphasize the "institutional bias"
of nineteenth-century American political scientists, and in
this, one must agree they are right as far as they go.

But there was much more to juristic political science than
simply "narrow institutionalism." While institutionalism *does*
serve to differentiate early political science from its later phases
and to highlight Arthur Bentley's contribution in *The Process
of Government* (1908), other aspects of jurisprudence relate
very directly and in theoretically important ways to the group
theory of politics. Paradoxically, it is these ways that are largely
ignored by contemporary group theorists who prefer to attack
the straw man of nineteenth-century institutional focus.

This is not to belittle the constraints that nineteenth-century
institutionalism placed on political science. Bentley was merely
one author among a great many who recognized this more
than half a century ago. Among the most influential in those
years was not Bentley, who was little known, but rather James
Bryce. In his presidential address to the annual APSA meeting
in 1908, Bryce stated (1909: 6-8), "Political institutions . . . used
to be treated as abstract entities, if the term be permissible:
things existing *in vacuo,* like the Platonic ideal, with a definite
and permanent type."

In place of this perspective, Bryce called on political scientists
to study not only formal institutional aspects of politics, but
also (1) "the needs it was meant to meet and the purposes it
actually serves," (2) "the character of the men who work it,"
and (3) "the traditional color of the institution." These approaches, which today would be called functional, social psychological, and political cultural respectively, were very broad.
Bryce noted (1909: 6-8), "You may ask: Are we then to study
everything in the light of everything else? and if so, what limit

can be set to investigation? The answer is: No limit. Every political organism, every political force, must be studied in and
cannot be understood apart from the environment in which it
is plays."

One senses in the phrase "No limit" the sense of liberation
that came with the turn away from institutionalism in political
science. Yet the debate about jurisprudence and the theory
of sovereignty continued in the forefront of attention for more
than a decade after the writings of Bentley and Bryce in 1908.
Why was this so? I shall argue that it was not because of some
mere residual inertia, but rather that jurisprudential theory
continued as a vital center of political thought precisely because
its major theoretical concerns went beyond institutionalism alone.

The reader may wonder here what relation this has to group
theory. Among the most important theoretical concerns to
which I have alluded was the problem of the proper relation
of groups in the state. In traditional jurisprudential theory that relation was prescribed as one of subordination. Moreover, traditional theorists customarily distinguished between this relation as
norm and as practice. As Theodore Woolsey noted (1893: 203),
"The quality of sovereignty, however, does not necessarily
imply unlimited power or unchecked power; much less un-
delegated power."

On subjects such as the relation of the state to religious groups,
much attention was given to comparison of normative models
in relation to divergent national practice (Woolsey, 1893a:
Ch. 12). Moreover, the symbolic uses of sovereignty were recognized, as was the gap between a power unchecked in theory
and that power not expressed in practice (Woolsey, 1893b:
203). Finally, the relation of the state to various interests was
discussed under the rubric of theories of representation.

Juristic political scientists wrestled, for example, with John
Calhoun's theory of the state as based on interests. This view,
Calhoun wrote (Mulford, 1881: 212; Woolsey, 1893c: 292),
"regards interests as well as numbers, considering the community
as made up of different and conflicting interests, as far as the
government is concerned, and takes the sense of each through

its appropriate organ, and the united sense of all as the sense of the entire community." This problem was discussed not only in terms of Calhoun's reference to the South as an interest, but also in terms of narrower groups such as the cotton interest or the sugar interest. In other contexts, even informal groups such as the family received extended treatment (Mulford, 1881a: Ch. 15).

Contrary to the impression given by Bryce and later political scientists, nineteenth-century authors routinely brought in historical and political evidence of a concrete nature to illuminate their normative theories, whether to support their applicability in practice or to demonstrate the divergence of theory and reality. As W. W. Willoughby wrote (1896: 382-383),

> It is thus seen that a complete system of Political Science includes three main divisions: first, the determination of fundamental philosophical principles; second, the description of political institutions . . . and third, the determination of the laws of political life and development, the motives that give rise to political action, the conditions which occasion particular political manifestations, the circumstances when certain forces are applicable either for the good or for the bad.

Willoughby, whom modern interest-group theorists have sometimes characterized as an extreme legalist (Zeigler and Peak, 1972: 6), was in no small part also an empiricist. He held, for example, that "Not until a sufficient number of facts have been observed, and the consequences of cause and effect in political life remarked, is the formation of adequate philosophical conceptions possible. When formed, however, these conceptions serve to explain and harmonize the facts that have appeared confused and contradictory" (Willoughby, 1896b: 383).

In considering the twentieth-century reaction against jurisprudence among American political scientists, one must remember that the theoretically important contrast at the time (and now) was not the shift in substantive focus (governmental bodies and political parties remained the central emphasis) nor even the rise of empirical description as a preferred style. Rather, controversy centered on the crisis of the normative theory of the state advocated by most juristic political scientists. More specifically, the crisis was precipitated by changing views about the relation of organized groups to the sovereign state.

Latham (1952: 376-397) is absolutely correct in emphasizing the origins of the modern group theory of politics in the pluralist critique of sovereignty. That critique, however, is less interesting for its rebuttal of the straw man of the absolutist state into which the pluralists (and implicitly, Latham) simplified the theory of sovereignty than for its implications for the normative theories of the day. Contrary to frequent assumptions, the pluralist critique assumed importance because of its prescriptive rather than descriptive aspects, though the two were intertwined. Before turning to this subject, however, it is necessary to treat two additional, more popular intellectual currents that underlay pluralism and gave it no small part of its momentum.

Pressure Politics, Economic History, and Pluralism

With the consolidation of corporate capitalism and the rise of organized labor in the late nineteenth century, American social scientists were increasingly confronted with the contesting claims of economic groups as these vied for popular support, institutional position, and the mantle of government power. The activities of these groups seemed to contravene with some frequency the norms of political process held by political scientists and, indeed, most Americans.

Among some of the earliest works that dealt explicitly with interest groups in the pages of the *American Political Science Review* were those treating pressure politics. Although called "muckrakers" by their opponents, these authors shared many of the perspectives found in the writings of leading political scientists such as James Bryce (Filler, 1968: 17). For example, in a review of Lincoln Steffens's *The Struggle for Self-Government* (1906), S. E. Sparling (1908: 658-659) endorsed the call for reform, noting "The value of Mr. Steffens' volume consists largely in a vivid portrayal of conditions which have made possible the work of the system—a composite of social, political, and business interests. . . . The alertness of business interests in politics coupled with the supineness of the people, has done much to make possible the conditions pictured in this volume."

The new attention given to pressure politics was not an abstract methodological change but was associated with a quite specific historic moment. In his *The American Commonwealth* (1894), Bryce had forecast that the time would come when "the chronic evile and problems of old societies and crowded countries will have appeared on this soil." In the 1910 edition of the book, Bryce felt it appropriate to add that "the demand of the multitude to have a larger share of the nation's collective wealth may well have grown more insistent." Henry Jones Ford (1911: 476-477), in reviewing this edition, drew attention to this insertion, stating, "The remark notes a sign of the times that portends a new pressure upon our political institutions which is already manifesting itself and which must deeply affect constitutional development."

This "new pressure" soon translated itself into new perspectives on American government. By 1915 one may find a basic text such as James T. Young's *The New American Government and Its Work* (1915) starting not with the discussion of the legal framework that was nearly universal among earlier texts, but rather with a discussion of the influence of business groups on political processes, contrasting actual practices with legal norms. In this shifting perspective, the normative emphasis of the nineteenth century was retained not at the level of legal philosophy, but rather at the more practical level of political reform.

In his presidential address to the 1916 meeting of the American Political Science Association, Jesse Macy (1917: 1-11) called on his colleagues to reflect the new "scientific spirit in politics." By this Macy meant not value-free methodology, but the contrary idea of applying the knowledge of political science to the great tasks of reform, notably the attempt to control selfish interest groups. Similar views were then being expressed in sociology by Macy's contemporary, Albion Small, one of Arthur Bentley's teachers at the University of Chicago.

A more elegant theoretical framework for the study of economic pressures was presented in the work of Charles A. Beard, later a president of the American Political Science Association. Contrary to popular conceptions, Beard was neither an economic determinist nor a Marxist, but instead professed belief in the views of Madison in *Federalist No. 10* excerpted below (Beard, 1913: 14-15):

> The diversity in the faculties of men, from which the rights of property originate, is not less an insuperable obstacle to a uniformity of interests. The protection of these faculties is the first object of government. From the protection of different and unequal faculties of acquiring property, the possession of different degrees and kinds of property immediately results; and from the influence of these on the sentiments and views of the respective proprietors, ensues a division of society into different interests and parties.

Beard's influential views were expressed in *An Economic Interpretation of the Constitution of the United States* (1913), *Economic Origins of Jeffersonian Democracy* (1915), *The Economic Basis of Politics* (1922), and later works. Beard interpreted party development in terms of group interests, attacking Bryce's idealist emphasis on political principles (e.g., centralism versus states' rights). He noted that parties were prone to switch rhetorical ideals when interest dictated (Beard, 1922: 158-9).

In addition to Beard, four other economic historians had their works reviewed in the *American Political Science Review* during this period, including Alvord (1917: Vols. I and II) who likewise emphasized American politics as a reflection of factional interest apart from principle. Finally, other related historical works not reviewed, such as Gustavus Myers's *The Great American Fortunes* (1910), achieved widespread popularity at this time and may, therefore, be presumed to have contributed to the intellectual climate of American political science when Harold Laski was presenting the pluralist critique of sovereignty to this audience.

At the core of the pluralist critique was the argument that the state was not sovereign as jurisprudential theory held, but rather that the state was one of many associations in society. Associations other than the state, such as the church, could be shown empirically to be sovereign over important matters in which the state could not in fact intervene, contrary to traditional theory about absolute sovereignty being vested in the state. The writings on pressure politics and economic history dovetailed nicely with pluralist theory, documenting the weakness of the state in exerting jurisdiction over economic interests.

The Rise and Fall of Classic Pluralism

Because of the intellectual currents just discussed, much of the pluralist critique of sovereignty was accepted implicitly even before Laski performed the pleasant task of rendering explicit an idea whose time had come. The pluralists portrayed the jurisprudential theorists as believing that absolutist state jurisdiction was both desirable and actual. This portrayal was an injustice, because the jurists devoted a large proportion of their attention to discussing the desirability of limited government and to the distinction between ideal and reality. Only by an unrepresentative selection from their works is it possible to portray them as advocating "a sort of mystic monism as the true path of thought" (Laski, 1917).

In contrast to this alleged monism, Laski (1917, in Browne, 1946: 120) presented the "pluralist theory of the state" as a more scientific view:

So I would urge that you must place your individual at the center of things. You must regard him as linked to a variety of associations to which his personality attracts him. You must on this view admit that the State is only one of the associations to which he happens to belong, and give it exactly that preeminence—and no more—to which on the particular occasion of conflict its possibly superior moral claim will entitle it. In my view, it does not attempt to take that preeminence by force; it wins it by consent. It proves to its members by what it performs that it possesses a claim inherently greater than, say, their church or trade union. It is no dry *a priori* justification which compels their allegiance, but the solidity of its moral achievement.

In reviewing Laski's work, Walter Shepard (1917: 582-583), who was later to become American Political Science Association president, called it "an important contribution" representing a "brilliant school of political writers" who were developing a "more satisfactory theory of the nature of the state."

On the surface, pluralism was a devastating rebuttal of traditional theory. The jurists *did* claim the state was sovereign absolutely; partial sovereignty *was* considered a contradiction in terms. Yet, as Laski showed (1916: 437-464), the Hegelian concept of the omnicompetent state was abandoned in practice during nineteenth-century struggles over such matters as the independence of religious groups from state invervention. Moreover, this conception of the state created a framework for interpretation of the increasingly important economic pressure groups that appeared at this time. Finally, and not least in Laski's own motivation, it provided a rationale for protecting the growth of trade unionism from the intervention of a generally conservative and unsympathetic state. Later, when progressive preferences emphasized the need for a liberal government to intervene in business affairs, Laski adapted his views accordingly, abandoning the pluralist defense of group autonomy.

At a deeper level, however, the pluralist critique was premised on insufficiently examined assumptions about "absolutist" theories of sovereignty. In a relatively short space of time American political scientists recognized this and abandoned the theory, though in the process juristic political science suffered blows from which it never recovered.

The concept of "absolute sovereignty" put forward by nineteenth-century scholars was akin to what would later be called "ideal type." It was neither a normative model nor a description. The normative theory of these scholars, not only American political scientists but also classic theorists such as Bodin and Hegel, led them to constitutionalism, not absolutism. Further distinction was made between constitutional theory and actual practice, though perhaps not to the degree scholars today would desire.

For Laski and the pluralists to say that "absolute sovereignty" was not an accurate description was to misconstrue the nature of jurisprudential theory. Moreover, what Laski presented as an accurate description was *itself* a normative model. In the passage excerpted above, for example, it is not a simple observation of fact to assert that the state gains the allegiance of and preeminence over its citizens by "consent" in a form of transaction in which it "proves" the superiority of its benefits, achievements, and performance in comparison to other groups. This concept of government by uncoercive consent through the citizen's rational calculation of comparative group achievements is a sort of neo-utilitarian normative model, not an empirical description.

The normative model latent in classic pluralism suggests an important element in understanding the evolution of American political science. The jurisprudential approach had the potential for evolving the following paradigm: (1) to clarify the nature and utility of ideal types in political science; (2) to define more rigorously both alternative normative models of the state, and the role of groups within it; and (3) to compare the degree to which various social systems combined various degrees of fulfillment of the different models. Instead, after Laski, pluralism led to the search for the one accurate descriptive framework, to the obscuring of distinctions between norm and practice, and to the isolation of political theory from much of the rest of political science. The banner of empirical description was raised, frequently masking, as in Laski's case, an implicit and unexamined normative system.

LASKI ABANDONS PLURALISM

The group theory of the classic pluralists provided a defense of associational autonomy. While pluralism was at first hailed by American political scientists as superior in its descriptive aspects, this quickly ceased to be the issue (not surprisingly, since the jurists refused to consider the pluralist description as antagonistic to their normative constructs) and debate turned to the implicit normative aspects of pluralism. Ironically, these prescriptive implications gave the controversy its depth and greatest theoretical significance.

In Laski's day, American political scientists were not generally oriented toward theories of group autonomy. Rather, they shared some version of the jurists' norm of the pre-eminence of the state over factions and groups within it, albeit constrained by vaguely defined rights of individuals and groups. In this they were in some ways closer to Bertrand Russell than to Laski, specifically Russell's emphasis (1917) of the danger of political power in the hands of undemocratic private groups. The norms of scientific reform were not those of pluralism.

Thus, in reviewing Laski's subsequent work, *Authority in the Modern State* (1919), Walter Shepard posed the question (1919: 493), "How, it may be asked, are conflicts between opposing groups to be adjusted except upon the basis of the supreme will of the state? It is in affording an answer to this question that Mr. Laski is perhaps least convincing." Not only did questions arise regarding the normative premises of pluralist group theory, but its description fell under attack as well. In an article on "The Pluralistic State" the following year, Ellen Deborah Ellis (1923: 584) acknowledged that pluralism was "timely in that it calls attention to the present bewildering development of groups within the body politic, and to the fact that these groups are persistently demanding greater recognition in the governmental system." But then she added that pluralism as a description was inaccurate, applying only to a polity in "a very advanced state of disorganization."

A sharper critique by Francis Coker appeared a year later. Coker (1921: 194-195) noted that the limited status of government was beside the point: *everyone* agreed on that. To construe the theory of sovereignty as holding government to be unlimited was to misinterpret it. Coker (1921: 197) went on to find in pluralism the normative models underlying professional representation, administrative democracy, administrative syndicalism, distributivism, guild socialism, and syndicalism.

The latent radical implications of pluralism had some influence in political science in the early 1920s. Group autonomy, if it were not to be the private tyranny forecast by Russell, had to be accompanied by democratization of hitherto autocratic organizations. Laski (1922: 130-131) himself avoided commitment to this path, phrasing his advocacy of pluralism in more abstract terms that implied only some sort of functional democratic organization. Traces of Laski's philosophy are discernible in work in this period on international law (Korff, 1923: 404-414), administrative democracy (McMullin, 1923: 216-230), and guild socialism (Carpenter, 1922). These traces of influence were few, however, compared with the general criticism of pluralism on both normative and descriptive grounds.

In this debate, George Sabine (1923: 34) tried to stake out a middle ground, holding "The one clear lesson from these disputes is that both monism and pluralism are inescapable aspects of our world." Monism was faulted for implying that conflict among groups was settled by law, while pluralism was criticized for implying such conflict was settled by negotiation, when in fact both processes occurred. "For my part, then," Sabine wrote (1923a: 54), "I must reserve the right to be a monist when I can and a pluralist when I must." Yet this formulation clearly favored "monist" norms while finding both approahces inadequate in terms of empirical description.

The last major articles on pluralism to appear in the *American Political Science Review* (1907-1927) returned to Coker's linkage of pluralism to radicalism, criticizing both. Ellis (1923: 584), for example, noted the connection between pluralism and guild socialism, associating these ideas with discontended groups who naively seek the overthrow of the state as well as the government, not understanding the difference. W. Y. Elliot (1924: 259-260) also analyzed Laski's work in terms of its radical implication, concluding, "It is curious that Mr. Laski can arrive at a conclusion which strips the majesty from the law without seeing that he is rendering the very individuals

helpless whom he set out to protect against the absolute sovereignty of the absorptive state." With the growing anxiety over
fascism and communism, Elliot (1925: 499) returned to this
theme in a later essay in 1925, castigating pluralism "as appeal
to that violence which M. Sorel has eulogized, whose only
immediate issue is the reappearance of a sovereign equally
despotic, whether he be black-shirted or red."

By the time Elliot's second attack appeared, however, Laski
himself had abandoned pluralism. In *A Grammar of Politics*
(1925: 9), Laski's focus had shifted away from the sovereignty
of groups to the way groups exert "the thousand varying influences which go to shape the sovereign will." Rather than advocate guild socialism, much less the revolutionary syndicalism
implied by Elliot, Laski moved toward favoring government
regulation of the private sector through representative councils
made up of management, worker, consumer, and government
delegates. The orders of these councils would require the ap-
proval of a central Ministry of Production and would be subject
to the control of the parliament. In later years, Laski moved
increasingly toward a state planning solution to the problem
of coordination of groups within the sovereign state, embracing
"monist" concepts far more than most of his earlier critics.
The new concern for descriptive political science in the 1920s
had roots in the comparison of practice with ideal in jurisprudence, in the practical concerns of the reformers, and in
the empirical historical research of the economic historians
and of the pluralists (e.g., the history of their church-state
relations). Precedents could be found, for example, in Woodrow
Wilson's *Congressional Government* (1885: p. xv) and its attempt
to de-emphasize law in order to focus on "realistic analysis
of the most characteristic practical features of the federal system."

Another forefather of descriptive science (1909) was Bentley's
teacher, Albion Small. Like Beard and Laski, Small was an
exacting historical scholar. But where Wilson (1885a: 331-
334, bk. 3) treated fragmentation in *government,* Small (Small
& Vincent 1894) focused on the social fragmentation of every

large *society* made up of groups, each having particular ideas and feelings.

Small's writings contain many of the central points of interest-group theory: (1) society conceived as composed of a large number of groups; (2) no one of which can claim to represent the general will; hence, (3) the need for elections to determine a rough approximation of the collective volition; (4) determined by group forces at various stages of the political process; (5) in the context of a state characterized as a relatively neutral agency for determining and implementing collective decisions made through this process; and (6) which was seen as neutral in the sense of absence of elite or class domination.

Also prefiguring later interest-group theory was Small's contrast between normal group process and the debilitating effects of political protest outside conventionally accepted channels. Indicative is Small's treatment of labor strikes and other social movement forms (1894a: bk. 4) under the heading of "The Pathology of Social Organs—Characteristics of Social Disease." The "pathology" of labor strikes, for example, was contrasted with the "genuine reform" associated with "social amelioration," philanthropy, and specific efforts such as Civil Service reform. Small warned fellow sociologists (1894b: pp. 74, 239) not to become "social agitators" but to emulate the role of "scientific social reformer." Although in later years Small (1924: p. 285) abandoned group theory, which he had never labeled as such, in favor of a more elitist concept of America as "an aristocracy of political pull," this earlier orientation was quite similar to that of Macy and the political science reformists of the period before World War I.

INFLUENCES ON BENTLEY

A last set of writings, originating in German scholarship, influenced Bentley directly. The American introduction to Ludwig Gumplowicz's *The Outlines of Sociology* (1899), written on behalf of the American Academy of Political and Social Science, described the work as "distinguished from all earlier sociological works by the character of the sociological unit upon which it is based, which is the group" (Moore, 1899: 5).

While this may seem unexceptional today, its importance derived from two aspects of its historic context. First, group theory was a clear alternative to class analysis and its radical implications. (Gumplowicz himself incorporated major elements of class theory, but these aspects were largely ignored by his American interpreters.) Equally important, group theory was an attack on individualism in sociology. Individualism was tied both to concepts of free will, and to the reification of abstract "needs," "wills," and "feelings" as causal social "forces" difficult to define, much less observe. Either as free will or as social force, individualism seemed to frustrate the development of scientific sociology. In contrast, group theory seemed to hold the key. "The fate which befalls the individual in society," Moore stated in the introduction to Gumplowicz's volume, "is not the fate which he merits always, but it is necessarily that which his group makes inevitable" (Moore, 1899a: 6).

A second German scholar influencing Bentley was Rudolph von Jhering, whose work also emphasized the role of interest groups. Von Jhering (1877: 40) argued that "Being interested in a purpose, or briefly, interest, is an indispensable condition for every action." One finds in von Jhering's work a theory of political change based on social (not individual) action, which is conditioned by individual interests that are grouped in associations, the "social mechanics" of which determine what group theorists would today call homeostatic equilibrium.

REASONS FOR THE NEGLECT OF BENTLEY IN HIS OWN TIME

Bentley was an early advocate of a descriptive political science based on a group conception of political life. He wrote (Bentley, 1908: 172):

> We must deal with felt things, not with feelings, with intelligent life, not with idea ghosts. We must deal with felt facts and with thought facts, but not with feelings as reality or with thought as truth. We must find

the only reality and the only truth in the proper functioning of the felt
facts and the thought facts in the system to which they belong.

Statements such as "We must not deal with thought as truth"
were out of touch with the mood of political science prior to
World War I. The pluralist critique of juristic normative theory
had not yet done its work, nor had postwar disillusion undermined the capacity of reformism to present itself as the heir
to the mantle of science.

Arthur Bentley's *The Process of Government* (1908) was
ignored by political scientists for some two decades before
it achieved any significant recognition. Almost without exception discussion on groups in politics in the *American Political
Science Review* omitted mention of Bentley until he was resur-
rected by modern group theorists nearly half a century later.
Then, as in the 1967 edition of Bentley's work, he was praised
for developing a theory of government as "a process in which
interest groups are the players and protagonists. They are not
individuals but groups; for the individual himself is but the
product of group action and conditioning" (Odegard, 1967).

At this point, the student of political science may well wonder
what was exceptional about this viewpoint and why Bentley's
contemporaries were not right in attaching to his work far
less importance than was done in retrospect by contemporary
group theorists. His view was unexceptional insofar as "group"
was defined sweepingly as any relationship among two or more
individuals, ranging from a family to a nation or a race. "Interest"
was equated with "group" (Bentley, 1908a: 211). At this basic
level, Bentley's thesis was controversial only for those who
wished to interpret political change in terms of the personalities
of great individuals apart from their relation to family, race,
class, ethnicity, religion, educational affiliation, or other "group"
traits. Since virtually no one (and certainly not Albion Small,
whom Bentley grossly misrepresented) defended such an extreme
"great man" theory it is not surprising that political scientists
of the day did not find this view controversial. Though the
attack on individualism in sociology was then timely, it was

not perceived as being important in a political science weighted toward institutionalism, not individualism.

The Nation (1908: 94) found Bentley's work "critical rather than constructive," and Charles Beard (1908: 739-741), reviewing the volume for the *Political Science Quarterly,* also found the volume unoriginal in theory or argument. Its tone was characterized in various reviews as "flippant," "impatient," and "unjudicial," and, as Beard noted, "unnecessarily rude to his predecessors."

The Process of Government did make two contributions in Beard's view: presenting an alternative to Marxist class analysis and going beyond formal descriptions of politics. While neither was sufficiently original to place the work in the main-stream of political science discussion at that time, its contemporary importance warrants a brief discussion of these two points.

In discussing the development of group theories of politics, Bentley wrote (1908b: 465), "The starting-point for practical purposes is, of course, Karl Marx." In Marx, Bentley found "a very crude form of group interpretation." Bentley considered the working class and what Marx termed the ruling class to be simply two more interest groups, ones which happened to find "unusually vehement verbal expression" in the mid-nineteenth century, thereby causing Marx to mistake them as the primary groups in the political process (Bentley, 1908c: 465-467).

Leaving aside Bentley's misinterpretation of Marx as holding all political conflict to be class conflict, one can see that the importance of this argument to later group theory lay in its view of working class and elite groups as simply other types of groups, not more deserving of discussion than families, farm organizations, racial groups, political parties, discussion societies, interest associations, and other groups. Implicit is the image of government as "the steady appeasement of relatively small groups." In contrast, elite theorists have generally argued that business, for example, is a pre-eminent group whose institutional position cannot be placed in the same category with, say, voluntary associations for purposes of political analysis.

On the second point, that of going beyond formal description, Bentley's work was part of a long-standing trend away from institutionalism, preceded by Wilson and Bryce and followed by Beard and Laski. In Bentley's time this tendency was being accelerated by the work of the "muckrakers" on pressure politics. But where most political writers drew out the reform implications of this new literature on groups, Bentley ignored it. Thus it is hardly surprising that reform forces such as *The Nation* found *The Process of Government* "not constructive."

In his introduction to a reissue of Bentley's work, Peter Odegard expressed his failure to understand how Bentley could have neglected bringing the evidence of the "muckrakers" to bear on his theory of interest groups since they had already established the importance of such interests as Standard Oil and other trusts. Far from being surprising, however, this omission was a direct corollary of Bentley's rejection of prevailing definitions of the terms "interest" and "opinion."

Popular theories of governmental process emphasized the role of elites, using "interest" to refer to elite will and "opinion" to refer to popular will. This popular definition cast governmental process as interest-group politics to be sure. Odegard was correct in this regard, but he neglected to determine (as Bentley did not) that this usage cast interest groups as elite groups, viewing routine politics on important decisions to be elite conflict. Where the popular view emphasized public opinion and social reform movements as mediating instruments between the mass of active citizens and political elites, Bentley redefined (1908: 244) "interest group" to comprehend both elite interest and public opinion blocs, social movements, the family, lobbies, etc. "Nothing turns on the distinction between interest and opinion," he misleadingly wrote. Bentley's redefinition obscured important theoretical distinctions therefore emphasized in political writing, serving its intended purpose of defining out of existence the elite theory premises of discussions of "interest groups" in that period. This obfuscation was another factor in Bentley's neglect.

Closely related were Bentley's attitudes toward social change. Where Bentley's foil, Albion Small, had linked "genuine change" to social crises, Bentley's mentor, von Jhering, had interpreted historical change in terms of laws of "social mechanics" operating through interest-based associations. The vagueness, self-contradiction, and changing views of all authors concerned warns against portraying this difference in emphasis as an unambiguous contrast, but that difference was nonetheless sufficient for Bentley to praise the "power" of von Jhering's thinking in contrast to the "confusion" of Small's thought on social psychology and social change (Bentley, 1908e: 56).

While Bentley was condemning research on psychological "soul stuff," the general trend in political science was in precisely the opposite direction, discovering the importance of the individual as interpreted by social psychology. In this regard, Graham Wallas's *Human Nature in Politics* (1909) was seminal. Between 1908 and 1928, twenty-five articles and book reviews on psychology and politics appeared in the *American Political Science Review,* including works by illustrious names such as Wallas, Merriam, Lasswell, MacIver, and Ellwood. Charles Merriam (1921: 173-85), in his review of "The Present State of the Study of Politics," emphasized the importance of psychological approaches and the influence of Albion Small, omitting mention of Gumplowicz, von Jhering, or Bentley. Bentley's reference to psychological factors as "spooks" flew in the face of an important push toward interdisciplinary research in political science.

David Easton wrote (1953: 177) that "Bentley stands as the watershed between the simple realism of Wilson and the more complex realism of the group approach." It is difficult to see how, in turning away from a focus on political change in terms of periodic social crises and toward the equilibrium theory of German jurisprudence that Bentley was drawing closer thereby to "complex reality." Insofar as psychological factors, social movements and crises, and elite theory embody an important part of that "complex reality," Bentley was a force in the divergence between interest-group theory and the study of collective behavior.

In itself, this evolution of group theory might not have been harmful to political science had it not become eventually the dominant political science approach to informal political processes. While undercurrents and exceptions could be cited, it is more indicative to note that within the structure of academia, courses on social movements, social change, and collective behavior fell to the departments of sociology and social psychology. It was adherents of these disciplines who developed the pertinent theories to the greatest depth. The "group" theory of politics came to focus in practice on normal lobbying processes, rarely treating social movements and crises. The period in which Bentley wrote was one of increasingly intense concern over labor, anarchist, socialist, and bolshevist movements, however, and Bentley's perspective was therefore not one whose time had come.

Finally, the neglect of Bentley was also attributable to his position on public interest theories of the state. Bentley (1908f: 222) held that "we shall never find a group interest of the society as a whole . . . the society itself is nothing other than the complex of the groups that compose it." This attack on the idea of democracy as founded on what Rousseau called the general will set the stage for a redefinition of democracy. As Pateman (1970) has demonstrated lucidly, the redefinition of democracy by later group theorists gave prime importance to group processes rather than accountability to policy preferences of an electoral constituency. Thus, pluralist group conflict within electoral machinery and civil liberties became the defining characteristic of democracy. As Bachrach (1967) has noted, this emphasis stripped democratic theory of normative standards which might be used to judge the degree of attainment of democracy as an ideal construct. Moreover, by interpreting democracy as a social relationship already fulfilled in normal group processes, scholars eventually came to relate democracy to the equilibrating processes of group conflict rather than to a conflict theory perspective emphasizing tensions between the state and elites on the one hand and democratic aspirations of various groups on the other.

Group Theory and Descriptive Political
Science in the 1920s

Bentley's work cannot be characterized as being in advance of its time, ignored because of the shortsightedness of his contemporaries. This is so with regard to his attack on normative theory, his critique of the relevance of social psychology, his advocacy of a mechanistic equilibrium model, his discussion of the theory of public interest, and his obscuring of the issues raised in elite theory interpretations of the state.

Prior to Bentley's resurrection by modern group theorists, the only significant endorsement of his work in the pages of the *American Political Science Review* came from a sociologist, Harry Elmer Barnes (1921: 487-533), representing the quite different concerns of another discipline. Moreover, Barnes's apparent enthusiasm for Bentley grew from his incorrect equation of Bentley's views on *governmental* process with Ratzenhofer's and Gumplowicz's views of *society* as a complex of competing interest groups over which the state imposed necessary restraint, which did not derive from the sum of conflicts among interests. Even with Barnes's high praise, Bentley remained largely ignored during this period.

Much later, Bentley was remembered less for his particular theories than for his general orientation toward the importance of groups and the methods of "empirical theory" (Dowling, 1960: 951; Golembiewski, 1960: 961). In terms of operationalization of definitions and measurement of critical variables, Bentley's work did not constitute a useful guide (Dowling, 1960a: 949-950; Hale, 1960: 956), but political scientists such as Golembiewski have been prone to credit Bentley for his contribution to scientific orientations in political science.

Nonetheless, Bentley did not play a significant role in the development of a political science constructed around descriptive or empirical theory. Indeed, much of this credit must go to the nineteenth-century "institutionalists" such as Willoughby who spelled out the role of descriptive research in a comprehensive political science. There one finds a more sophisticated and certainly more influential view than Bentley's.

In the early years of the twentieth century, the felt need to focus empirically on groups was widely shared among American political scientists. Summarizing popular ideas on government, for example, Albert Hart (1907: 558) noted that "more and more people tend to accept the theory that all government in America—national, state, municipal or local—springs from one source, the American people as a whole, who choose to exercise their power through a variety of organizations." At the same time, a reform element felt that "individual interests without number have been built up" and "they have not been harnessed to a common cause" (Wilson, 1911: 5).

Given such concerns, these years were characterized by a search for the common, uniting interest. This humane orientation was sometimes coupled with a distaste for the concept of political "science," as in the writings of Woodrow Wilson (1911a: 10-11):

> I do not like the term political science. Human relationships, whether in the family or in the state, in the countinghouse or in the factory, are not in any proper sense the subject matter of science. . . . I prefer the term politics. . . . Know your people and you can lead them; study your people and you may know them. But study them, not as congeries of interests, but as a body of human souls, the least as significant as the greatest,—not as you would calculate forces, but as you would comprehend life.

Yet the reformers were very much advocates of empirical research, and Wilson himself is correctly cited by later group theorists as being among those who guided political science in the direction of realistic description of political process. Statements such as that quoted above are properly understood not as attacks on empiricism but as a call to link continually pragmatic study with normative concerns—a call that merely rephrased similar views of institutionalists such as Willoughby.

It was only with the disillusion following World War I that advocacy of a non-normative science of politics came to the fore and that the concepts prefiguring modern, "value-free" empirical theory received their real development. Ironically, from the point of view of those who emphasize Bentley, the push for descriptive science after World War I first became prominent in relation to the development of social psychology and public opinion research. Later, its development was associated with such theorists as Michels, Catlin, Ellis, Munro, and Dickinson, and reflected in group studies by authors such as Herring, Odegard, and Rice.

James Mickel Williams's *Principles of Social Psychology* (1922: 715) appeared in 1922 and was reviewed favorably for its emphasis on "the standpoint of the conflict of interests which shows itself in economic, political, professional, family, cultural and educational relations." The following year, Horace Kallen's (1923: 203) essay on "Political Science as Psychology" appeared in the *American Political Science Review,* criticizing radical pluralism and saying of behaviorist psychological analyses that "what is important is that they cannot formulate a variant conception of political society without at the same time grounding it upon a variant definition of human nature whose variant trait is established in the special group interest to be advanced, defended, and vindicated. So, then," Kallen asked, "if political science is not psychology, what is it?"

In 1924, in reporting the results of a survey taken by a committee of the American Political Science Association, Charles Merriam (1924: 485-486) noted that psychology seemed to hold "rich possibilities" for political analysis, writing, "As social psychology develops, the whole study will be correspondingly enriched by the addition of the analysis of groups, of group relations, and individual-group relations, and indeed the whole interlocking series of cycles in the complex social process." Merriam linked this projection to an appeal to develop these promised new avenues of insight through empirical analysis, not through traditional theoretic consideration. Likewise, Ellwood's *The Psychology of Human Society* (1925) presented a more detailed framework for the empirical study of "the origin, development, and structure of group life." Works by

Lasswell, Floyd Allport, and Sorokin (all 1925) added fuel
to this perspective.

Among the most important of the areas studied empirically
was that of public opinion. Here was the empiricist's domain
that corresponded to the focus of earlier theorists on the concept
of the public interest or general will. Lippman's work on public
opinion was most influential in spreading the newly discovered
facts about the relative absence of rationally or intelligently
held common opinion on most issues (Lippman, 1922; 1925).
The role of imitation, suggestion, and emotions was also emphasized in Lowell's *Public Opinion in War and Peace* (1923).
Bernays (1923; 1928) reported the rise of public relations as
a new profession, and Weeks's concerns in *The Control of
the Social Mind* (1923) became generally accepted. Allport's
empirical research on the convertibility and similarity of extrem-
ists further supported this orientation (Allport and Hartman,
1925: 735-760).

This new wave of psychologically oriented, empirical work
on public opinion both reflected and reinforced the new pes-
simism about the common man, a view given further impetus
by the rise of fascism in Italy. At one pole, the new empiricism
seemed to lead to the conclusion that political scientists must
"face squarely the fact that the voice of the people is usually
the voice of Satan" (Angell, 1927: 695). At the other end of
the spectrum were those, such as Eldridge, who sought to deal
with the problem of "the phantom public" raised by Lippman
through grand reform proposals for civic education (Eldridge,
1929; Garson, 1973a: 50-77; Garson 1973b: 25-38).

One of the outstanding political scientists of that day, George
E. G. Catlin, looked to psychological studies of opinion for
a possible key to the scientific measurement of influence. "Politics," Catlin (1927: 257) held, "must . . . be founded on the observation of some distinguishable political 'process' . . . and this,
it may be tentatively suggested as a focus for convenient study,
is to be detected in the recurrent situation of the relationship
of wills in a fashion of control." These behavior patterns were
seen as " 'lines of conduct' of an individual or interest-group

character, pursued in relation to other individuals or groups" (Catlin, 1927a: 255). The scientific problem for political scientists was to find a measure of the strengths of opposing individual and group wills in any given case. After a quite modern critical discussion of the problems of measuring influence, Catlin (1927b: 262-268) indicated that his hope for quantification of political science lay along lines suggested by the psychological studies of opinion.

By this point, Ellis could characterize political science as being "at the crossroads," turning away from law and jurisprudence toward descriptive science. In contrast to the traditional idea of "the sovereign state," the new concept of "the political state" was viewed as a scientific advance. "All that it (the concept of the political state) seeks to do," Ellis (1927: 789-790) wrote, "is to describe and account for political organization, leaving to the moralist the justification or otherwise of the use made of political power."

When MacIver's *The Modern State* (1926) appeared, its reviewer, W. Y. Elliot (1927: 432-434), criticized it for failing to clarify that the state still retained ultimate sovereignty over the groups within it. Traditionalists within political science perceived the growth of the movement for a purely descriptive science and condemned it roundly. W. W. Willoughby attacked Krabbe's *Modern Theory of the State* for its critique of the concept of sovereignty as resting on a confusion of ethical and descriptive studies of the state (Willoughby, 1926: 509-523). Sabine (1928: 553-575) defended Krabbe against Willoughby, but in the process also emphasized the continuing need for normative theory. Edwin Corwin (1929: 591) pleaded that political science "must still retain its character as a 'normative,' a 'telic' science." And in his presidential address to the American Political Science Association, Jesse Reeves (1929: 16) defended political philosophy, holding that "each group has something to receive from the other."

In spite of pleas for mutual tolerance on the part of men like Sabine and Reeves, the enthusiasm for descriptive science was pronounced and its practitioners were not inclined to relate

their work to the more theoretical work on groups that had
gone before. Citing the example of physics, Munro (1928:
10) told his colleagues in a presidential address to the American
Political Science Association that "our immediate goal, therefore, should be to release political science from the old meta-
physical and juristic concepts upon which it has traditionally
been based. . . . It is to the natural sciences that we may most
profitably turn." Similarly, in discussing how modern courses
of introductory political science should be taught, Spencer
(1928: 10) warned against political scientists playing the role
of reformer. Instead, he wrote, "It is the function of the political
scientists to observe political phenomena and to tell what he sees."

In illustration of the new descriptive approach and its relation
to group theory, one may cite the brilliant work of John Dickinson. Dickinson (1929: 299) used historical and anthropological
evidence to argue that "conflict between interests is inevitable"
and that order is not suppression of conflict; order is the read-
justment of human relations in the course of conflict, which
is a never-ending process. In this view, "Government, like the
human will, is motivated by the very forces which it governs;
its function is only to arrange them in a more orderly pattern"
(Dickinson, 1929a: 619). Conflict is partially resolved through
voluntary group agreements, but the inequities of unchecked
application of these means alone are inadequate. Custom, therefore, plays a major role in social control, and the state is constrained by its own habits or culture. Custom and voluntarism
resolve most conflicts, but authority backed up by force is
held in reserve. Indeed, "an important element in the art of
governing is to predict successfully whether such voluntary
and natural adjustments will occur" (Dickinson, 1929b: 625).

Dickinson's work, based on theoretical inference from historical and anthropological data, presented an interpretation
of politics revolving around group interests. It transcended
Bentley's mechanistic model by emphasizing the role of culture
and the use of authority as social control. Other important
studies of a modern, descriptive nature focusing of groups,
were Odegard's *Pressure Politics* (1928), Herring's *Group*

Representation Before Congress (1929), and Rice's *Farmers and Workers in American Politics* (1924). Of these, Rice's study, with its emphasis on culture areas and psychological traits in analyzing group interests in legislation, was the most theoretically complex. As Zeigler (Zeigler and Peak, 1972b: 12) has noted, Odegard's work was "essentially a descriptive study with little or no emphasis on theoretical problems," a characterization that applied to Herring's volume as well.

In *The Science and Method of Politics*, George Catlin (1927: 210-211) wrote that "politics, as a theoretical study, is concerned with the relations of men, in association and competition, submission and control, insofar as they seek, not the production and consumption of some article, but to have their way with their fellows." Thus, with the rise of descriptive political science in the 1920s the study of politics came to be viewed as the study of influence and power, not the study of government and the state. The crucial distinction between the two lay in the abandonment of normative theory by the empirical students of group power.

This difference was not primarily one of institutional focus or even of emphasis on the importance of group interests in politics. Extra-institutional concerns such as the family and religion had been treated by the jurists. And few gave more importance to the role of groups in political life than the later generation of scientific reformers. To be sure, the increasing importance of organized economic groups was reflected in increasing attention to this phenomenon over the years by writers of all orientations, but the crucial shift was in the questions that were asked about these groups.

While a traditional "theory of politics" was obliged to wrestle with the question of how groups within a society ought to be coordinated, relating these models to historical origins, ethics, practice, and many other concerns, the new descriptive approach merely sought to establish what practice was. Where descriptive studies were extrapolated into a generalized description of political process, as in the work of John Dickinson, that model was so broad that virtually any normative model from monarch-

ism to socialism could be contained within it. Because many
polities in varying degrees fulfilled many different normative
models of how groups ought to be coordinated within the state
(the "problem of order"), the search for a descriptive theory
of politics in relation to interests and groups was reduced to
a search for lowest common denominators, such as the uni-
versality of interest conflict or the universal relevance of custom
and culture.

Of course, the descriptive orientation was inevitably violated
by frequent implicit and sometimes explicit normative statements. Dickinson's work, for example, implied the desirability
of the state's deferring to voluntary resolution of conflict and
to custom in most matters, a model strikingly in contrast to
that implied by advocates of social planning as it was developed
in the decade that followed (cf., Garson, 1973a), and Lippman's
work was deeply imbued with conservative principles. But
more important than the reintroduction of relatively unexamined normative theories through the back door was the
acquiescence of political science in the post-World War I mood
and its shift from prescription to description. Its importance
lies not only in the neglect of enduring issues and questions,
but also in the theoretical setback that political science suffered
by the artificial divorce of normative theory from empirical
research on American politics.

Conclusion

The study of the origins of group theory is important because
the shortcomings of the past recur in the present. The reasons
that Bentley was ignored in his day, for example, are at the
core of contemporary criticisms of group theory. For example,
Rothman's critique of Truman's *The Governmental Process*
emphasized the relative neglect of social movements, crises,
change, and the rejection of Marxist analysis while reintroducing
economic explanations standing in tension with a purely group

explanation of politics, criticisms that would apply to Bentley as well as Truman (Rothman, 1960: 24, 29; Truman, 1960: 494-495).

Similarly, R. E. Dowling (1969b: 953) wrote, "We can see in Truman, that is, over and above his observations about the place of groups and their pressures in the matter that comes to the political scientist, a faith in something called 'the group interpretation of politics.' This faith has had an influence on his political science which has been, if I am not mistaken, almost wholly evil." Dowling observed that this appeared most clearly where Truman sought to defend interest-group theory from the charge that it "leaves something out." "He does not see that the *merit* of a 'group interpretation' of politics," Dowling (1969c: 953) wrote, "would, if it were worked out, be precisely that it does *'leave something out'*." The concept of theory is lost by making "value-free" political science more "accurate" through including all considerations within it.

The purpose of theory is to simplify reality. That everything is related to everything else, and that groups are important in politics is a view that may be accurate, but it is not helpful in advancing the discipline. Bentley's mechanistic physics of group pressures was less accurate, but it was, like Marxism, a relatively strong construct. That it was not developed, like jurisprudential models, as a normative type among a set of types reflects the underlying drive in political science for the one correct theoretical framework, a drive that misunderstands the literally essential role of normative theory in social science methodology, and leads to a literature that sustains a high level of generality through concentration on lowest common denominators. The effect has been less than intellectually satisfying to many, precipitating factions within the discipline that seek to reassert normative theory on methodological as well as moral grounds.

The history of political science, it was stated at the outset, has been one of gradual encroachment of ideas rather than the sequential building of scientific study upon scientific study. Jurisprudence fell to the "facts" marshalled by the pluralists and their counterparts in the 1920s not because the facts refuted their theories (the facts were largely irrelevant to the normative questions raised by the jurists), but because the new perspectives were in accordance with the more pessimistic mood and hopes for science after World War I.

Reformism, perhaps because of its untheoretical articulation, was not so much rejected as ignored. While reformism earlier had seemed to be closely allied to science, after World War I it could be dismissed by Spencer as moralism in obvious conflict with the serious study of political phenomena. Pluralism itself fell, partly from its insecure foundations on a caricature of jurisprudence, but also from the equation of its normative implications with radicalism. With the emergence of descriptive science in the 1920s came an optimism about the vast possibilities for a science of politics now that the discipline had been freed from the fetters of metaphysics. But these possibilities went unrealized and were forgotten in the main, thereby enabling the discovery anew of "value-free" science after the next world war.

The history of ideas inevitably conveys a greater sense of coherence and sequence than actually existed. The change is better categorized under the term "accretion" than that of "development." Development connotes either change by explicit choice, or growth in accordance with some inner telos. The change of political science was neither of these for the most part; rather, the discipline spread in response to outside stimuli such as the rise of economic groups, the tides of progressivism and disillusion, the birth and excitement of modern psychology, and many other factors.

This is not to deny that much may be found in the way of explicit analysis of this or that tenet or belief. But in the debates, the shift in basic premises and questions was all too often overlooked, and political science changed in accord with these unacknowledged premises. This change is not one of deterioration from a golden age of juristic political science. Much was genuine advance: increasing scope, and depth of study in terms of subject matter; increasing sophistication of technique; increasingly interdisciplinary borrowings from psychology, sociology, anthropology, economics, and other disciplines.

But the change in political science cannot be seen as simple advance; in the shifts in mood and predisposition, opportunities were lost as well—losses from which we are only now recovering. With the passing of jurisprudence, the normative debate over integration of ideal constructs of the state in relation to practice faded as a possibility. This stripped political science of carefully formulated norms by which to categorize practice, as Bachrach has shown, obscuring the critical role of ideal types in social science research.

With the turning away from reformism, not only was the discipline drained of much compassion and vision, but an implicitly dynamic focus on political change gave way to a static focus on describing political life as it existed. Though pluralism was rejected for logical reasons in part, its contribution to historical approaches to political science and its relevance to normative theory (even if from an ostensibly "descriptive" stance) tended to drop from sight with the rise of descriptive political science after World War I. This orientation too passed in turn, leaving for later political scientists the rediscovery of its contribution in scientific method, social psychology and socialization, political culture and custom, and group interests conceptions of political process.

Representatives of all orientations emphasized the role of group interests in politics in one manner or another. A group interest conception of the state, going back to Madison was a perennial problem for the jurists, especially with the consolidation of enormous economic interests toward the end of the nineteenth century. The jurists emphasized the importance of group interests in exacerbating the gap between practice and various normative models of the state. Like the social planners of the 1930s they were optimistic about the ability of the state to insulate itself from these interests and to control them autonomously when necessary.

The reformers' view of group interests was closely allied to this perspective, though often implying elitist rather than constitutionalist models of the state. The pluralists showed how the expanding center of private power posed a growing challenge to the pre-eminence of the state, reducing the state to merely one among many groups. The fact of developing private power eventually led Laski to Marxism and social planning, while other lines of influence may be traced toward advocacy of democratization of groups and guild socialism on the one hand, or to acceptance of the beneficial effects of competing private powers and laissez-faire on the other. It is more difficult to summarize the orientation of the empiricists toward groups in politics, but they shared a highly influential focus on the irrational nature of group identifications and the negative consequences of this for public opinion and democracy.

The cases for the pre-eminence of the state, for social planning, for liberal reform, for organizational democracy, for laissez-faire, or for resignation to the mixed blessings of group process may still be made. In fact, all these normatively premised perspectives are still advocated under new labels. And the actual operation of American politics displays in varying degrees the practice associated with each perspective. What has not yet come to the fore is the explicit comparison of normative models of the state and their integration with empirical study. Rather than adopt a systematically multifaceted orientation that incorporates the many strands of our discipline's past, most political scientists remain predisposed to select one or another orientation as "the most nearly correct framework."

REFERENCES

ALLPORT, F. (1924) Social Psychology. New York: Houghton Mifflin.
——— and D. A. HARTMAN (1925) "Measurement and Motivation of Atypical Opinion in a Certain Group," American Political Science Review, Vol. 19, No. 4 (November): 735-760.
ALVORD, C. W. (1917) The Mississippi Valley in British Politics. Cleveland: Clark, 2 vols.
Anonymous (1908a) Review of Bentley (1908) in The Nation, Vol. 87 (July, 30): 94.
——— (1908b) Review of Bentley (1908) in Outlook, Vol. 89 (May 30): 263.

———— (1922) Review of James Mickel Williams, *Principles of Social Psychology* (New York: Knopf, 1922), in *American Political Science Review*, Vol. 16, No. 4 (November): 715.

———— (1927) Review of Norman Angell, *The Public Mind* (New York: Dutton, 1927), in *American Political Science Review*, Vol. 21, No. 3 (August): 695.

BACHRACH, P. (1967) *The Theory of Democratic Elitism: A Critique.* Boston: Little, Brown.

BARNES, H. E. (1921) "Some Contributions of Sociology to Modern Political Theory," *American Political Science Review*, Vol. 15, No. 4 (November): 487-533.

BEARD, C. (1908) Review of Bentley (1908), *Political Science Quarterly.* Vol. 23, No. 4 (December): 739-741.

———— (1913) *An Economic Interpretation of the Constitution of the United States.* New York: Macmillan.

———— (1922) *The Economic Basis of Politics.* New York: Vintage, 1957.

BENTLEY, A. (1908) *The Process of Government.* Peter Odegard, ed. Cambridge: Harvard Univ. Press, 1967.

BERNAYS, E. L. (1923) *Crystallizing Public Opinion.* New York: Boni and Liveright.

———— (1928) *Propaganda.* New York: Liveright.

BLAISDELL, D. C. (1940) *Economic Power and Political Pressures.* Monograph No. 26 of the Temporary National Economic Committee. Washington, D.C.: USGPO.

BROWNE, W. R., ed. (1946) *Leviathan in Crisis.* New York: Viking.

BRYCE, J. (1909) "The Relations of Political Science to History and to Practice," *American Political Science Review*, Vol. 3, No. 1 (February): 1-19.

CARPENTER, N. (1922) *Guild Socialism: An Historical and Critical Analysis.* New York: Appleton.

CATLIN, G.E.G. (1927a) "The Delimitation and Measurability of Political Phenomena," *American Political Science Review*, Vol. 21, No. 2 (May): 255-269.

———— (1927b) *The Science and Method of Politics.* New York: Knopf.

COKER, F. (1921) "The Technique of the Pluralist State," *American Political Science Review*, Vol. 15, No. 2 (May): 186-213.

CORWIN, E. S. (1929) "The Democratic Dogma and the Future of Political Science," *American Political Science Review*, Vol. 23, No. 3 (August): 569-592.

DICKINSON, J. (1929) "Social Order and Political Authority," *American Political Science Review*, Vol. 23, No. 2 (May): 293-328 and Vol. 23, No. 3 (August): 593-632.

DOWLING, R. E. (1960) "Pressure Group Theory: Its Methodological Range," *American Political Science Review*, Vol. 54, No. 4 (December): 944-954.

EASTON, D. (1953) *The Political System.* New York: Knopf.

ELDRIDGE, S. (1924) *Political Action.* Philadelphia: Lippincott.

ELLIOT, W. Y. (1924) "The Pragmatic Politics of Mr. H. J. Laski," *American Political Science Review*, Vol. 18, No. 2 (May): 251-275.

———— (1925) "Sovereign State or Sovereign Group?" *American Political Science Review*, Vol. 19, No. 3 (August): 475-499.

———— (1927) Review of R. M. MacIver, *The Modern State* (New York: Oxford Univ. Press, 1926), in *American Political Science Review*, Vol. 21, No. 2 (May): 432-434.

ELLIS, E. D. (1920) "The Pluralistic State," *American Political Science Review*, Vol. 14, No. 3 (August): 393-407.

—— (1923) "Guild Socialism and Pluralism," *American Political Science Review*, Vol. 17, No. 4 (November): 584-596.

—— (1927) "Political Science at the Crossroads," *American Political Science Review*, Vol. 21, No. 4 (November): 773-791.

ELLWOOD, C. (1925) *The Psychology of Human Society*. New York: Appleton.

FILLER, L. (1968) *The Muckrakers: Crusaders for American Liberalism*. Chicago: Regnery, orig. 1950.

FORD, H. J. (1911) Review of James Bryce, *The American Commonwealth* (New York: Macmillan, 1910; orig. 1894), in *American Political Science Review*, Vol. 5, No. 3 (August): 476-477.

GARSON, G. D. (1973a) "Research on Policy Alternatives for America in the 1930's," *Political Inquiry*, Vol. 1, No. 1 (Winter): 50-77.

—— (1973b) "Citizenship as Ideology," *Maxwell Review*, Vol. 10 (Winter): 25-38.

GOLEMBIEWSKI, R. J. (1960) "The Group Basis of Politics: Notes on Analysis and Development," *American Political Science Review*, Vol. 54, No. 4 (December): 962-971.

HART, A. B. (1907) "Growth of American Theories of Popular Government," *American Political Science Review*, Vol. 1, No. 4 (August): 531-560.

HERRING, E. P. (1929) *Group Representation Before Congress*. Baltimore: Johns Hopkins.

JHERING, R. von (1877) *Law as a Means to an End*. New York: Macmillan, 1913.

KALLEN, H. M. (1923) "Political Science as Psychology," *American Political Science Review*, Vol. 17, No. 2 (May): 181-203.

KORFF, B.S.A. (1923) "The Problem of Sovereignty," *American Political Science Review*, Vol. 17, No. 3 (August): 404-414.

LASKI, H. J. (1916) "The Political Theory of the Disruption," *American Political Science Review*, Vol. 10, No. 3 (August): 437-464.

—— (1917) *Studies in the Problem of Sovereignty*. New Haven: Yale Univ. Press.

—— (1921) *The Foundations of Sovereignty*. New York: Harcourt, Brace.

—— (1925) *A Grammar of Politics*. New Haven: Yale Univ. Press.

LASSWELL, H. (1925) "Two Forgotten Studies in Political Psychology," *American Political Science Review*, Vol. 19, No. 4 (November): 707-717.

—— (1929) "The Study of the Ill as a Method of Research into Political Personalities," *American Political Science Review*, Vol. 23, No. 4 (November): 996-1001.

LATHAM, E. (1952a) "The Group Basis of Politics: Notes for a Theory," *American Political Science Review*, Vol. 46, No. 2 (June): 376-397.

LEISERSON, A. (1951) Review of Truman (1951), in *American Political Science Review*, Vol. 45, No. 4 (December): 1192-1193.

LIPPMAN, W. (1922) *Public Opinion*. New York: Harcourt, Brace.

—— (1925) *The Phantom Public*. New York: Harcourt, Brace.

LOWELL, A. L. (1923) *Public Opinion in War and Peace*. Cambridge, Mass.: Harvard Univ. Press.

McIVER, R. M. (1917) *Community: A Sociological Study*. London: Macmillan.

—— (1926) *The Modern State*. New York: Oxford Univ. Press.

MACY, J. (1917) "The Scientific Spirit in Politics," *American Political Science Review*, Vol. 11, No. 1 (February): 1-11.

MERRIAM, C. (1921) "The Present State of the Study of Politics," *American Political Science Review,* Vol. 15, No. 2 (May): 173-185.

——— (1924) "The Significance of Psychology for the Study of Politics," *American Political Science Review,* Vol. 18, No. 3 (August): 469-488.

MICHELS, R. (1958) *Political Parties.* New York: Free Press.

MOORE, F. W. (1899) "Introduction," in Ludwig Gumplowicz, *The Outline of Sociology* (Philadelphia: American Academy of Political and Social Science).

MULFORD, E. (1870) *The Nation: The Foundations of Civil Order and Political Life in the United States.* Boston: Houghton Mifflin, 1881.

MUNRO, W. B. (1928) "Physics and Politics: An Old Analogy Revised," *American Political Science Review,* Vol. 22, No. 1 (February): 1-11.

ODEGARD, P. (1967) "Introduction," to Bentley (1908).

——— (1925) *Pressure Politics.* New York: Columbia Univ. Press.

PATEMAN, C. (1970) *Participation and Democratic Theory.* Cambridge: Cambridge: Univ. Press.

REEVES, J. S. (1929) "Perspectives in Political Science, 1903-1928," *American Political Science Review,* Vol. 23, No. 1 (February): 1-16.

RICE, S. A. (1924) *Farmers and Workers in American Politics.* New York: Columbia Univ. Press.

ROTHMAN, S. (1960) "Systematic Political Theory: Observations on the Group Approach," *American Political Science Review,* Vol. 54, Vol. 1 (February): 15-33.

RUSSELL, B. (1917) *Political Ideals.* New York: Century.

SABINE, G. (1923) "Pluralism: A Point of View," *American Political Science Review,* Vol. 17, No. 1 (February): 34-50.

——— (1928) "Political Science and the Jurist Point of View," *American Political Science Review,* Vol. 22, No. 3 (August): 553-575.

SHEPARD, W. J. (1917) Review of Harold J. Laski (1917), in *American Political Science Review,* Vol. 11, No. 3 (August): 582-584.

——— (1919) Review of Harold J. Laski, *Authority in the Modern State* (New Haven: Yale Univ. Press, 1919), in *American Political Science Review,* Vol. 13, No. 3 (August): 491-494.

——— (1922) Review of Harold J. Laski (1921) in *American Political Science Review,* Vol. 16, No. 1 (February): 130-131.

SMALL, A. (1909) *The Cameralists: The Pioneers of German Social Policy.* Chicago: Univ. of Chicago Press.

——— (1924) *Origins of Sociology.* Chicago: Univ. of Chicago Press.

SMALL, A. and G. VINCENT (1894) *An Introduction to the Study of Society.* New York: American Book.

SOROKIN, P. (1925) *The Sociology of Revolution.* New York: Lippincott.

SPARLING, S. E. (1908) Review of Lincoln Steffens, *The Struggle for Self-Government* (New York: McClure, Phillips and Co., 1906), in *American Political Science Review,* Vol. 2, No. 4 (November): 658-659.

SPENCER, R. (1928) "Significance of a Functional Approach in the Introductory Course in Political Science," *American Political Science Review,* Vol. 22, No. 4 (November): 954-966.

TRUMAN, D. (1951) *The Governmental Process: Political Process and Public Opinion.* New York: Knopf.

——— (1960) "On the Invention of Systems," *American Political Science Review,* Vol. 54, No. 2 (June): 494-495.

TURNER, J. M. (1923) "Democracy in Administration," *American Political Science Review,* Vol. 17, No. 2 (May): 216-230.

WALLAS, G. (1962) *Human Nature in Politics.* Lincoln, Neb.: Univ. of Nebraska Press.

WEEKS, A. (1923) *The Control of the Social Mind.* New York: Appleton.

WILLOUGHBY, W. W. (1896) *An Examination of the Nature of the State.* New York: Macmillan.

——— (1926) "The Jurist Theories of Krabbe," *American Political Science Review,* Vol. 20, No. 3 (August): 509-523.

WILSON, W. (1885) *Congressional Government.* Boston: Houghton Mifflin, 1971.

——— (1911) "The Law and the Facts," *American Political Science Review,* Vol. 5, No. 1 (February): 1-11.

WOOLSEY, T. (1893) *Political Science, or The State.* New York: Scribner's.

WOOTTON, G. (1972) "Interest Groups in Britain and the United States: Contributions to Public Policy," American Political Science Association, annual meeting, Washington, D.C., 5-9 September 1972.

YOUNG, J. T. (1915) *The New American Government and Its Work.* New York: Macmillan.

ZEIGLER, L. H. and G. W. PEAK (1972) *Interest Groups in American Society.* Englewood Cliffs, N.J.: Prentice-Hall.

Chapter 2

Pluralist, Statist, and Corporatist Elements in the Emergence of Group Theory

In a recent article Norman H. Keehn argued for corporatism rather than pluralism as both interpretation and ideal for the American system of politics. Pluralism, he contended, reinforced the erosion of sovereignty and undermined the capacity to govern. Fortunately, he believed, technology is carrying society away from pluralism, making the "joint government" of public and private sectors a necessity. "Both sides are losing their distinctive characteristics," Keehn wrote, "government has acquired certain rights over the control of property while public functions have devolved upon private interests" (Keehn, 1976: 38). In this view, the stage is thereby set for "bringing the representatives of the producer groups and government together for the purpose of securing the broadest possible consent to an acceptable division of the national product" (Keehn, 1976: 36).

Pluralism and corporatism are similar but rival models of consensual politics. In the former, consensus emerges from the play of interests in the marketplace game of politics; in the latter, consensus emerges from the self-subordination of special interests to a commonly developed conception of the public interest, enforced by the state.

Though pluralism has emerged as a leading variant of group theories of politics, students of interest groups have long had a love-hate relationship with corporatism. Though obscured by the strong contrast Keehn draws between the two, a tight bond of logic connects them and facilitates a strange and fascinating sort of mutual intercourse that will be traced in this essay. An appreciation of the corporatist strands *within* the pluralist tradition may provide a greater insight into the strengths and weaknesses of both theories than may be gained through a simple contrast.

Corporatism and Classic Pluralism

In its first modern incarnation, around the time of World War I, the pluralist theory of the state was pitted against alternatives that posited a strong view of the public interest or some similar concept. These theories were normatively premised against group autonomy. At base, they were fundamentally dissimilar to later "free marketplace" images of political process such as those with which pluralism was to become associated. For example, one work published at the time classic pluralism was about to be popularized in the United States by Harold J. Laski and others was Heinrich von Treitschke's *Politics* (1916). Treitschke's view of the state as the objectively revealed will of God implicitly opposed group challenges to the state. Another example was Bertrand Russell's *Political Ideals* (1917). Its emphasis on the dangers of private tyranny and the need for democratization of private corporations was a radical contrast to von Treitschke's work, but it, too, accepted the legitimate hegemony of the state over the corporate bodies within its domain.

Laski and other pluralists argued against traditional concepts of state sovereignty. To them, absolute sovereignty was a myth rendered increasingly inappropriate by the growing de facto power of modern corporate bodies. Laski's studies portrayed the state as a corporate personality like other corporate persons (Laski, 1917). "Is the state," he asked, "but one of many, or are those many but parts of itself, the one?" (Laski, 1916: 438). In Laski's early formulations, the answer seemed to be clearly the former. In *The Foundations of Sovereignty* (1921), for example, Laski presented an image of politics as the harmonized articulation of complex group interaction. In this view, the concept of the public interest virtually vanished. Reviewing one of Laski's works, Walter Shepard, a president of the American Political Science Association, noted warily that Laski implied an "articulate public opinion as would be capable of eventually through its own nongovernmental organs of enforcing a will which will supersede the sovereign will of the state . . ." (Shepard, 1919: 493).

Yet even in *The Foundations* one may find foreshadowed a sort of functional democratic organization of a corporatist sort. The recurrent issue of classic pluralism was that of coordination. The need for coordination in a society of many corporate persons led back to the idea of negotiation and collective decision-making in a setting convened by the state. Laski's *A Grammar of Politics* (1925) made this explicit. Here he argued that, while the propensity of the state to serve the interests of the governors requires a continuous check by associated interests of citizens, and while there are a "thousand varying influences which go to shape the sovereign will," ultimately there is a necessary and legitimate sovereign will. Specifically, Laski advocated new corporate-democratic institutions whereby the state could regulate industry through a council of producers and public representatives very much like that put forward by Keehn in his corporatist prescription mentioned earlier.

When Laski asked if the state was one of many corporate bodies in society or if all were part of the state, he was counterposing pluralism and absolute sovereignty as polar opposites. Yet his own thoughts on the issues of coordination within the polity led him to neither the one nor the other. There are three general solutions to the problem of coordination: (1) authoritative decisions made by or under the auspices of the state, however composed; (2) authoritative decisions made collusively in the private sector; and (3) distributive decisions made through marketplace mechanisms. Laski's pluralism never embraced the latter two. Both his "pluralist" and "Marxist" writings were similar in being founded ultimately on decision-making under state auspices.

True, Laski's early writings in a pluralist vein take such delight in crushing into dust the cornerstones of traditional political architecture that the coordinative processes of his vision lay in ambiguity. Consequently, it is possible to read into Laski's early work many anti-statist themes, ranging from guild socialism and syndicalism on the left to laissez-faire and libertarianism on the right. Laski's vision was none of these. What he was erecting under the clarion call of pluralist theory was a plan of a different process of decision-making, still under state auspices. As spelled out in later works, the state would not find its sovereignty evaporating as mere myth. Rather, it would exercise its sovereignty in a far more delegative manner consistent with the complexity of modern political economy. Such delegation would require functional or corporate participation.

Thus, in a "pluralist" way, churches, labor unions, and other corporate bodies were taking on the capacity to make authoritative decisions, eroding traditional concepts of sovereignty vested solely and absolutely in the state. At times Laski's defense of group autonomy, as of nascent unions from conservative governments, seemed to hint of anarchism, as William Yance Elliot (1925: 499) warned. But Laski's "Marxism" was a corporatism of the left, far removed from the revolutionary syndicalism that Elliot had in mind. That corporatism was a direct and necessary corollary of Laski's pluralist theory, given his rejection of marketplace and other private mechanisms of decision-making combined with his fear that traditional state centralism would be far too conservative.

Scientism, Planning, and Corporatism

Laski's vision was largely misunderstood and ignored in the United States, but classic pluralism came to be remembered as a necessary revolt against neo-Hegelianism, which permeated so much of late nineteenth-century political thought. As such, its orientations if not its prescriptions were continuous with the new scientific mood that swept social science after World War I (see Wahl, 1925).

This mood was illustrated, for example, in the work of George E. G. Catlin. Catlin, in a quite modern discussion of the problem of measuring influence, foresaw a new science of politics built on observation of "the recurrence of specific behavior patterns . . . of an individual or interest group character" (Catlin, 1927: 255). Similarly, Ellis declared political science was at a cross-roads, leaving behind the metaphysics of "the sovereign state" and marching toward scientific description of "the political state" (Ellis, 1927: 788).

In this period from roughly 1925 to 1935, corporatism exerted a significant appeal within American political science. It was the appeal of ostensible enemies who, in mobilizing to combat each other, begin to assume unanticipated similarities. That similarity centered on a concept already familiar in Laski: government operating through interests institutionalized as part of the structure of the state. The basis for the corporatist appeal had been laid in the years immediately after World War I. The rise of a descriptive political science and the discrediting of jurisprudential approaches undermined the concept of rule of law superior to social interests. Postwar disillusion with reformism weakened the call to insulate the state from the pressures of its constituent interests, quite in contrast to the independent regulatory agency model that had dominated "good government" thinking for the previous half century.

Increasingly, scientistic political science revealed the importance of interests as part of the processes of state. Scientism, particularly as the apparent challenge to democracy intensified during the 1920s, became associated with the study of political control and planning. In his presidential address to the American Political Science Association (APSA) in December 1925, Charles Merriam stated, "The whole rationale and method of government is involved in these days of Lenins, Mussolinis, and Ghandis on the one hand and Einsteins and Edisons on the other. Out of what material shall be woven the fabric of the next era, if not from more intelligent and scientific understanding and appreciation of the processes of social and political control? If scientists cannot help, there are many volunteers who will offer their services, and some may be both pig-headed and rough-handed" (Merriam, 1926: 11). To mobilize political science for purposes of social and political planning became a common theme in the following decade.

The scientism for which Merriam is today remembered was put to work in the National Resources Planning Board, which Merriam headed, and other activities of government. Political scientists began to condemn the "ramshackle character of our national legislative machine," as Edward Corwin put it in his 1931 presidential address to the APSA (Corwin, 1932: 27). Corwin called on political scientists to put aside questions of influence and concentrate instead on issues of government function and management in order to use their scientific skills in analyzing government from a policy rather than political standpoint.

This orientation was epitomized by the invitation in the following year to Henry S. Dennison, president of Dennison Manufacturing Corporation, to present his views to the APSA on the topic of "The Need for the Development of Political Science Engineering" (Dennison, 1932). Related groups such as the Brookings Institution pointed toward the planning models of French and German advisory economic councils (Lorwin, 1931). By 1934, a vast amount of literature on social planning was available (see Brooks and Brooks, 1933, 1934), ranging from Chamber of Commerce reports to Harry Laidler's *Socialist*

Planning and a Socialist Program (1932). George E. G. Catlin wrote, "The blessed word Mesopotamia of the last decade was 'rationalization'; of this decade, it is planning " (Catlin, 1932: 730).

In a decade, social planning emerged from a concept bordering on sedition to one accepted by nearly all segments of American society. Moreover, in spite of divisiveness on the left, there was relative consensus in the planning literature on the general vision of the use of state power to achieve regulation, security, and fairness. Charles Beard labelled him the "philosopher of the New Deal," but Rexford Tugwell's *Industrial Discipline and the Governmental Arts* (1933) expounded principles, if not techniques, held by most advocates of social planning during the 1930s.

In the common view illustrated by Tugwell, government was to take a positive role to end the economic downturn. Business leaders were not to be overthrown, but were to join in some cooperative movement to effect the social program of the nation. Regulation was necessary because of the rise of giant corporations and the progressive obliteration of the small employer, discussed by Laidler, Catlin, and others. The vision was not one of class conflict, or even of the pluralist competition of one group against another. Rather, social planning was a cooperative vision of consensus around values such as "fairness." Implicitly, it was a vision influenced by the nationalist and corporatist ideas then rising in Europe. It was corporatist in the sense of national unity and planning through the drawing-in of powerful social groups directly into the affairs of government. Social planning under the New Deal, as in the Blue Eagle code authorities, the Tennessee Valley Authority (TVA), or Agriculture Department "grass-roots democracy" program, routinely incorporated aspects of corporatism. Governmental authority was worked through interests, primarily economic, institutionalized under new organs of government.

Walter Shepard, in his presidential address to the APSA in 1934 wrote, "There is a large element of fascist doctrine and practice that we must appropriate," albeit with greater attention to civil liberties (Shepard, 1935: 19). The power of private economic groups that had been the focus of early reformers, classic pluralists, and descriptive scientists now served to render ambiguous the difference between corporatism and American pluralist practice. For example, E. Pendleton Herring, the famous interest group specialist, reviewed Haider's and Child's work on labor in this light. Herring noted the similarity of Haider's study of labor under fascism with Child's study of labor in American politics: "Both books demonstrate the fact that the processes of government are not confined to the institutions labelled political but also manifest their power through various agencies of social control" (Herring, 1930: 761). Pluralism in practice was not so dissimilar from corporatism in theory—interest groups worked through and even took on the delegated authority of the state.

Then, too, there was the appeal of corporatism by way of its perceived necessity. Einzig (1933) foresaw national planning via functional corporate groups as a likely replacement of laissez-faire. Shepard (1933) called attention to the decline of legislative bodies and urged the study of functional and proportional systems of representation. European authors such as Manoilesco (1934) were often more dire, predicting a "century of the corporate state."

Indicative of the mood of this period was George Norlin's endorsement of the "golden mean" between fascism and individualism (Norlin, 1934). The "golden mean" was a new version of nationalist power. In Europe, Karl Mannheim called it "authoritative democracy" (Mannheim, 1935). In the United States, Karl Loewenstein (1937) and Max Lerner (1938) termed it "militant democracy." Loewenstein, for instance, argued that liberal democracy must decline in favor of " 'disciplined' or even—let us not shy from the word—'authoritarian' democracy" (Loewenstein, 1937: 657).

In his presidential address to the 1936 meeting of the APSA, Arthur Holcombe stated, "There seems to be a conspiracy . . . to force mankind to choose between two types of leadership. Professional students of politics will not be stampeded by any such conspiracy" (Holcombe, 1937: 11). As the "twin" dangers of fascism and communism to which Holcombe alluded grew in menace during the 1930s, explicit discussion of the attractions of corporatism waned among political scientists. But by then, positive government was widely accepted as was the acquisition of a share in government operations by corporate interests (see Jenkin, 1945; Bone, 1946: 816).

Instead, the late 1930s saw a tide of new books concerned not with the problems of coordination in a complex pluralist society (the issue that had brought corporatism to the foreground), but with the defense of liberal democracy against fascism (see Swabey, 1937; Leighton, 1937; Heimann, 1938). The new literature on the defense of democracy obscured the relation of pluralism to corporatism, but it laid the basis for interest-group theory after World War II. The new intellectual task seemed to be one of revising democratic theory to better accord with the resurgent belief in the common man (see Friedrich, 1942), but to do so in a way that seemed consistent with the negative findings about citizen competence and rationality popularized a decade earlier in such works as Walter Lippman's *The Phantom Public* (1925).

Group Theory in the Defense of Democracy

In spite of its attractions, corporatism never became a dominant approach to coordination among American students of interest groups. By the end of the 1920s, leading American political scientists had formulated a different conception of political process in a liberal democracy. This conception distinguished liberal democracy from statism, emphasizing the role of interest groups in each. It provided a continuing thread connecting earlier group theories (e.g., Bentley's group theory, classic pluralism) with modern ones, while also providing a powerful alternative model to corporatism at the time of its most intense appeal.

Of these authors, John Dickinson was the most sophisticated. Dickinson taught that statism was inferior to democratic government because it futilely sought to suppress rather than reflect the underlying interest structure of society. But by absorbing interests into the "orderly processes of democracy" Dickinson did not mean corporatism. On the contrary, Dickinson held that making "intelligence effective in government requires primarily that the members of government shall be guaranteed a certain independence, a certain freedom to rise above the special interests and make positive contributions of their own toward the adjustment of such interests" (Dickinson, 1930: 305). It was better, he wrote, that "the influence which the various interests and purposes in the community exert on government should be organized into the orderly processes of democracy than allowed to assert themselves irregularly and sporadically through the methods of absolutism" (Dickinson, 1930: 304).

Dickinson held a view of the liberal democratic state as neither a statist suppressor of interests nor a marketplace reflector of group forces. Instead, the democratic state was seen as an adjuster of interests. It played an educational role by bringing about new avenues of adjustment. This position recalled the rule of law as an integrator of broad social interests as nineteenth-century jurists had taught. But in Dickinson's model, integration was to be effected in close interaction with, rather than isolation from, such interests (compare Sandelius, 1931: 17-19). Dickinson tried to thread a line between corporatist absorption of state power by private interests on the one hand, and the use of state power to suppress interests on the other. These views harmonized with the heightened awareness of the dangers of centralism, a common theme of the early 1930s.

THE DANGERS OF CENTRALISM

In his presidential campaign, Herbert Hoover had warned that "The centralization of government will undermine responsibilities and will destroy the system" (Hoover, 1932: 40). This theme was not at all limited to Republican orthodoxy, however. Similar views were repeatedly expressed by contemporary political scientists. "Authority," Lewis Rockow wrote, for example, "no matter how reached, if centralised, is dangerous to freedom. Hence it is suggested to reserve as great as possible an arena of self-government to functional and territorial units" (Rockow, 1931: 584). In functional democracy and the linking of "the entire industrial system with the structure of government," one easily discerns the appeal of corporatism. But at the same time such ideas prefigured the modern pluralist concept of multiple centers of power in a system whose decentralization preserves freedom.

In his presidential address to the APSA in 1932, William F. Willoughby outlined "A Program for Research in Political Science." Its first topic was the issue of centralization as a reversal of the trend toward democratization. In particular, Willoughby was concerned with how this harmed efforts centered on how popular government "is to be justified" (Willoughby, 1933: 3).

The work of Charles Beard was one such effort. Writing in response to the question, "Is representative government in any form competent for the tasks of modern society?", Beard and his collaborator John Lewis took the occasion to warn against trends toward centralization, precisely in the vein Willoughby had in mind:

> When both economy and politics are centralized and cannot proceed effectively without cooperation from top to bottom—wise consideration for popular welfare at the top and loyal cooperation at the bottom— then it becomes doubly doubtful whether it is possible to keep the organism long in motion from heat generated merely at the center (Beard and Lewis, 1932: 239).

The issue of decentralization in the context of classic pluralism fifteen years ealier had been the point of departure for serious consideration of new, even radical programs for the *restructuring* of power (e.g., for guild socialism). But in sharp contrast, this newly revived concern over centralism in the early and mid-1930s was a basis for theoretical justification of the *existing structure* of representative democracy.

Compared to fascism or communism, the greater decentral-ization of liberal democratic politics was seen as the cornerstone of its defense. Through this concern for the justification of democracy, political scientists of the 1930s reintroduced through the back door the normative dimension they had sought to expunge in the years following World War I. Ironically, in later years the heritage of this progressive effort to defend liberal democracy was to seem a conservative disposition to defend the status quo.

HERRING'S GROUP CONCEPT OF THE PUBLIC INTEREST

Decentralism by itself, however, was an insufficient base for the intellectual defense of democracy. The very basis of democratic theory had been severely damaged by research after World War I on the limitations of public opinion (Lippman, 1922, 1925; Angell, 1927), on the potential of the new science of propaganda (Bernays, 1923, 1928; Lasswell, 1927) and, later, on opinion control and psychological warfare (Lasswell et al., 1935; Childs, ed., 1936; Smith, 1939; Albig, 1939; Doob, 1948; Gosnell and Moyca, 1949). Traditional theory, with its assumptions of interested and rational citizens, seemed irrev-ocably rebutted by studies that showed apathy, ignorance, and prejudice widespread.

Two intellectual strategies were possible to defend liberal democracy within the context of this pessimistic research. The first was to seek to change the individual citizen through civic education to fit the expectations placed on him by tradi-tional democratic theory. Merriam (1931, 1934), Pierce (1933),

Krey (1934), and Friedrich (1942) were among those to explore this alternative (for further discussion see Garson, 1973). Far more important, however, was the second strategy, involving a revision of democratic theory along group lines to better fit the realities of American political life. The criticism of interest-group theory after World War II by Peter Bachrach (1967) and others centered on just such a "downward" revising of democratic standards. But the redefinition of democracy first occurred during the 1930s, not in the 1950s.

The central question in this redefinition was how participation was to be viewed. Classical theory taught that rational citizen participation was an intrinsic good serving the ends of self-actualization and education. Without rational discussion, participation, and decision, democracy did not exist. But how could these tests of democracy be met if research showed citizens irrational, low in information and interest, and lacking in the skills and means to participate in decisions that modernization was making increasingly remote and complex?

Francis Wilson was among the earliest to indicate the answer to this question. Wilson accepted that participation was the crucial test of the existence of a "public," and, therefore, of democracy. And he acknowledged that opinion and propaganda research showed no clear and informed "public" capable of mandating government policies. It might even be granted that voting proceeded from emotional and irrational bases. But Wilson argued that the *individual* vote and the *individual* response to an opinion questionnaire were not the most accurate way of understanding a "public." These methods yielded a misleading perception of the "public," and of the public interest.

In this view participation remained the test of a democratic public, but voting was not the only or main criterion of participation. "Many historic reforms in government," Wilson wrote, "have been attempts to reorganize participation, and many new ways of making participation effective, especially by organized or conflicting groups or interests, have been developing" (Wilson, 1933: 375). Public opinion research like Odegard's (1930) had already drawn attention to the influence of pressure groups, churches, media, and other interests on public thought. Wilson extrapolated these findings to conclude that "the public" could be better known and understood through its expression in groups than through voting or that modern form of plebiscite, the public opinion poll. Wilson's formulation seemed to retain the essence of the classical definition of a democratic public (participation), but within a group rather than individual context.

E. Pendleton Herring extended this to the argument that the public interest could be known only through the group life of the public. Herring, today remembered primarily for his seminal Brookings Institution survey of interest-group lobbying in Congress (Herring, 1929), was also a frequent contributor to the *American Political Science Review* during the 1930s. Among his articles relating group theory to democratic theory was a noteworthy two-part article that directly pre-figured post-World War II group theory:

> The conception of the public welfare draws its content in any given case from the substance presented by certain special interests, not in terms of some abstract ideal, but rather in terms of the parties at conflict and in relation to the law. . . . Hence the public interest cannot be given concrete expression except through the compromise of special claims and demands finally effected. Special interests cannot then be banished from the picture, for they are the parts that make the whole . . . 'pressures' of such groups can be directed to useful ends and the influence of parti-sanship subdued by a salutary functionalism (Herring, 1933: 916-917).

If the reference to functionalism again invoked the connection between group pluralism and corporatism, Herring's thesis was nonetheless useful in shoring up the political theory of liberal democracy. His picture of government caught in "the tug and pull of economic and social forces" was a timely accom-modation to the rise of conflict theory, including Marxism, in the discipline at that time. But Herring's work interpreted that conflict as a matter of compromise, not class antagonism.

And, he defended that compromise as the *only* manner in which the public interest could find expression. "The bureaucrat selects from the special interests before him a combination to which he gives official sanction. Thus, inescapably in practice, the concept of public interest is given substance by its identification with the interests of certain groups" (Herring, 1936a: 23). But, like Truman later, Herring avoided a simplistic marketplace-of-interests model by vaguely leaving open the possibility of the state "directing" and "selecting" group pressures.

Through this group theory one could defend representative democracy as a system that effected the public interest through the accommodation of conflicting interests. The ideological function of this theory may be seen clearly in Herring's later work, *The Politics of Democracy* (1940):

> In contrast to the totalitarian state, democracy tries to retain both integration and liberty. To succeed under democracy, party government must achieve a working alliance of interests and bring support to leaders who desire both to control the government and to tolerate a loyal opposition. . . . Fundamentally, however, government by parties means the control of government by alternating groups (Herring, 1940: 55).

Herring's work, which justified democracy and differentiated it from totalitarianism on the basis of group theory, was received with enthusiasm. E. E. Schattschneider wrote, "This book is required reading . . . *The Politics of Democracy* is written in a new mood. Confronted with the prospect of losing our institutions, we look at them with new eyes and discover that even the faults of the system have something to be said for them . . . (Herring) repudiates the conventional attitudes of uncompromising criticism and substitutes for it a more charitable set of standards . . . producing what is probably the most thoroughgoing defense of American politics ever written by a reputable scholar" (Schattschneider, 1940: 788-799).

Herring's "more charitable set of standards" required only that the group process as a whole be regarded as rational, not citizens at the individual level. Almost in passing, Herring noted this view of politics was normative. In practice, political decisions were strongly affected by nongroup factors like the individual personalities of bureaucrats (Herring, 1934: 1029). And the "pressure politics" Herring advocated also required a balance of countervailing group forces. In practice, actual influence patterns often took the form of one-sided "compliance politics" (Herring, 1936b: 375). Although these considerations represented drastic adjustments of Herring's group theory, they were barely discussed. As it evolved in the 1930s under Herring's tutelage, the group conception of politics served as an ostensibly empirical defense of democracy. It was based not on the discredited notions of rational public opinion and responsible elections, but rather on the social rationality emerging from the decentralized conflict of interest groups.

Corporatism and Wartime Consensus

The foremost reason for the welcome given to Herring's *The Politics of Democracy* was, of course, its consistency with the positive and patriotic assessment of American democracy common by the late 1930s. The shift toward patriotic and consensual imagery was described by Francis Wilson: "Roosevelt's doctrine is, withal, a doctrine of conservative nationalism. There is authority, legitimate authority, in the nation because of the moral contribution it makes to the life of each citizen. . . . The morality of a national society expresses itself in a unified will" (Wilson, 1942: 459). Similarly, Harwood Childs, then the foremost student of American opinion, wrote, "The public opinion problem . . . is a problem of rallying the American people, and the people of the world for that matter, behind a philosophy of life, a democratic way, which gives sense and meaning to the rapidly shifting scenes of international events" (Childs, 1943: 67).

Consensus came to be seen as the prime political need. In reviewing Merriam's *A Prologue to Politics* (1939), Carl J.

Friedrich noted, "Merriam recognizes the organization of consent as the greatest problem of our day. This is very true" (Friedrich, 1940: 348). Authors like Dillon popularized Herring's view that interest-group politics could be the progenitor of consensus on basic rules of the game. "Pressure groups are the modern expression of democracy," Dillon wrote, "by the people and for the people" (Dillon, 1942: 481). Odegard's conclusion a decade earlier that "It is through such organizations that the ordinary citizen finds his true representation" (Odegard, 1930: 168) now could be quoted to buttress this viewpoint. And to round out the argument, group politics could be cast as a critical test of the difference between liberal democracy and either fascism or communism. For instance, Lederer's *State of the Masses: The Threat of the Classless Society* (1940) concluded that "The destruction of all social associations was even more important than the suppression of political parties. The result is a dissolution of the whole fabric of society" (Lederer, 1940: 222). Through its organic connection to a complex group process democracies could expect to enjoy consensus born of interest conflict, while alternative systems suffered deterioration caused by interest suppression.

The mood of consensus blended with a revived scientism, just as it had for similar reasons after World War I. The wartime push to demote theory, to be practical and descriptive, fit in with attempts to minimize disunity. Writing "A Challenge to Political Scientists" in a 1943 issue of the *American Political Science Review*, William Foote Whyte argued, "Political scientists should leave ethics to the philosophers and concern themselves primarily with the description and analysis of political behavior . . . politics should be viewed not as a struggle between good and evil, but as a struggle among individuals and groups for power and priority . . ." (Whyte, 1943: 699). Implicit was the idea that in ethics lay division and ideology, while in empirical description lay tolerance for varied interests and scientific unity as a discipline beyond ideology.

Finally, consensus and scientism blended easily with incrementalism, forming the triune godhead of post-World War II interest-group and pluralist theory. Though commonly identified with David Truman's 1951 work, *The Governmental Process*, this viewpoint had already been well formed by the 1940s. Illustrative was Arthur Macmahon's 1947 presidential address to the American Political Science Association convention:

> But the outstanding fact is the consistency of cumulative policy. Conflict plays its role in a moving consensus which conditions and absorbs it. The resulting steadiness of confirmed trends permits us to view more confidently than we might otherwise do the ability of the modern democratic state in the setting of the multiple interests of a free society to avoid a dilemma which, if it were real, might be fatal either to the method or to the program of the democratic state (Macmahon, 1948: 2).

Furthermore, Macmahon stated, "Basic values must underlie an advancing consensus worked out among the diverse groups of a plural society" (Macmahon, 1948: 7). The image of an advancing consensus effected through cumulative policy decisions and based on group conflict was one that was to dominate political science for two decades.

Political Science Chooses Interest Group Liberalism

The new faith in group accommodation within a consensual value system, though powerful in the years after World War II, still left a wake of unbelief. It was not universally accepted that this vision of political order realistically dealt with the problems of coordination toward which corporatism and the social planning of the "authoritarian" or "militant" democrats had been addressed a decade before. Skeptics abounded.

More important, much research supported this skepticism. Garceau's *The Political Life of the American Medical Asso-*

ciation (1941), for example, showed consensus in that interest group to be a spurious cover for the suppression of dissent in the medical profession. Contrary to Macmahon, Blaisdell's study *Economic Power and Political Pressures* (1940), prepared for the Temporary National Economic Committee of Congress, concluded that government policy *lacked* consistency precisely due to interest-group pressures, particularly business insistence on advantageous terms for cooperation. Wiltse found no progress toward public interest representation as a balance to special interest dominance of the regulatory agencies. As a remedy, Wiltse argued for a regularized, institutionalized integration of government agencies with interest representatives "consciously and intelligently" developed by administrators (Wiltse, 1941: 516). Stuart Chase's *Democracy Under Pressure* (1945) found monopolization increasing group imbalances in politics. For reform, however, Chase urged media publicity rather than the corporatist implications of Wiltse.

In a more theoretical vein, some of the leading political scientists of the day attacked the emerging arguments of interest group liberalism. E. E. Schattschneider, for instance, in his *Party Government* (1942) emphasized the inherent incapacity of pressure groups to promote the general interests of state. Instead of reliance on group consensus, what was necessary, Schattschneider said, was the formation of truly national political parties. (This, of course, prefigured the ill-fated postwar efforts of an APSA committee to promote more responsible political parties.)

Also prominent in critiquing the emerging pluralist theory of politics was Herman Finer. Though he admitted that "this is the age of government by bargaining and adjustment among interests," he argued that reconciliation (coordination with consent) of interests "cannot occur simply at the level of group representation." This lesson Finer derived from "the short, brutish record of the Italian corporate system." Instead of either corporatism or interest-group liberalism, Finer pleaded for a vaguely defined "pattern of state that commends itself to the individuals . . . who are at once members of the lesser groups and members of the all-inclusive group" (Finer, 1945: 255).

Skepticism toward group theory did not carry the day. Not only did the new group theory ride on favorable currents of the period, such as decentralism, consensus imagery, incrementalism, and scientism, but whatever weaknesses the "new" theory might have in terms of the problem of coordination, the alternatives were weaker still. Corporatism was discredited by its association with fascism. The appeal for direct social planning now seemed cliche.[1] Suggestions of "more and better" regulation seemed likely to repeat the failed reforms of the past, while even in the immediate postwar period the idea of responsible political parties was not well accepted. Finer's hopes for a revitalizing individualism seemed removed from the mainstream of political analysis. There seemed no real alternative to interest-group liberalism.

If there was an alternative, hopeful, and exciting program for coordination of state it lay in the laissez-faire revival on the right. By the end of the war, a strong conservative anti-planning movement was in full swing. It was represented by von Mises's *Bureaucracy* (1944), Hayek's *Road to Serfdom* (1944), and other works by Crider (1944) and Baker (1945). In this school the concept of "democratic planning" was viewed as a contradiction in terms. The limits of human rationality precluded genuinely rational planning or, indeed, regulation. The superiority of coordination through marketplace mechanisms free from government interference was asserted with vigor.

Needless to say, liberal social scientists regarded this as something akin to throwing the baby out with the bath. In reviewing Hayek's work, for instance, Friedrich noted that it "has made a deep impression in certain circles." He condemned its profoundly antidemocratic implications: "The will of the people," he wrote, "is not the road to serfdom" (Friedrich, 1945: 579). Similarly, Herman Finer called Hayek's work "the most sinister offensive against democracy to emerge from a democratic country in many decades" (Finer, 1945).

For many political scientists the alternative to statist or corporatist social planning on the one hand, and to laissez-faire on the other, seemed to be coordination through indirect economic controls. Keynesian fiscal and monetary mechanisms such as those recommended in Edwin Nourse's Brookings Institution study (Nourse, 1944) seemed full of promise. While the combined inflation and stagnation of the period since 1965 have now dimmed enthusiasm for this approach, it then seemed capable of accomplishing everything that had been claimed for direct social planning, yet still allowing decentralism and incrementalism to continue to characterize American politics. Agencies of direct planning, such as the National Resources Planning Board (NRPB), was dissolved. The Full Employment Act of 1946 created the Council of Economic Advisers (CEA) to fill the gap. Wayne Coy wrote, "The National Resources Planning Board is gone, but its place has been filled in part by the President's Council of Economic Advisers" (Coy, 1946: 1132).

Where Charles Merriam, a political scientist had been the leading intellect of the NRPB, in 1946 the torch was passed to the economists of the CEA. This passage marked the formal abandonment of the vision of direct national social planning. The structures of social planning in the 1930s had been too limited, imperfect, and weak to withstand the pressures that undercut their meaning. More important, the shift to indirect planning removed much of the controversy over corporatist versus other methods of integrating interest groups with state planning. Instead, it seemed the science of economics could guide the state with but little and indirect interventions of a sort far less likely to embroil government in endless group controversy. (Some of the flavor of the enthusiasm for Keynesian controls may be derived in reading S. Harris, ed., *Saving American Capitalism,* 1948, a collection by two dozen economists, political scientists, historians, and public officials.)

In practice, however, the issues of corporatism versus pluralism in how an agency should relate to its interest-group public arose in the CEA as well. The CEA had been given an intentionally small staff, for example, and therefore was forced to rely on staff in other federal departments and in private groups like the Brookings Institution, the Twentieth Century Fund, and the National Industrial Conference Board (Nourse and Gross, 1948: 294). In addition, the CEA established and regularly met with six advisory councils drawing on representatives from industry, agriculture, labor, and consumers. CEA members and staff "actively sought, as far as time allowed, to maintain an open-door policy on consultation with private group representatives" (Gross and Lewis, 1954: 123). At the same time the CEA members were reluctant to testify before Congress, insulating themselves from influence through elected representatives (Silverman, 1959). Thus, the CEA, like many other agencies of government, came to be characterized by a mixed bag of strategies for relating its operations to interest groups: (1) statist—group influences screened through a central executive charged with independently estimating the public interest; (2) corporatist—group influences directly institutionalized through representation within the agency in the form of staff and advisers; and (3) pluralist—group influences competed for attention and influence while taking advantage of the administrator's "open door" policy of access.

When what Theodore Lowi later labeled interest-group liberalism was eloquently popularized in David Truman's *The Governmental Process* (1951) and Earl Latham's *The Group Basis of Politics* (1952b), these three strategies of coordination were not clearly distinguished. Though often equated with pluralism, the group theory of politics of the early 1950s was far more eclectic. It was more an orientation than a closely argued theory.

The emergent group theory was an orientation that defended the legitimacy of positive government against the renascent laissez-faire conservatives and that argued against radicals who wanted that form of direct social planning which, in the name of the "public interest," overrode and reshaped rather than reflected interests. Group theory tottered on the brink of Bentley's physics of group forces, a view of government as a passive register of the pressure of lobbies. But though a few such as Charles Lindblom (1959, 1965, 1968) were comfortable with assertion of the incrementalist group bargaining model as both simple description and prescription, the general trend was far more ambiguous.

Writers such as Truman and Latham were misrepresented when cast as either describing of prescribing a system in which political outcomes were determined by the relative strength of group forces. These authors held out the possibility that decisions might be made on bases other than pluralist. For instance, a statist strategy was implicit in their concepts of "constituency interests" and "potential groups." Latham placed constituency interests as a factor in addition to and, hence, different from organized interest-group forces. Truman's analogous concept was that of "potential groups"—defined as "any mutual interest" or "any shared attitude" (see Latham, 1952a: 391-392; Truman, 1951: 52, 511). In both cases the door was opened for the public official to make decisions not on the physics of organized forces but rather on the basis of a judgment about the common interest of all existing *and* conceivable interests. By opening group theory to all things, the simplicity and force of Bentley's theory was sabotaged. As Dowling observed of Truman's use of the "potential group" concept, "Truman's political science, then, is quite consistent with my conception of the common good" (Dowling, 1960: 953). The reintroduction of the public interest concept through the back door mixed pluralist and statist strategies of coordination.

In an indirect way, the breadth of the new group theory left room not only for pluralism and statism, but for corporatism as well. Though corporatism as such had fallen from the terms of discourse, a related concept appeared: private government. Alpheus Mason, for instance, had written in 1950 on the dangers of allowing business to "replace government with a power system of its own" (Mason, 1950, 342). Latham put a more favorable light on this. He wrote, "private government is not only a legitimate but a much-neglected subject of inquiry by political science" (Latham, 1952a: 382-383). Latham argued that both state and nonstate associations were in the same category of power, as Laski and the classic pluralists had contended. "The state as an association (or group)," he wrote, "is not different from other associations" (Latham, 1952a: 382).

What distinguished public and private governments was merely the badge of officiality. "It is part of the political consensus—the understood and agreed conditions of life in civilized society—that certain groups will be permitted to act like badge-wearers," Latham held. "The groups so privileged collectively make up the instrumentalities of the state and such groups are distinguished from others only in their possession of the characteristic of officiality" (Latham, 1952a: 389). The concept of the equality of groups in terms of power status and of the group basis of officiality hinted at corporatism. These and other group-theory concepts were not corporatist, of course, but the ideas of officiality of selected groups and agencies as interest groups were not far removed from acceptance of the corporatist strategy of coordination: direct incorporation of interest groupings into government structure.

Conclusion

Later critics of interest-group liberalism were to condemn its link to "conservative doctrine" (Walker, 1966: 285-286) and "implicit and unrecognized conservative themes" (McCoy and Playford, 1967: 3; see also Connolly, 1969; Lowi, 1969; Baskin, 1971; Dolbeare and Edelman, 1971: ch. 2; Wolfe and McCoy, 1972: ch. 4). Radical critics have been prone to cast group and pluralist theory as a reaction against Marxist and class interpretations of politics (Domhoff, 1970: 310). Conventional political scientists, in contrast, have generally portrayed group theory emerging as a reaction against "the formalism and static quality of the institutional approach to political analysis that was prevalent during the early twentieth century" (Young, 1968: 80).

As Avery Leiserson pointed out at the time Truman's classic work, *The Governmental Process* (1951), was published, the function of the new group theory was different from either of these. Political scientists would receive the work enthusiastically, Leiserson correctly predicted, because it set forth a framework for presenting "the great mass of empirical, historical, and descriptive materials that political science has accumulated about the 'realities' of political organization" (Leiserson, 1951: 1193).

Group theory introduced to political science a common vocabulary compatible with virtually any model of political process, whether pluralist, statist, or corporatist. Dowling faulted Truman for this indiscriminate all-inclusiveness, saying, "the merit of a 'group interpretation' (meaning by that a Bentleyan methodology) would, if it were worked out, be precisely that it does 'leave something out' " (Dowling, 1960: 953). The commonality of group theory was its appeal and its weakness.

Group theories of politics, including pluralism, cannot be contrasted easily with corporatism for purposes of analyzing American politics. Primarily, this is because corporatism is a theory of political coordination, while group theory is not properly termed theory at all. Rather, it is an eclectic set of images of a decentralized but consensual democratic polity.

Group theory served the intellectual purpose of aiding in the redefinition of democracy to avoid the seemingly unrealistic assumptions about individual rationality and motivation. It served the ideological purpose of defending contemporary democratic practice against the surge of fascist and communist philosophy. And it served the cultural purpose of revitalizing the values of decentralism and consensus. But group theory was not intended to be a theory of coordination of state, or even a theory in the predictive sense at all, as Truman himself warned his would-be followers and critics (Truman, 1960: 494-495).

NOTE

1. This is evidenced by the dismantling of Merriam's National Resources Planning Board, and the lack of impact of the call in 1945 by a founder of the National Economic and Social Planning Association for national unity behind social planning (Lorwin, 1945).

REFERENCES

ALBIG, W. A. (1939) *Public Opinion.* New York: McGraw-Hill.

ANGELL, N. (1927) *The Public Mind.* New York: Dutton.

BACHRACH, P. (1967) *The Theory of Democratic Elitism: A Critique.* Boston: Little, Brown.

BAKER, J. R. (1945) *Science and the Planned State.* New York: Macmillan.

BASKIN, D. (1971) *American Pluralist Democracy: A Critique.* New York: Van Nostrand Reinhold.

BEARD, C. A. and J. LEWIS (1932) "Representative Government in Evolution," *American Political Science Review,* Vol. 26, No. 2 (April): 223-240.

BERNAYS, E. L. (1923) *Crystallizing Public Opinion.* New York: Boni and Liveright.

——— (1928) *Propaganda.* New York: Horace Liveright.

BLAISDELL, D. C. (1940) *Economic Power and Political Pressures.* Monograph No. 26 of the Temporary National Economic Committee. Washington, D.C.: USGPO.

BONE, H. A. (1946) Review of Thomas Paul Jenkin (1945) in *American Political Science Review,* Vol. 40, No. 4 (August): 816.

BROOKS, E. C. and L. M. BROOKS (1933) "Five Years of 'Planning' Literature," *Social Forces,* Vol. 11, No. 2 (March): 430-465.

——— (1934) "A Decade of 'Planning' Literature," *Social Forces,* Vol. 12, No. 2 (March): 427-459.

CATLIN, G.E.G. (1927) "The Delimitation and Measurability of Political Phenomena," *American Political Science Review,* Vol. 21, No. 2 (May): 255-269.

——— (1932) Review of Charles A. Beard, ed., *America Faces the Future* (Boston: Houghton Mifflin, 1932), Harry Laidler, *The Road Ahead* (New York: Crowell, 1932), and George Soule, *A Planned Society* (New York: Macmillan, 1932), in *American Political Science Review,* Vol. 26, No. 4 (August): 730-733.

CHASE, S. (1945) *Democracy Under Pressure: Special Interests versus the Public Welfare.* New York: Twentieth Century Fund.

CHILDS, H. L., ed. (1936) *Propaganda and Dictatorship.* Princeton: Princeton Univ. Press.

——— (1943) "Public Information and Opinion," *American Political Science Review,* Vol. 37, No. 1 (February): 56-68.

CONNOLLY, W. E., ed. (1969) *The Bias of Pluralism.* New York: Atherton.

CORWIN, E. S. (1932) "Social Planning Under the Constitution—A Study in Perspectives," *American Political Science Review,* Vol. 26, No. 1 (February): 1-27.

COY, W. (1946) "Federal Executive Reorganization Reexamined: Basic Problems," *American Political Science Review,* Vol. 40, No. 6 (December): 1132.

CRIDER, J. H. (1944) *The Bureaucrat.* Philadelphia: Lippincott.

DENNISON, H. S. (1932) *American Political Science Review,* Vol. 26, No. 2, (April): 241-255.

DICKINSON, J. (1930) "Democratic Realities and Democratic Dogma," *American Political Science Review,* Vol. 24, No. 2 (May): 283-309.

DILLON, M. E. (1942) "Pressure Groups," *American Political Science Review,* Vol. 36, No. 3 (June): 471-481.

DOLBEARE, K. and M. EDELMAN (1971) *American Politics.* Lexington, Mass.: Heath.

DOMHOFF, G. W. (1970) *The Higher Circles.* New York: Vintage.

DOOB, L. (1948) *Public Opinion and Propaganda.* New York: Holt.

DOWLING, R. E. (1960) "Pressure Group Theory: Its Methodological Range," *American Political Science Review,* Vol. 54, No. 4 (December): 944-954.

EINZIG, P. (1933) *The Economic Foundations of Fascism.* London: Macmillan.

ELLIOT, W. Y. (1925) "Sovereign State or Sovereign Group?" *American Political Science Review,* Vol. 19, No. 3 (August): 475-499.

ELLIS, E. D. (1927) "Political Science at the Crossroads," *American Political Science Review,* Vol. 21, No. 4 (November): 773-791.

FINER, H. (1945) *Road to Reaction.* Boston: Atlantic—Brown.

——— (1945) "Towards a Democratic Theory," *American Political Science Review,* Vol. 39, No. 2 (April): 249-256.

FRIEDRICH, C. J. (1940) Review of Merriam (1939) in *American Political Science Review,* Vol. 34, No. 2 (April): 347-348.

——— (1942) *The New Belief in the Common Man.* Boston: Little, Brown.

——— (1945) Review of Hayek (1944) in *American Political Science Review,* Vol. 39, No. 3 (June): 579.

GARCEAU, O. (1941) *The Political Life of the American Medical Association.* Cambridge, Mass.: Harvard Univ. Press.

GARSON, G. D. (1974) "Citizenship as Ideology," *Maxwell Review,* Vol. 10, No. 1 (Winter): 25-38.

GOSNELL, H. and C. D. MOYCA (1949) "Public Opinion Research in Government," *American Political Science Review,* Vol. 43, No. 3 (June): 564-572.

GROSS, B. and J. P. LEWIS (1954) "The President's Economic Staff During the Truman Administration," *American Political Science Review,* Vol. 48, No. 1 (March): 114-123.

HARRIS, S. (1948) *Saving American Capitalism.* New York: Knopf.

HAYEK, F. (1944) *Road to Serfdom.* Chicago: Univ. of Chicago Press.

HEIMANN, E. (1938) *Communism, Fascism or Democracy?* New York: Norton.

HERRING, E. P. (1929) *Group Representation Before Congress.* Baltimore: Johns Hopkins Univ. Press.

——— (1930) Review of Carmen Haider, *Capital and Labor Under Fascism* (New York: Columbia Univ. Press, 1930) and Harwood L. Childs, *Labor and Capital in National Politics* (Columbus: Ohio State Univ. Press, 1930), in *American Political Science Review,* Vol. 24, No. 3 (August): 760-763.

——— (1933) "Special Interests and the Interstate Commerce Commission," *American Political Science Review,* Vol. 27, No. 5 (October): 738-751, and Vol. 27, No. 6 (December): 899-917.

——— (1936a) *Public Administration and the Public Interest.* New York: McGraw-Hill.

——— (1936b) Review of E. E. Schattschneider, *Politics, Pressures, and the Tariff*

(New York: Prentice-Hall, 1935), in *American Political Science Review*, Vol. 30, No. 2 (April): 374-375.

——— (1940) *The Politics of Democracy*. New York: Norton.

HOLCOMBE, A. (1937) "The Political Interpretation of History," *American Political Science Review*, Vol. 31, No. 1 (February): 1-11.

HOOVER, H. (1932) "The Consequences of the Proposed New Deal," *Opposition Politics*, Joseph Boskin, ed. (Beverly Hills, Cal.: Glencoe, 1968): 37-43.

JENKIN, T. P. (1945) *Reactions of Major Groups to Positive Government in the U.S., 1930-1940*. Berkeley: Univ. of California Press.

KEEHN, N. H. (1976) "A World of Becoming: From Pluralism to Corporatism," *Polity*, Vol. 9, No. 1 (Fall): 19-39.

KREY, A. C. (1934) *Conclusions and Recommendations: Report of the Commission on the Social Studies*. New York: Scribner's.

LAIDLER, H. (1932) *Socialist Planning and a Socialist Program*. New York: Falcon.

LASKI, H. J. (1916) "The Political Theory of the Disruption," *American Political Science Review*, Vol. 10, No. 3 (August): 437-464.

——— (1917) *Studies in the Problem of Sovereignty*. New Haven: Yale Univ. Press.

——— (1921) *The Foundations of Sovereignty*. New York: Harcourt, Brace.

——— (1925) *A Grammar of Politics*. New Haven: Yale Univ. Press.

LASSWELL, H. D. (1927) "The Theory of Political Propaganda," *American Political Science Review*, Vol. 21, No. 3 (August): 627-631.

——— et al. (1935) *Propaganda and Promotional Activities: An Annotated Bibliography*. Minneapolis: Univ. of Minnesota Press.

LATHAM, E. (1952a) "The Group Basis of Politics: Notes for a Theory," *American Political Science Review*, Vol. 46, No. 2 (June): 376-397.

——— (1952b) *The Group Basis of Politics: A Study in Basing-Point Legislation*. Ithaca, New York: Cornell Univ. Press.

LEDERER, E. (1940) *State of the Masses: The Threat of the Classless Society*. New York: Norton.

LEIGHTON, J. (1937) *Philosophies in Conflict*. New York: Appleton-Century.

LEISERSON, A. (1951) Review of Truman (1951) in *American Political Science Review*, Vol. 45, No. 4 (December): 1192-1193.

LERNER, M. (1938) *It Is Later Than You Think: The Need for Militant Democracy*. New York: Viking.

LINDBLOM, C. (1959) "The Science of Muddling Through," *Public Administration Review*, Vol. 19 (Spring): 79-88.

——— (1965) *The Intelligence of Democracy*. New York: Free Press.

——— (1968) *The Policy-Making Process*. New York: Prentice-Hall.

LIPPMAN, W. (1922) *Public Opinion*. New York: Harcourt, Brace.

——— (1925) *The Phantom Public*. New York: Harcourt, Brace.

LOEWENSTEIN, K. (1937) "Militant Democracy and Fundamental Rights," *American Political Science Review*, Vol. 31, No. 3 (June): 417-432; and Vol. 31, No. 4 (August): 638-658.

LORWIN, L. L. (1931) *Advisory Economic Councils*. Washington, D.C.: Brookings Institution.

——— (1945) *Time for Planning*. New York: Harper.

LOWI, T. (1969) *The End of Liberalism*. New York: Norton.

McCOY, C. A. and J. PLAYFORD, eds. (1967) *Apolitical Politics: A Critique of Behavioralism*. New York: Crowell.

MACMAHON, A. (1948) "Conflict, Consensus, Confirmed Trends and Open Choices," *American Political Science Review*, Vol. 42, No. 1 (February): 1-15.

MANNHEIM, K. (1935) *Mensch und Gesellschaft im Zeitalter des Umbaus*. Leiden: Sijthoff.

MANOILESCO, M. (1934) *Le Siecle du Corporatisme*. Paris: Felix Alcan.

MASON, A. T. (1950) "Business Organized as Power: The New Imperium in Imperio," *American Political Science Review*, Vol. 44, No. 2 (June): 323-342.

MERRIAM, C. (1926) "Progress in Political Research," *American Political Science Review*, Vol. 20, No. 1 (February): 1-13.

——— (1931) *The Making of Citizens*. Chicago: Univ. of Chicago Press.

——— (1934) *Civic Education in the United States*. New York: Scribner's.

——— (1939) *A Prologue to Politics*. Chicago: Univ. of Chicago Press.

MISES, L. von (1944) *Bureaucracy*. New Haven: Yale Univ. Press.

NORLIN, G. (1934) *Fascism and Citizenship*. Chapel Hill: Univ. of North Carolina Press.

NOURSE, E. G. (1944) *Price-Making Together in a Democracy*. Washington, D.C.: Brookings Institution.

——— and B. GROSS (1948) "The Role of the Council of Economic Advisers," *American Political Science Review*, Vol. 42, No. 2 (April): 283-295.

ODEGARD, P. (1930) *The American Public Mind*. New York: Columbia Univ. Press.

PIERCE, B. L. (1933) *Citizen's Organizations and the Civic Training of Youth*. New York: Scribner's.

ROCKOW, L. (1931) "The Doctrine of Sovereignty of the Constitution," *American Political Science Review*, Vol. 25, No. 3 (August): 573-588.

RUSSELL, B. (1917) *Political Ideals*. New York: Century.

SANDELIUS, W. (1931) "National Sovereignty versus the Rule of Law," *American Political Science Review*, Vol. 25, No. 1 (February): 1-20.

SCHATTSCHNEIDER, E. E. (1940) Review of Gerring (1940) in *American Political Science Review*, Vol. 34, No. 1 (August): 788-789.

——— (1942) *Party Government*. New York: Farrar and Rinehard.

SHEPARD, W. J. (1919) Review of Harold J. Laski, *Authority in the Modern State* (New Haven: Yale Univ. Press, 1919), in *American Political Science Review*, Vol. 13, No. 3 (August): 491-494.

——— (1933) "Legislative Assemblies," in E.R.A. Seligman et al., eds., *Encyclopedia of the Social Sciences*, Vol. 9, 355-361.

——— (1935) "Democracy in Transition," *American Political Science Review*, Vol. 27, No. 1 (February): 1-20.

SILVERMAN, C. (1959) *The President's Economic Advisers*. University, Alabama: Univ. of Alabama Press, Inter-university Case Program No. 48.

SMITH, C. W. (1939) *Public Opinion in a Democracy: A Study of American Politics*. New York: Prentice-Hall.

SWABEY, M. C. (1937) *Theory of the Democratic State*. Cambridge, Mass.: Harvard Univ. Press.

TREITSCHKE, H. von (1916) *Politics*. New York: Macmillan.

TRUMAN, D. (1951) *The Governmental Process: Political Process and Public Opinion*. New York: Knopf.

————— (1960) "On the Inventions of Systems," *American Political Science Review*, Vol. 54, No. 2 (June): 494-495.

TUGWELL, R. (1933) *Industrial Discipline and the Governmental Arts.* New York: Columbia Univ. Press.

WAHL, J. (1925) *Pluralist Philosophies of England and America:* London: Open Court Publishing.

WALKER, J. L. (1966) "A Critique of the Elitist Theory of Democracy," *American Political Science Review*, Vol. 60, No. 2 (June): 285-295.

WHYTE, W. F. (1943) "A Challenge to Political Scientists," *American Political Science Review*, Vol. 36, No. 4 (August): 692-697.

WILLOUGHBY, W. F. (1933) "A Program for Research in Political Science," *American Political Science Review*, Vol. 27, No. 1 (February): 1-23.

WILSON, F. (1933) "Concepts of Public Opinion," *American Political Science Review*, Vol. 27, No. 3 (June): 371-391.

————— (1942) "The Revival of Organic Theory," *American Political Science Review*, Vol. 36, No. 3 (June): 454-459.

WILTSE, C. (1941) "The Representative Function of Bureaucracy," *American Political Science Review*, Vol. 35, No. 3 (June): 510-516.

WOLFE, A. and C. McCOY (1972) *Political Analysis: An Unorthodox Approach.* New York: Crowell.

YOUNG, O. R. (1968) *Systems of Political Science.* Englewood Cliffs, N.J.: Prentice-Hall.

Chapter 3

1950-1960: The Golden Era of Interest-Group Theory—Its Rise and Passage

Like Marxism and other great conceptions of political process, the roots of contemporary group theories of politics may be traced almost endlessly into the past. Nonetheless, for most American political scientists, the group theory of politics is associated primarily with the decade of the 1950s. The influence of group theory rose to a peak between 1950, when Bertram Gross hailed the republication of Arthur Bentley's *The Process of Government* (1949) as one of "the most important books on government ever written in any country" (Gross, 1950: 742), and 1960, when the *American Political Science Review* carried a series of articles reappraising Bentley, but now in a fundamentally critical fashion (Rothman, 1960; Dowling, 1960; Hale, 1960).

Yet at the end of the decade, David Truman, the foremost exponent of group theory, saw fit to disassociate himself from the many who had seen in his *Governmental Process* (1951) the basis for a systematic, scientific theory of politics (Truman, 1960). The seemingly sudden entrance of the group-theoretic approach was counterbalanced by its equally rapid passage. Three alternative hypotheses may account for this. First, one may assert that group theory was "an idea whose time had come" in the postwar period, and that changed sociopolitical circumstances made it "an idea whose time had passed" by the end of the decade. Alternative to this social determinism, one may follow Sorokin's depiction of social science as a field dominated by scholars guided by the "Columbus complex" to be first, to draw the outlines on maps later to be filled in by those of lesser stature. In this view, the causes of the rise and passage of ideas is part of the field of collective behavior, encompassing, for instance, the study of fads and fashions.

Both hypotheses are quite different from a third: the view that the evolution of social scientific ideas follows the paradigm of natural science. Popularized by Kuhn, this belief anticipates that major theoretical frameworks will be displaced by newer organizing paradigms in a "scientific revolution" marked by the explicit confrontation of old and new ideas, and that the new will prevail primarily because of a better correspondence to empirical evidence (Kuhn, 1970). These three viewpoints may be termed the social, the psychological, and the rational, respectively. The present essay explores their relative explanatory power in the case of the rise and passage of interest-group theory.

1950-1952: A Revival and Restatement

The revival of interest-group theories of politics in the early 1950s drew support from its foundation on two critical bases: the wartime mood of social consensus, and the rise of behavioralism in the social sciences.

Consensus was in many ways the more important. In the 1930s and 1940s, E. Pendleton Herring and others had worked out a defense of empirical democratic theory that relied on a group explanation. Democracy was justified in terms of the rationality of group process, not the fitness of individual voters (Herring, 1940). Lederer (1940) and others centered their critique of totalitarianism precisely on the obliteration of independent-interest associations in such states. By midwar, pressure-group process was equated with "the modern expression of democracy by the people and for the people" (Dillon, 1942: 481). And, after the war, the consensual conflict of interest groups commonly was viewed as the heart of democratic practice. In his 1947 presidential address to the American Political Science Association, for instance, Arthur Macmahon chose consensual conflict as a theme. "Basic values," he stated, "must underlie an advancing consensus worked out among the diverse groups of a plural society" (Macmahon, 1948: 7).

The themes of consensus and group process were articulated in greater detail two years later, in Quincy Wright's presidential address to the APSA. Wright argued that an education to the viewpoints then common in American political science "tends to develop a spirit of moderation" (Wright, 1950: 7). It would be inconsistent, Wright thought, for one to be a political scientist and still believe in communism or fascism. Rather than accept such unconsensual beliefs, the rational individual continually synthesizes group pressures. "In our complicated world," Wright said, "each human mind must continually synthesize the claims of family, nation, church, business, cultural associations, local community, and world society . . . A world with millions of small conflicts in the minds of individuals and in the discussions of small groups is likely to be more peaceful and prosperous than a world divided into two opposing groups each of which commands the exclusive, intense, and blind obedience of the population" (Wright, 1950: 11). Thus, Wright's presidential address illustrated the then-common view that the politics of small group conflicts represented both description and prescription of democratic practice. This group politics was cast as the cornerstone of free society.

Given this background it is hardly surprising that the republication of Bentley's The Process of Government was hailed as one of the most important books ever written about government. It seemed as timely and controversial as ever. R. M. MacIver had criticized Bentley for portraying legislation as the mere calculable result of pressure group struggles, apart from reasoned decisions about opposing concepts of national welfare. But Bertram Gross, reviewing Bentley, called this criticism misdirected. Conceptions of the national interest,

in Bentley's work, were *embodied* in interest-group programs
(Gross, 1950: 747).

Gross's response to MacIver reflected a revolution in thought.
For social scientists like Gross, the group basis of democracy
was the living tissue of American politics. The group conception
removed the veil of rhetoric that obscured the actual operation
of government behind abstractions like "the national interest."
In the group theory of politics was found a rationale for analyzing politics in terms of empirical behavior, not political
philosophy. If Bentley understood his work to be merely a
beginning, and if Bentley led in part to his own neglect by moving
off in the direction of philosophy himself, Gross and others
recognized in his work the basis for a more concrete and scientific approach to political science.

The rise of behaviorism in the social sciences was the other
major basis on which the revival of interest-group theory was
founded. As with the descriptive political "science" that flowered
after World War I, World War II bred another version of
"value-free" scientism, albeit garbed in more sophisticated
technology. Postwar behaviorism rested in part on the scientism
of Merriam, Munro, and Catlin a generation earlier. But in
a more direct way, behaviorism rested on a variety of diverse
forces: large-scale federal funding of the "behavioral sciences";
expansion of survey research data and techniques; the desire
to emulate the seeming advances made in economics and other
social sciences, as well as frustration at the low value attached
by the federal government to previous political science expertise;
the inability to successfully apply American public administration to underdeveloped countries after the war; and, for that
matter, the inability to explain the rise of fascism and communism (see Somit and Tanenhaus, 1967: 184-185).

Behavioralism, as it came to be loosely termed, derived partly
from a behavioristic approach to psychology. The individualistic
focus of the latter stood in some tension to a group theory of
politics. This problem was not critical, however, because behavioralism was more a mood or style than a precise body of scientific
thought in political science. Behavioralism dovetailed with

group theory in several ways. Both, in particular, emphasized description rather than normative theory. In a controversial article, William Foote Whyte had written "a challenge to political scientists," declaring, "Political scientists should leave ethics to the philosophers and concern themselves primarily with the description and analysis of political behavior" (Whyte, 1943: 697). Although this challenge was vigorously criticized (Hallowell, 1944; Almond, 1946) and a committee of the American Political Science Association urged continuing prescriptive efforts (McLean, 1945: 743), the challenge proved compelling.

In practice the behavioral approach was less different from previous political science than it was portrayed. Though its promise of providing the technical methods through which empirical hypotheses, such as those of group theory, might be confirmed created a new mood of enthusiasm and expectation in the discipline, the behavioral revolution as applied to group theory fell far short of creating a wholly new terminology for analysis of government. Earl Latham's effort to delineate the framework of a group theory of politics, for example, created a new concept of "officiality" that was not greatly different from that cornerstone term of the "old" political science, sovereignty (Latham, 1952a: 389-390). Likewise, David Truman's notion of "taking account of potential group interests" seemed to sanction government intervention in the public interest as perceived by officials of state, something that was at the core of the prescriptive approach (Truman, 1951: 510-524).

Just as the group approach was not entirely new, neither was it uniquely American. In France, for example, Maurice Duverger's *Les Partis Politiques* (1951) centered on the argument that parties tended to become centralized over time. As prescription, Duverger emphasized the need to overcome the insulation of parties (and government) from group process and pressure. Ironically, at the same time American political scientists from an older tradition were urging a more responsible party system more resistant to group pressures (APSA Committee on Political Parties, 1950: 2). These scholars explicitly denied the Bentleyan notion that something akin to the public interest would emerge from the claims of competing pressure groups. This effort, however, was soon subject to intense dissent (Turner, 1951) and fell by the wayside.

The ill-fated efforts of the APSA Committee on Political Parties serves, nonetheless, as a reminder that group theory was *not* generally accepted by political scientists as an "idea whose time had come" when Truman's *The Governmental Process* appeared. On the contrary, most research on group behavior upheld the traditional view that the evils of pressure groups dictated their regulation by government acting in terms of an independently conceived national interest. Illustrations abound. Alpheus T. Mason examined the National Association of Manufacturers and the Liberty League, concluding that "To escape anarchy, politics must be dominant over economics" (Mason, 1950: 342). Stephen Kemp Bailey's study of the National Farmers' Union, the Chambers of Commerce, and other groups concluded that economic policies were "formulated by a kaleidoscopic and largely irresponsible interplay of ideas, interests, institutions, and individuals" (Bailey, 1950, quoted by Zeller, 1950: 470). Schriftgiesser's *The Lobbyists* (1951) popularized the findings of the Buchanan Committee on the dangers of unregulated lobbying. Knappen's study of the politics of the shipping industry (Knappen, 1950) and Shott's study of the railroads (Shott, 1950) also portrayed the results of group process in an unfavorable light. And, the very possibility of representativeness of interests in the group process was called into question by early opinion data showing that less than a third of Americans said they belonged to *any* organization taking stands on national issues (Woodward and Roper, 1950: 874).

Notwithstanding the enduring tradition of the "public interest" viewpoint, Truman's *The Governmental Process* was well received. Avery Leiserson, reviewing it for the *American Political Science Review,* rightly forecast that it would be adopted enthusiastically by teachers of political science because it contained a framework for presenting "the great mass of empirical, historical, and descriptive materials that political science has accumulated about the 'realities' of political organization" (Leiserson, 1951: 1193). But the proper way to understand this is by emphasizing the work "framework" rather than "empirical, historical, and descriptive materials." Indeed, what is striking on reading *The Governmental Process* is precisely that this was *not* an inductive work based on empirical research. The bulk of such research was, as indicated, contrary to the value premises Truman held. Rather, the appeal of *The Governmental Process* lay in the realm of theory.

Truman's work was not distinguished simply because of its emphasis on the eufunctional role of interest groups; other works (e.g., Griffith, 1951) said much the same. Herring had laid the groundwork for this orientation over a decade earlier and by World War II such views were common, if not dominant, in political science. Rather, what distinguished Truman's writing was the systematic way in which the entire compass of American government was reviewed from a group-process perspective. *The Governmental Process* showed what Leiserson hailed in his review: the group theory of democratic politics provided the framework for organizing discussion of the bulk of what American political scientists were concerned with. The omnipresence of group conflict and interest accommodation provided the running theme for political analysis.

Equally important, this theme filled a relative void. The traditional line of analysis, focusing on the law, had long since passed from favor. While Truman, Latham, and other postwar group theorists found utility in contrasting their orientation with that of the jurisprudential approach, this resembled the beating of a dead horse. Similarly, though class analysis of politics enjoyed some revival in the 1930s, its general impact on American political science was not great. A few, such as Oliver Garceau (1951: 79), still urged further research on the relation of politics to the status and class systems, but these were exceptions. The alternative unifying theme urged by the right, rooted in laissez-faire economics and a faith in the wisdom of the marketplace in allocating public goods, enjoyed a revival in the 1945-1949 period. It too, however, was denounced bitterly by leading political scientists (Friedrich, 1945: 579; Finer, 1945) and remained even more peripheral to the discipline than Marxism. The weakness of alternative organizing frameworks for analyzing American politics, combined with the revived interest in *science* in political science (Spengler, 1950; Appleby, 1950), made the desire for the sort of framework Truman presented irresistible for many scholars.

Of course, other political scientists condemned the revival of scientism in the strongest terms (Waldo, 1952; Morgenthau, 1952). And other new frameworks *were* being proposed at this time (e.g., functionalism: see Parsons, 1951; and power analysis: see Lasswell and Kaplan, 1950), but these found much less popularity among political scientists. The high level of abstraction of these new frameworks and their endless terminological exercises were far less in harmony with contemporary political science than the pragmatic and concrete group approach of Truman.

If group theory was merely a restatement of ideas long common in political science, it must be appreciated that it was a powerful restatement. This was brought home in Earl Latham's classic article in 1952, "The Group Basis of Politics: Notes for a Theory" (Latham, 1952a). In this article, Latham showed how the group approach could be used to subsume a wide range of social science insights (Weber, Pareto, Mosca, Michels, Mannheim, and Parsons among sociologists; Horney in psychology; Commons, Veblen, Clark, and Andrews among economists). Moreover, the group approach grew out of a solid body of literature in political science itself (Bentley, Herring, Schattschneider, Munro, Odegard), including numerous specific studies in areas of legislation (Bailey, Young), political parties (Key), public policy (Chase, McCune), and administration (Leiserson, Almond, Dahl). In Latham's view, group theory spanned stratification theory (Whyte, Warner, Lynd), theories of leadership (Roethlisberger and Dickson, Mayo, Barnard, Simon), and various theories of power (Berle and Means, de Grazia, Galbraith). There seemed to be little it did *not* incorporate. The revival of the group theory of politics seemed to promise to provide a common home for most of the important centers of theorizing that were then working in isolation from each other.

1953-1956: The Challenge of Stratification Theory

Neither Truman nor Latham was concerned with rebutting alternative theories of the political process. Given the relative absence of rival paradigms, this was not necessary. Truman's work operated at a concrete level, eschewing theory except insofar as it was implicit in the categories of his analysis. Latham cast a wide net, encouraging theorists and scholars of many stripes to accept the usefulness of group theory as a unifying, overarching framework. Strange bedfellows were thereby proposed: Schattschneider, whose work had cast business as a danger and pressure groups as incapable of directing the nation's affairs (Schattschneider, 1942) with Galbraith, who argued that the nation's major group coalitions, together with government, formed a benign system of countervailing powers (Galbraith, 1952), for instance. To maintain this breadth, Latham's central findings tended toward the uncontroversial and trivial. "The conclusion emerges," he wrote, for example, "from an inspection of the literature dealing with the structure and process of groups that, insofar as they are organized groups, they are structures of power" (Latham, 1952a: 382). In reviewing Latham's *The Group Basis of Politics* (1952b), on which the previously mentioned article had been based, James MacGregor Burns found that expansion to book length carried "group theory no further than where it left off at the end of chapter one" (Burns, 1953: 236). Thus, even from the start, group theory displayed weaknesses when considered as a theory rather than as a framework. It was more useful for organizing research findings than for extending predictive theory, as Burns found evident in Latham's own attempt to apply group theory.

At the same time, empirical studies of specific interest groups continued to come to conclusions disconcertingly in tension with the felicitous view of American democracy implicit in the group approach. Charles Hardin's study of *The Politics*

of Agriculture (1952) was one example. In this study of the
Farm Bureau, Hardin found not countervailing power, but
corporatist collusion. Hardin found that the U.S. Department
of Agriculture was working hand-in-glove with established
farm interests through an extensive system of support (extension services, government advisory committees, appoint-
ments, local boards) to perpetuate a particular structure of
power (Hardin, 1952). The class foundations of rural life were
found to be the ultimate object of the struggle for power in
rural America. In this setting, analysis easily might proceed further
through stratification theory than through a theory portraying
politics as the competition of many groups under the neutral
umpireship of the government.

Such studies did not, however, carry the weight in political
science of the more general and theoretical works. This was
a period when the same forces that had favored the rise of
group theory in political science were fostering related approaches in other disciplines (in sociology, see Nisbet, 1953,
for a normative theory of community as pluralist democracy;
in history, the "consensus school" represented by Boorstin,
1953). And in political science, too, related approaches were
both extending and splintering the group approach. For example, David Easton's *The Political System* (1953) appeared,
introducing systems analysis as an even more general framework
for political science analysis. Its input-output categories provided a new and rival terminology, though its core concept
of politics as an equilibrating system was generally compatible
with the group-process view. Similarly, Dahl and Lindblom
(1953) presented a systematic effort to apply political economy
as a framework, analyzing politics in terms of four control
systems: market prices, hierarchy, polyarchy, and bargaining.
These categories also presented a rival terminology, though
the control systems discussed could easily be analyzed in group-
theoretic vocabulary as well. Indeed, scholars such as Easton,
Dahl, and Lindblom perceived their work as partial efforts
to construct a science of politics, just as Truman's had been,
none necessarily contradicting the other. The differences in

frameworks had more to do with the relative utility of their operating concepts than with any issue of one being "correct" and another "incorrect."

In contrast, stratification theory, which received a major forward thrust with the publication of Floyd Hunter's *Community Power Structure: A Study of Decision-Makers* (1953), did represent a clear challenge to the group approach. Indeed, the counterposition of the group/pluralist approach with the stratification/elite approach was to be the dominant focus of contention in the discipline for the next decade. Not only did stratification theory imply that group process was auxiliary to prior elite patterns of conflict and accommodation, but its very methods of studying power were not those of Latham, Truman, Herring, and other adherents to the group-process school.

Hunter's methodology was based on survey research of the reputational aspect of power. Though elite analysis was a well grounded approach in political science (long advocated by Harold Lasswell, for instance; see Strong, 1954: 236), the reputational methodology was not. Later, as the findings of stratification theorists like Hunter slowly filtered across the divide separating sociology from political science, it was to be the methodological rather than substantive aspects that were the object of attack by group theorists and related scholars.

The reputational approach was condemned for putting words into respondents' mouths. By asking "Who has power?" Hunter seemed to assert that someone did indeed "have power." Others questioned whether survey respondents' knowledge was a useful guide to the distribution of power in the first place; one might be documenting simply the prevailing myths of society. Hunter's response was partly to combine reputational research with a study of actual policy decisions in his later work, *Top Leadership USA* (1959). In addition, of course, stratification theorists could argue that the respondents were associational leaders whose appraisal of local influence patterns was akin to that of a panel of experts. Moreover, because people act in terms of their perceptions, reputation for power would lead to deference and accommodation; it would be self-fulfilling even if one were to grant a mythic element.

What is most striking about the emergence of stratification theory as an alternative paradigm, however, is not the methodological debate briefly highlighted above. What stands out is the relative *lack* of cross-disciplinary impact of stratification research. It was not until after publication of C. Wright Mills' *The Power Elite* (1956) that the debate was really joined. Between 1953 and 1956 research on group theory grew by a slow and eclectic process of accretion. Most works neither addressed Truman and Latham on the one hand, nor Hunter on the other, except occasionally, in passing. In keeping with the tone of Truman's *The Governmental Process,* students of group process favored the concrete and the untheoretical.

Empirical researchers concentrated on several issues, often coming to conclusions that severely revised the image of group politics presented earlier. One such issue was whether government was to be viewed as an arbiter among competing interest claims. Ralph Huitt, in a study of the House Committee on Banking and Currency, found that congressmen "were not sitting as arbiters of the group struggle, but as participants" (Huitt, 1954: 364). All groups fought in the name of the general interest, and congressmen fought alongside groups of their choosing. Similarly, Keefe found that political parties acted "in the capacity of pressure groups, advancing and opposing legislation and other legislative matters primarily on the basis of their effect upon the party organizations. In this respect, they hardly differ from the NAM, the CIO, or the American Legion" (Keefe, 1954: 462). Through findings such as these, group theorists increasingly reoriented their approach to emphasize governmental actors *as interests* in the group process, not arbiters. The media, of course, were viewed in the same way (Ferguson and Smuckler, 1954).

If agencies of state were but some among many political groups in society, as Laski had long before contended, then how could coordination be attained? What was the group theory of coordination? Out of these questions grew the interest in responsible party government, mentioned earlier (see Ranney, 1954). Advocates of responsible parties accepted the emerging group-theory description of American political process, but they believed group theory foundered on the prescriptive issue of coordination. Rather than trust the ultimate social rationality of group conflict, they sought order in party discipline.

A parallel and more influential course was charted by those who sought coordination through administrative regulation. Students of administration, noting Latham's work, recognized that greater attention had to be given to consideration of the role of groups in governmental process. But leading thinkers like Emmette Redford were concerned that the new focus on groups supplement, not supplant, traditional administrative orientations (Redford, 1954: 1104-1105). Rather than indicate ability to accept passively the group process, what group research seemed to show was the need for new administrative mechanisms that would give adequate attention to *inclusive* interests (Redford, 1954: 1113). Studies such as that of the steel industry (Stocking, 1954) were demonstrating the correctness of the group process *description* of American politics while underscoring the need for a new *prescriptive* theory that would address the social problems of government by group pressure. The more management-oriented American Society for Public Administration (ASPA) favored prescription along the lines of neutral competence of state administrators, while administrationists in the American Political Science Association (APSA) tended to prescribe a stronger executive institution (Kaufman, 1956: 1073). In either event, there was support for acceptance of the group theorists' description of politics, but also support for reforms to alter the evils it seemed to embody.

Thus the mid-1950s was not a period of simple acceptance of the group approach to political science. Rather, this was a time of intense interest in overcoming the problems of coordination posed by the newly reemphasized group-process approach. Walter Lippman was urging a revival of the philos-

ophy of public interest (Lippman, 1955). His condemnation
of moral relativism was by implication an attack on the early
group-theory view that government was merely one interest
among a morally equal many. Similarly, Louis Hartz's influential *The Liberal Tradition in America* (1955), in its documentation of an underlying American consensus on norms such
as freedom and equality, seemed to lay the basis for reasserting
the notions of a public morality and public interest. This seemed
all the more urgent as empirical group studies continued to
show the evils of unregulated group conflict and the need for
"constant, unrelenting search for the public interest" (Wengert,
1955: 66).

It was in this context that a major new work appeared in
stratification theory: C. Wright Mills's *The Power Elite* (1956).
While never widely accepted in political science, this work
by an American sociologist of Weberian persuasion served to
crystallize discussion of group theory. *The Power Elite* relied
on positional analysis (inferring the distribution of power
from the class distribution of governing positions) combined
with distributional analysis (inferring patterns of power from
the distribution of social benefits) to show an elitist image
of American politics. Its discussion of "the higher immorality"
in America was not so far removed from what others were
saying about the need for a revitalized public philosophy, but
Mills' sharp pen traced the inability to act in the public interest
not to mere passivity in the face of intense group pressures,
but to an active effort by elites to control the outcomes of major
decisions in their collective interest. Administrators and interest-
group leaders alike were portrayed as lesser operators at middle
levels of power.

The radical tone of Mills's work provoked sharp criticism.
Reviewing *The Power Elite* for the *American Political Science
Review,* H. Malcolm MacDonald castigated Mills' scholarship
as "absurdity," "over-exaggeration," and "labor(ing) points
well-known to most men" (MacDonald, 1956: 1168). Yet,
indicative of a dialogue in the ensuing decade in which the pro-

tagonists were to talk past each other continually, what was striking about this review was that, for all its vehemence, not a single point of empirical criticism was cited with which Mills might disagree. Rather, the tone of moderation was pitted against the tone of radical criticism. The confrontation of stratification theory with group theory and its variants (pluralism, decision-making theory, systems analysis) was to be a battle of ideological perspective, not really dependent on the fit of paradigms to evidence.

1956-1959: The Rise of Modern Pluralism

In the same year that *The Power Elite* appeared, Robert A. Dahl published *A Preface to Democratic Theory* (1956). Starting the following year and until 1959, Dahl and his associates undertook the decision-making study of New Haven that was to culminate in the pluralist classic, *Who Governs?* (1961). Pluralism was a reformulation of group theory. Unlike classic pluralism at the time of World War I, modern pluralism was not a defense of group autonomy from the state. Nor was it simply a revival of Bentley's physics of group forces or an equivalent to Truman's *The Governmental Process*. Pluralism's claim to be differentiated from earlier group theory lay in its perspective on governmental structure.

The difference was a subtle one. Earlier group theorists had emphasized the role of *groups* in democratic process. That is, the social (associational) structure of the nation was viewed by Lederer, for example, as the crucial factor differentiating democracy from fascism and communism. Dahl concurred with this in his view of democracy as government by minorities (groups) (Dahl, 1956: 133). But in an emphasis that contrasted with the group theorists, Dahl focused on the role of *government structure* in democratic process. After tracing the debate over Madisonian democracy and the compromises embodied in the checks and balances of the American system of government, Dahl concluded that an essential aspect of every polyarchal (pluralist) state was a system in which government machinery was divided and subdivided, a fragmented polity with "numerous groups of officials in competition and conflict with one another" (Dahl, 1956: 137). This, in turn, was grounded on an underlying social consensus on basic values and norms (Dahl, 1956: 135).

Where postwar group theory emphasized the fragmentation and conflict of public and private interests, it did not preclude the faith, so strongly rooted in the New Deal generation, that groups might be coordinated through a centralized, positive state (e.g., by administrative regulation or disciplined parties). Group theory was, of course, in tension with aspirations toward policy coordination and planning, but it could be treated, as Redford had done, as a body of literature helpfully indicating political obstacles to reform. Pluralism, in contrast, made a virtue of governmental fragmentation and the endless bargaining and compromise it involved. Comprehensive planning was viewed as a utopian ideal not compatible with the pluralist view of how American politics worked. Though pluralism and earlier postwar group theory were very similar in many respects, this difference in emphasis rendered pluralism far more conservative in its normative implications. Though the difference in emphasis seems to have been largely unrecognized at the time, it was sufficient to bring down on pluralist writers a far greater share of criticism.

On the other hand, the pluralist emphasis on the ultimate grounding of group politics in consensus on "the rules of the game" was compatible with the revived interest in public philosophy discussed earlier. Samuel H. Beer, for example, strongly criticized the group theorists for their neglect of political culture. Referring to group theory, Beer wrote, "The principal failing of such an approach is that by concentration upon groups and their diverse interests, it fails to direct analysis to the cultural context within which interests emerge and act. In the study of American and British politics, such neglect means passing over important elements of consensus which we shared throughout the political system and which involve not only 'rules of the game' but also positive social and political values" (Beer, 1956: 2). Specifically, Beer found that British political parties were not simply reflectors of group interests (admittedly strong and effective), but also were bearers of class values and carriers of the effects of thought and research (e.g., of the Fabian Society). What Beer was stating was not far removed from Dahl's belief that "The extent of consensus on the polyarchal norms, social training in the norms, consensus on policy alternatives, and political activity: the extent to which these and other conditions are present determines the viability of a polyarchy itself" (Dahl, 1956: 135).

Dahl's perspective on the role of value consensus was not, however, identical to that of advocates of public philosophy. Where discussion of a philosophy of public interest usually led into discussions of governmental action outside the realm of group pressures, Dahl viewed consensus on values as something that emerged from group process. Consensus was articulated through a decision-making process "made by endless bargaining" (Dahl, 1956: 150). Once formed, it set the parameters of government; consensus was viewed as the fundamental restraint on government and the basic protection of a democratic form of politics. In contrast, consensus in public philosophy was viewed as a sort of mandate to government to constrain group interests, not constrain the state. For the two schools of thought, the discussion of value consensus seemed similar in giving it paramount importance, but the perspectives with which consensus was approached differed fundamentally.

In a benchmark article titled " 'The Public Interest' in Administrative Decision-Making," Glendon A. Schubert (1957) outlined the views of these schools. On the one side he put the "administrative rationalists" and "administrative Platonists"; and the other, the "administrative realists," including the advocates of group theory and pluralism. The former included Emmette Redford (1952), an advocate of administrators' maximizing their ability to manipulate areas of pliability for community ideals, and Paul Appleby (1950), a spokesman for the view that administrators should inject consideration of public interests apart from the views pressed as being in the public interest by representatives of private interests. The latter included Bentley, Truman, and others in the group-theory tradition who tended to deny that any public interest existed apart from compromise emanating from group process (see Truman, 1951: 51). Schubert sided with these, defining the public interest as the "maximal accommodation of the affected interests in comparison with the relative capacities of alternative structures for making the same decisions" (Schubert, 1957: 368).

If the public interest was the social rationality emerging from group accommodation, it was not simply the interest of the strongest group. This was primarily because all actors in the group process were socialized to varying degrees of accept- ance of the prevailing political culture. This notion meshed with the theories of E. E. Schattschneider, an influential analyst of group process who had often been critical of Trumanesque group theory. "The important point about pressure politics," Schattschneider wrote, "is not that it is a conflict of private interests, but the fact that private conflicts are taken into the public domain. Pressure politics is therefore a stage in the socialization of conflict" (Schattschneider, 1957: 942). Dahl's pluralist version of group theory, therefore, differentiated itself from Truman's version by directing attention not only to group conflicts but to the socialization aspect of conflict as well. This was a perspec- tive then being popularized in sociology also through Lewis Coser's *The Functions of Social Conflict.* (1956).

A Preface to Democratic Theory and the pluralist theory it embodied thus represented a more subtle and convincing version of group theory. However, the continuing appeal of earlier paradigms, the proliferation of research in political science attending the mushrooming of the profession, and the conservative and therefore controversial implications of plural- ism itself combined to assure that interest-group research would not be unified under a pluralistic umbrella. First, traditionalists like Douglas Morgan (1957) scorned Dahl's work for its sci- entistic avoidance of ethical concerns (like the philosophy of the public interest). Second, even more radical thinkers now found a progressive virtue in reasserting that old juristic chestnut, the sovereignty of the state over the private interests in its domain (see Roelofs, 1957). This, of course, cast the state as the rational constrainer of selfish groups, not as the culture-constrained reflector/participant in group process. Third, more conservative theorists such as Andrew Hacker (1957) preferred to analyze politics at an individual rather than group level, often, as in Hacker's case, emphasizing the dangerous *lack* of socialization of newly risen political participants to thus-far prevailing norms. Fourth, the individualistic focus combined with rationalist assumptions about human nature provided the basis for Anthony Downs' *An Economic Theory of Democracy* (1957). Downs' focus on individual choice diverged sharply from group theory, and his predication of politics on assumptions of maximizing incumbency through rational, self-interested decisions left little room for the new, pluralist considerations of culture and socialization. And, fifth, at the other extreme, some students of group behavior were saying that the mutual accommodation that characterized group process went beyond socialization to virtual functional representation. As Beer noted of British interest-group politics, "Vocational pressure groups do not merely advise; they are regularly brought into the heart of the policy-making process" (Beer, 1957: 649). Similarly, Ehrmann's study of French interest groups concluded, "the state has veered uneasily between collaboration with and submission to the groups" (Ehrmann, 1957: 1147). These findings could be taken in two directions: corporatism, making a virtue of existing practice; or what Schubert had called "administrative Platonism," calling for reforms that would reassert state supremacy. In either event, the conclusions did not support pluralist theories of politics.

Even among those more sympathetic to group theory and pluralism, basic problems could be perceived from the start. Of the International Political Science Association round table on interest groups at the 1957 Pittsburgh meeting, David Truman observed, "uneasiness regarding concept and theory was perhaps the most recurrent theme" (Truman, 1959: 727). It is true that the Pittsburgh convention and Henry Ehrmann's subsequent anthology, *Interest Groups on Four Continents* (1958), plus Almond's 1958 *American Political Science Review* article signalled a short period of enthusiasm for comparative study of interest groups. But in practice, comparative research (e.g., Stewart, 1958) tended to show that groups played a much more modest role than might be supposed on the basis of group or pluralist theory.

Similarly, some areas of research on American interest groups yielded the same finding. Roger Hilsman wrote, for example, "In reaction to the emphasis on pressure politics that followed the discovery of lobbyists and their activities, an observer today might also recognize that Congress has a greater freedom in the field of foreign policy than is ordinarily supposed" (Hilsman, 1958: 727). Likewise, when Field Haviland, Jr., sought to analyze the foreign aid policy process in terms of the "group interests which animate Congress," the groups he found worth discussing were not interest groups in the normal sense, but blocs of senators who voted similarly for reasons of ideology and party.

If this was true of foreign affairs, might interest-group pressures also *not* be the critical variables in other areas of government as well? Various research results indicated this. Donald Matthews' study of the importance of institutional norms in moulding congressional behavior, for example, suggested that this, like ideology and party, was one more among a constellation of variables, including group pressures, that determined legislative outcomes (Matthews, 1959).

On the other side of the coin, Milbrath's study of lobbying as a profession highlighted a number of reasons why one might *not* expect this aspect of interest-group influence (the one most discussed) to be as important as earlier writing suggested. As professionals, Milbrath pointed out, lobbyists merchandised "points of view." To maintain credibiliy as professionals articulating a reasoned viewpoint, lobbyists avoided party activism or involvement in directly partisan affairs. They were not executives or members of the power structure. Rather, the lobbyists worked with limited resources to provide ammunition to congressmen already disposed toward their cause. Conversion of congressmen, much less their corruption, was a rarity. Instead of being the behind-the-scenes manipulators, lobbyists emerged from Milbrath's study as relatively circumscribed actors playing auxiliary roles, reacting to rather than dictating the agenda of government.

Rather than seek to maintain the integrity of pluralist theory in the face of these problems, however, leaders of the pluralist school were preoccupied elsewhere. By the late 1950s the center of this particular stage was occupied by the debate between the pluralists, grounded primarily in decision-making studies by political scientists, and the elitists, grounded in stratification studies by sociologists. Often, great energies were expended in this debate in attacking straw men while sidestepping other more important criticisms such as those discussed above; the majoritarian perspective that pluralism frustrated the ability to make democratically supported, comprehensive changes (Spitz, 1958); and that interest groups themselves were not even representative of their own members (McConnell, 1958).

Robert Dahl's "A Critique of the Ruling Elite Model" (1958) was a major statement typifying one end of this debate. Addressing the work of Hunter and Mills, Dahl attacked elite theories of politics on conceptual rather than empirical grounds. Granting that stratification research would inevitably reveal inequalities of power, Dahl speculated that the distribution of inequalities would be pluralistic: groups high in influence in one area would not be high in another. Moreover, groups with a high potential for influence might not effect their power (for example, because of a low potential for unity). To test this speculation, Dahl proposed that elite theorists clearly define their intended elite, sample cases in which the preferences of the hypothetical elite are counter to other contending groups, and determine whether the elite regularly prevails (Dahl, 1958: 466). That is, Dahl proposed that the distribution of power be studied through a decision-making approach of government.

The central problem of the decision-making approach from an elite-theory perspective was its inability to take into account subtle matters of political consciousness. For instance, seeming support or acquiescence regarding elite policy might reflect manipulative socialization or pragmatic role acceptance, not popular support for government decisions. Moreover, the decision-making approach was biased toward taking at face value the possibly self-serving and rationalized statements of value and motivation made by elite decision makers. The danger was not simply that conspiracies might lurk behind the scenes, but even more that the study of influence would be tied to subjective considerations (e.g., assessment of the value of decision goals to actors, judgment whether the actor influenced or altered his or her behavior from "that otherwise intended") rather than objectives (e.g., the effect of the decision on distribution of benefits). The decision-making approach thus left open the possibility that government decisions might enhance elite positions in effect, but in decision-making methodology be judged nonelitist because of motivational and value-preference considerations.

Then, too, the decision-making approach seemed geared to the study of government decisions, whereas elite theorists (mostly sociologists) were disinclined to interpret power as an affair of government. What government refrained from doing, letting the economic, educational, social, cultural, and other systems operate as they were, had far more impact on the distribution of benefits in society than what government did overtly.

Finally, the decision-making approach displayed a functionalist bias. By studying government decision makers in close detail, the researcher might be led to assign priority to the actors occupying the decision-making role. That is, the decision-making approach could degenerate into functional teleology. In each area of decision, those who are most involved (by reason of occupational function) are seen as dominant. The logic of pluralism is completed by emphasizing that the division of labor assures that different people will hold different

positions, spreading power among many people in many decision-making areas. Power is identified with role, and holding
power with role incumbency. Though elite theorists obviously
must grant that in American politics political decision-making
is fragmented among a large number of office holders, they
would not grant that this dispersion parallels power dispersion
as pluralists hypothesize. Rather, they contend, power of office
is a function of social forces veiled by the effects of socialization
of citizens *and* officials to elite values. Marx held that,
in every age, the values of the ruling class became the prevailing
social values. But if this were admitted into the elitist-pluralist
debate, as the elite theorists (e.g., Mills) wished, then the pluralists' finding, that decisions were concentrated in scattered
governmental offices, becomes inconsequential to the central
debate.

In addressing this point Dahl argued that the elitists' formulation of the problem of value socialization removed it from
the possibility of empirical falsification. If popular values were
always elite values manipulatively socialized, then the false
but apparent consensus could not be distinguished from genuine
consensus. But assuming something less than universal elite-mass
consensus, then, Dahl wrote, for these areas the decision-making
test was the appropriate one (Dahl, 1958: 468-469).

If American corporations and banks were taken as the locus
of the ruling elite most often posited in the literature, Dahl
argued in subsequent works (Dahl, 1959a: Dahl, 1959b) then
the few decision-making studies that had been undertaken
did not support elite-theory views. The major work in this
area, Gordon's *Business Leadership in the Large Corporation*
(1945), had belittled the importance of interlocking directors,
for example, contrary to elitist suppositions that such interlocks
unified the ruling class. Latham's study of basing-point legislation (Latham, 1952b) was, of course, already a mainstay of
pluralist literature. Even peak business organizations, such
as the National Association of Manufacturers (NAM) seemed,
upon empirical study, to be relatively weak (Gable, 1953).
If the elitists were correct about the dominance of American
politics by a corporate-based elite, where was the evidence?

Floyd Hunter, in *Top Leadership USA* (1959), attempted to provide such evidence for the elite-theory point of view. Partly this work replicated on a national scale Hunter's earlier reputational study of Atlanta, using interviews with interest-group leaders to assemble a list of the "top two hundred" influentials in terms of reputation for power. This methodology, scorned by most political scientists as self-confirming (Scoble, 1959: 1132), was supplemented by a decision-making study of a business-government decision—the textile tariff issue. Hunter found, conforming to elite-theory expectations, that, studied in the manner indicated by Dahl, the reputationally defined elite was at the center of decision-making.

Perhaps because written by a practitioner of another discipline, or perhaps because his work was too closely identified with the unpopular reputational approach, Hunter's work had surprisingly little impact on political science or group theory. This was true even though in method (decision-making cases) and substance (the political aspects of business) it was precisely the sort of study Dahl was faulting the elite theorists for failing to undertake. Nonetheless, Hunter's later work was omitted from discussion in later pluralist attacks on his elite theories of politics (e.g., see Polsby, 1960; Herson, 1961). As Hunter came to be remembered in terms of study of community rather than national power, and as a plethora of community power studies revealed a diversity of findings, it seemed plausible to discount stratification theory as represented by Hunter on two grounds: (1) that its reputational method biased its conclusions—decision-making methodology would lead to more pluralistic results; and (2) communities vary in the pluralism or elitism of their respective power structures (and Atlanta happened to fit in with elite theory expectations held by Hunter). As a consequence, Hunter's work fell into relative obscurity among political scientists in the 1960s.

*1960-1961: How, When an Intellectual Current
Crests, It Has Already Begun to Die*

As the stratification theories of Hunter and Mills fell into
neglect in the early 1960s, modern pluralism reached the height
of its influence upon political science. Like a wave, its impressive
crest was part of its foundering and eventual ebb. Of course,
critiques of Hunter and Mills continued to be published (e.g.,
see Bell, 1960), but the major thrust shifted in tone. The major
pluralist statements of 1960 and 1961 were culminations of
research and debate a half-decade in preparation. Confident
in presentation, these works presented pluralism as a comprehensive political theory grounded in extensive empirical research. Robert Dahl's *Who Governs?* (1961) became the classic
representative of this phase of group theory, championing
the pluralist variant, but works by such scholars as Schubert,
Golembiewski, and Banfield were similar in perspective.

Schubert, in *The Public Interest: A Critique of the Theory
of a Political Concept* (1960), surveyed approximately 150
authors writing between 1930 and 1960. In this survey, the
development of political science was portrayed in terms of
the ascendancy of the "Realists" (e.g., group theorists) over
the "Rationalists" (those using the normative concept of the
public interest to justify regulation of group interests through
such devices as strong executive regulation, disciplined parties,
or popular participation) and "Idealists" (those emphasizing
the higher law of individual conscience as a safeguard against
selfish, group and party pressures). In this imagery, group
theory and pluralism emerged as realistic, avoiding the simplisms
of the rationalists or the unscientific sentimentalism of the
idealists. Moreover, the new group theory was portrayed as
the culmination of an intellectual process, remedying previous
faults. The categories used in Schubert's analysis of political
science seemed to indicate mere refinement of the new theories,
not their displacement by yet other paradigms. Rather, Schubert's works suggested that at last the theoretical groundwork
had been laid for a realistic and scientific approach to the study
of politics.

Similarly, Golembiewski defended group theory in terms of its scientific utility. Whatever faults Bentley may have had, Golembiewski argued, his work was a call to reorient the discipline around political analysis rather than political philosophy (Golembiewski, 1960: 962). Bentley had been interested in empirical theory in the modern sense. If Bentley had been oversold, he had seen his own work merely as preliminary. And, he had laid the basis for a scientific paradigm in political science. What his work and subsequent refinements of group theories of politics, including pluralism, made possible was a disciplinary transition to a new stage. It was now possible, Golembiewski proclaimed, to concentrate on a new theoretical need—not the formulation of a scientific paradigm (the basis for this was accomplished), but rather the next stage, the formulation of nominal and operational definitions of concepts (Golembiewski, 1960: 970). Banfield's *Political Influence* (1961), describing Chicago politics in terms of pluralism in the sense of dispersion of power and decentralization of decision-making, was published the following year, providing just such extensive and comprehensive attention to the definition of terms surrounding the study of political power.

Robert Dahl's *Who Governs?* (1961) thus appeared in the context of great expectations. Its publication was long anticipated as the first major community-power study providing an alternative to elite-premised stratification research. More important, Dahl and his associates at Yale had become central to a new approach to political science. *Who Governs?* was received as a text on political science as a discipline, not merely one more community power study.

Heinz Eulau, reviewing *Who Governs?* for the *American Political Science Review,* hailed it in just such a light. "For decades," Eulau wrote, "it has been fashionable to blame the practices of democratic politics rather than the theory for what were more or less vaguely felt as lasting shortcomings." (Eulau, 1962: 144). Dahl avoided this "trap" by redefining democracy to conform to America's politics of high fragmentation, reciprocal bargaining, and rival sovereignties. This redefinition emasculated that aspect of democratic theory that had undergirded a recurrent reform impetus (Bachrach, 1967; Pateman, 1970). At the same time, however, its empiricist orientation blended with behaviorism's rejection of normative theory. Dahl pronounced behaviorism a success, particularly as shaped by Truman (Dahl, 1961b: 766) and a group approach.

Pluralism and the group theory of politics rested on an insecure footing, however, and the hailing of its advent was matched by the din of criticism. This criticism had already caused Truman to disclaim his work as a basis for a general group theory of politics. Rather, he now wrote, it merely attempted "to examine interest groups and their role in the formal institutions of government in order to provide an adequate basis for evaluating their significance in the American political process" (Truman, 1960: 494; see also Truman, 1951: 505). The group approach was not a theory explaining the complexity of American politics, merely a useful entry point.

Truman was undoubtedly correct in his assessment of the state of group theory. Group theory, including pluralism, *was* more an orientation than a theory in the scientific sense of predictive capacity. Though a common theme (the fragmentation and decentralization of power) united group theorists, on many fundamental points there were differences. Indeed, most scholars eschewed the labels of "group theorist" or "pluralist" even when their work centered on this theme. There was little theoretical uniformity or cohesiveness.

For example, though Banfield's work took up the theme of decentralization of politics in Chicago in much the same manner that Dahl and his associates were doing in New Haven, Banfield's analytic gloss on essentially similar, factual findings was very different. Banfield portrayed Chicago politics resting not on group conflicts but on the drive of institutional leaders for self-preservation. Moreover, Banfield viewed the decision-making process whereby officials select among alternatives, using a concept of the public interest paramount over group interests, as an advantageous system not to be downgraded as Schubert suggested.

Similarly, other scholars attempting to apply a pluralistic, group approach found cause for reservation. Harry Eckstein, for example, undertook an insightful study of the British Medical Association in his *Pressure Group Politics* (1960), using the group approach as an analytic framework. While Eckstein found this framework heuristically useful, he noted its utility was greatest under a specific range of conditions. Group activity, he found, was greatest (and group analysis most pertinent) when issues centered on the contest of narrow technical policies in the context of basic agreement on underlying broader issues. That is, as Eckstein emphasized, the group approach was most valuable precisely when, from the point of view of democratic theory, it mattered least whether group influence was important!

Pluralism, in the sense of fragmentation of government structure (and power, contradicting elite theory), was *not* at issue. Numerous works in this period underlined the correctness of the new group theory in this regard (e.g., see Sayre and Kaufman, 1960). Most scholars, including those outside the group approach, could agree on this point. Andrew Hacker, for instance, documented the high circulation of the corporate elite and its social separation from political elites, contrary to the elite-theory image of a centralized merger of top business and top government (Hacker, 1961). Moreover, the emphasis by the pluralists on pragmatic factors of power was welcomed by many as a highly desirable counter to the abstractions of functionalism, game theory, and other scholastic exercises (see Wormuth, 1961).

The pluralist paradigm came under attack on other grounds: that it erred in its benign assessment of the group process and its cavalier dispensing with the public-interest concept; that groups were, in point of fact, much less important than pluralist imagery suggested; and that pluralist theory was not truly theory at all, and, therefore, was not a basis for a scientific approach to the study of political events. The wave of criticism on these grounds in the early 1960s, combined with the academic radicalization of the late 1960s, dealt the pluralist position blows from which it never recovered. Though lingering on as a description of fragmented politics contrasting with elite theory, pluralism's decline prefigured an onslaught of proposed new paradigms (e.g., communications theory, game theory, public-choice theory, rational-decision-making theory, phenomenology, and so forth) that were to splinter the discipline further without taking on half the influence of group theory.

The charge that normal group process was anything but benign was a position taken in a solid chain of political science literature stretching back into the nineteenth century. Typical was Philip Foss's *Politics and Grass* (1960), showing a "monopolitical" pattern in which entrenched economic interests lacked any significant competition in their attempt, largely successful, to dominate government policy in areas of concern to them. In a much more influential work, Robert Engler described the politics of the oil industry as a form of "private government," making the concept of the rule of law a mere myth and giving rise to the need for regulation in the public interest (Engler, 1961). The public-interest concept was then, moreover, a matter of high interest and popular support, pluralism notwithstanding, as evidenced by the work of the President's Commission on National Goals (1960). Of course, this commission was spawned by the Eisenhower administration and, therefore, tended not to be taken seriously by the pluralists, who were overwhelmingly liberal in persuasion. But this, in itself, was significant.

Liberalism was in crisis on this point, Henry Kariel argued in his modern classic, *The Decline of American Pluralism* (1961). In this work Kariel contrasted the traditional liberal vision of centralization, hierarchical accountability, and even nationalization with the pluralist vision of postwar liberals. This vision brought liberalism into crisis as private interests took on ever more public functions without being subjected to correspondingly meaningful public accountability. The decline of representative government was a function of the loss of power to the private power of corporations and unions. To bless this trend with the legitimacy of postwar liberal attitudes, such as those of pluralism, was to abdicate the essential responsibilities of democratic government.

A second line of criticism of pluralism was equally influential in its decline, but, ironically, was itself in more than a little tension with the public interest criticisms just outlined. This was the argument that interest groups were scarcely as important as pluralist theorists (much less those concerned with reasserting the public interest vis-a-vis selfish interests and pressures) had portrayed them. Donald Matthew's widely discussed work, *U.S. Senators and Their World* (1960), for example, emphasized the discretion of political decision makers. "You know, that's an amazing thing," Matthews quoted a senator. "I hardly ever see a lobbyist. I don't know—maybe they think I'm a poor target, but I seldom see them. During this entire natural gas battle (in which he was a prominent figure) I was not approached by either side" (Matthews, 1960: 177).

Similarly, John Wahlke and his associates found that state legislators saw themselves as being above the group process. Political culture, not direct group pressures, was the critical factor (Wahlke, Buchanan, Eulau and Ferguson, 1960). And in a study of bureaucrats, Joseph LaPalombara found that, not only did they continually explain their actions in terms of a national interest concept, but they also played a far more active role in the group process than one might expect on the basis of group theory. "The bureaucrat also tends to develop certain skills," he noted, "that permit him to manipulate the interest groups and to play them off against each other for his own purposes. It is for this reason that administrators often welcome group clienteles and, where such do not exist, will seek to create them" (LaPalombara, 1960: 48). LaPalombara went on to condemn group theory as "simplistic" in its attempt to account for political behavior in terms of interest-group conflict.

It might well be argued that these criticisms, while applicable against certain aspects of group theory, were misrepresentations if applied to pluralism. Dahl, for example, *did* discuss the active role of bureaucrats and politicians in the group process and *did* emphasize the importance of political culture as an intervening variable of critical importance. Thus, when the group approach fell under heavy attack in 1960, pluralist theory might be viewed as being something apart. Certainly Truman, Bentley, and group theory of a decade earlier took the brunt of criticism. But if pluralism was to be disassociated from group theory, what was left? What remained after the discrediting of group theory was pluralism not as a theory of political behavior, but merely pluralism in the sense of fragmentation of power, the importance of numerous power-related variables (not just groups, but culture, socialization, psychology, and virtually any other variable), and the decision-making method of studying politics.

In a 1960 symposium on "Bentley Revisited," the *American Political Science Review* published the strongest and most comprehensive attacks on group theory up to that time. The core argument of these articles was that group theory was not a true theory in the scientific sense, and that the great expectations of refounding political science on it were misguided.

"The failure of group theory to serve as an adequate guide to research," Stanley Rothman wrote, "is the result both of the logical inconsistencies of its propositions and its inability to explain what is purports to explain" (Rothman, 1960: 15). Building on Odegard's earlier criticism of the vagueness of group theory (Odegard, 1958), Rothman emphasized the core imprecision of group theory. Herring, Latham, and Truman, he noted, were referring to groups not just as interest groups, but as categoric groups (e.g., Jews, alcoholics) and, even, potential (unorganized) groups. As far as organized, group membership went, evidence by Wright and Hyman (1958) suggested, contrary to Truman, that Americans were not notably joiners, and groups seemed to affect their attitudes little.

More important, the notion of potential groups tended to render group theory tautological. Political attitudes are explained on the basis of group affiliations, but the pattern of group forces in a society is explained by the underlying pattern of potential groups, which in turn are based on categorical attributes, notably, shared attitudes. "In fact the whole concept of potential groups acts as a sort of *deus ex machina* which can be brought in for any purpose," Rothman observed. "Why are British trade unions socialist? Strong socialist potential group. Why did the Germans prefer a strong authoritarian regime? Strong authoritarian potential group. It can explain everything, but fundamentally it explains nothing" (Rothman, 1960: 23). Consequently, in *The Governmental Process*'s empirical sections, Truman rarely used a specifically *group* explanation for behavior. Rather, though groups are repeatedly referred to, Truman's work is built around a variety of types of political explanation: group theory, economic causation (e.g., Truman, 1951: 53, 67), individual-level analysis, to name a few.

This should bring us back to the question, "What *is* a group explanation of political behavior?" In simple and direct form, as expressed in Arthur F. Bentley's *The Process of Government* (1908), the group theory states that "all interests and all potential interests are a part of the governing process, since each interest is represented in proportion to its pressure" (Hale, 1960: 960). This "physics of group forces," by treating government decisions as a function of interest pressures, assumes an essentially neutral or "umpire" state. The government can never be charged with acting outside the "public interest"; one only may wish that groups other than those prevailing would exert more pressure.

Like most strong social theories on which prediction may be based, Bentleyan physics is a simple model of reality. It is also a profoundly conservative one, expelling not only the notion of the public interest, but also the very possibility that government might engage in long-range acts of foresight that transcend the pressures of the moment. Most social scientists would probably prefer a theory of government that gave greater discretion to decision makers, partly because one may judge this normatively to be beneficial to society, and partly because the acknowledgment of discretion makes better empirical theory. Government officials, as noted earlier, in fact do not act in terms of the physics of group forces. Bentley himself acknowledged this, as Hale has noted (Hale, 1960: 960), in his frequent assertions (Bentley, 1908: 301, 358-359, 449-458) that American government was out of balance with group forces and, hence, in need of reform. Given Bentley's theory in simple form, group theory made impossible such imbalance. To call for "rebalancing" was to call for government decisions on a nongroup basis. With this, Bentley implicitly sabotaged the shorings of the group basis of politics.

Recognizing the simplistic implications of pure Bentley, David Truman, although giving great honor to Bentley, rather clearly avoided a physics-of-group-forces model. Another critic, R. E. Dowling, asked in this context, "What, then, is his (Truman's) avowed debt to Bentley? It is, I suggest, little more than a realization that interest groups are 'very important' in the political process and that a lot of attention should be given to them" (Dowling, 1960: 951). But in avoiding Bentley's sometime simplicity, Truman presented no clear alternative. To say that the group process was an integral part of the political process was something deserving emphasis, but it fell far short of constituting theory in a predictive sense. One could not predict government outcomes as the resultant vector of opposing group forces, empirically measured. By introducing a more comprehensive view, emphasizing potential groups, economic factors, and various other variables, Truman's work better described the political process than did Bentley's. But, as Dowling argued pointedly, this was "a bit of very naive methodology." Truman "does not see that the *merit* of a 'group interpretation' of politics (meaning by that a Bentleyan methodology) would, if it were worked out, be precisely that it does 'leave something out' " (Dowling, 1960: 953).

The Passage of an Idea

Group theory and pluralism were not "rebutted" by the arguments just discussed. In a peculiar way, it did not matter if it was true that these ideas, which purported to represent a revolutionary new paradigm for a reconstructed political science, did not add up to scientific theory in the predictive sense. Or, that interest groups and lobbying might not be as important as initially portrayed. Or, even, that group theory was imbued with conservative implications at a time when practitioners in the discipline continued to see the urgent need for a reassertion of the "public interest" over transitory, selfish interests of the day.

What brought group and pluralist theory to a peak by the late 1950s and early 1960s was more a matter of mood and imagery than of science and evidence. Group and pluralist theorists were working neither inductively from comprehensively selected case observations, nor deductively from general principles of political behavior. Rather, their work sought to present a description of American politics sharply at variance with the pessimistic image put forward by elite theorists. At the same time, they were attempting to present a vocabulary of political analysis that contrasted with class-analytic terms without degenerating into traditional, uninspired institutionalism. Group and pluralist theories served a powerful purpose, as Leiserson, quoted earlier, noted: to provide an orienting framework to which a host of new studies and theories could be attached. The common theme was that American stability might be attributed to a rich, complex, and pluralistic pattern of interaction of groups, individuals, and strata in the context of a culturally legitimated, fragmented polity.

American political science, however, is as fragmented and pluralistic as that which it seeks to explain. Even at the height of its influence, the group approach was not dominant. Most studies of groups did not use a group- or pluralist-theory vocabulary to any significant degree (e.g., Block, 1960; MacKinnon, 1960; Lenczowski, 1960; Harbrecht, 1960). Those that did frequently arrived at conclusions inconsistent with the group approach (e.g., Foss, 1960; Engler, 1961; Wilson, 1961). More importantly, alternative (e.g., developmentalism—Deutsch, 1961) and contradictory (e.g., symbolic action—Edelman, 1960) paradigms were continually proposed, each attracting their own coteries of adherents and promoting new frameworks for discourse without explicitly confronting and rejecting earlier paradigms.

The fascinating process whereby ideas evolve in political science has little to do with "scientific revolutions" and the rational confrontation of paradigms popularized by Kuhn's work. Group theory after World War II did not spring fully grown from the womb of science, nor did it hatch from a Bentleyan egg unearthed by David Truman. The language and imagery of the group approach, rather, is rooted deeply in American political thought and may be traced back to Calhoun and Madison. The specific, Trumanesque revival of group theory emerged, moreover, from the wartime mood of consensus and the ideological defense of democracy against fascism, communism, and other elite conceptions of the state.

While serving an ideological function, the emphasis in the group approach upon the pragmatic and empirical also seemed to justify its identification with a more empirical, behavioral, and even scientific approach to the study of politics. This was compatible with the anti-ideological mood in social science following World War II, and with the "end of ideology" proclaimed by Bell, Lipset, and others.

The Governmental Process, Truman's classic postwar reformulation of the group approach, was a work of tone, not paradigmatic science. When Truman raised a framework to contrast with the group approach, he chose to deal with institutionalism. The institutionalist "paradigm," however, had long since passed from the scene (see Garson, 1974). It was, in short, a straw man. More serious, alternative paradigms, such as Marxism and elite theory, were largely ignored. There was no confrontation of paradigm with paradigm, evidence with evidence. Indeed, most specific group studies, then and later, continually came to conclusions inconsistent with Truman's work (e.g., showing the dangers of group process unregulated by a strong public interest in some areas, the importance of a public interest concept to decision makers, and the relative lack of impact of interest groups on political outcomes in other areas).

All of this might lead one to judge that, if the rational (scientific paradigm) explanation of the passage of ideas in political science is mistaken, perhaps a social explanation would fare better. That is, perhaps group theory would be interpreted better as an idea whose time had been prepared by sociopolitical events. Certainly this was *not* true in terms of the enduring importance of the public interest concept in scholarship on the group process. On the other hand, the revival of group theory *was* timely. As mentioned, it fit in with the postwar mood of consensus, anti-ideological pragmatism, and moderation.

Associations with fascism and communism had delegitimized elite theories, and group theory filled a relative void at a time when the discipline was again hearing strong calls to emulate scientific frameworks.

If the shift of political science ideas seemed faddish, each author seeking the psychological satisfaction of being the first to set forth the basic outlines for analysis, it is also true that there were many who endeavored to build upon the works of Truman and Dahl. Not infrequently, the laborers in this particular vineyard, like Eckstein, eventually came to conclusions emphasizing the limits of the group approach. But there was continuity of research, from Truman's restatement of the theory, to Dahl's formulation of the pluralist variant, to the drive to put group research on a comparative basis (Ehrmann, Almond), to Dahl's influential *Who Governs?* in 1961. If the diversity of the discipline allowed for the continual assertion of new frameworks (systems analysis, the economic theory of democracy, developmentalism), those identified with the group approach were not advocates of a faddish succession of frameworks.

The very development of group theory, however, contributed to its eventual decline. It is striking that the articulation of group theory, including pluralism, led to a "revolution of rising expectations." Truman's work, conceived as a descriptive exploration of the relation of group process to politics, was later cited as a classic exposition of paradigmatic theory. That Truman later disavowed such would-be accolades for his work is less important than that it, like Dahl's pluralism, came to represent a "theory" that could be counterposed to others, notably to elite theory. Once this expectation was established, it was then possible to attack group theory for failing to meet the expected standard: it could not be used as a basis for predictive scientific theory because group process was both less important and less benign than portrayed by Truman, Dahl, and other group theorists. The "golden rule" of social science was at work: as Truman had interpreted institutionalism as a straw man and foil for the group approach, now the theoretical expectations placed upon the group approach distorted its nature to serve similar purposes of other scholars.

As David Apter has noted, pluralism drew directly on the inheritance of institutionalism and it, was itself, interpretable as a form of elite theory (Apter, 1977: 374-375). The jurists and later institutionalists were concerned with questions such as the role of groups in the state; and all critics of group theory, such as Bachrach, accepted the pluralist description of American politics. The pluralists were concerned both to emphasize the jurists' central theme of the responsibility of the governor to the good of the governed, and to emphasize elite theory's central theme of the inevitability of hierarchy and the determining role of leadership in politics. Most critics of pluralism (e.g., Bachrach, Kariel, Pateman) dissented on grounds of normative theory, not empirical theory. But even here an artificial dichotomy was set up by the critics, portraying the group approach as merely a rosy rationale for the status quo, defining away the need for democratic reform. In fact, the concerns of the pluralists for the reform of democracy, such as community size and structure as prerequisites for the ideal democratic polity (Dahl and Tufte, 1973; Dahl, 1967) and workplace democracy (Dahl, 1970), were not so different from the concerns of the critics. These communalities became observable in retrospect only, however. At the time, there seemed to be a world of difference.

REFERENCES

ALMOND, G. A. (1946) "Politics, Science, and Ethics," *American Political Science Review,* Vol. 40, No. 2 (April): 283-293.

——— (1958) "Comparative Study of Interest Groups," *American Political Science Review,* Vol. 52, No. 1 (March): 270-282.

APPLEBY, P. H. (1950a) "Political Science, The Next 25 Years," *American Political Science Review,* Vol. 44, No. 4 (December): 924-932.

——— (1950b) *Morality and Administration in Democratic Government.* Baton Rouge: Univ. of Louisiana Press.

APSA Committee on Political Parties (1950) "Toward a More Responsible Two-Party System," *American Political Science Review,* Vol. 44, No. 3, Part 2 (supplement, September): 1-99.

APTER, D. (1977) *Introduction to Political Analysis.* Cambridge, Mass.: Winthrop Publishers.

BACHRACH, P. (1967) *The Theory of Democratic Elitism: A Critique.* Boston: Little, Brown.

BAILEY, S. K. (1950) *Congress Makes a Law: The Story Behind the Employment Act of 1946.* New York: Columbia Univ. Press.

BANFIELD, E. (1961) *Political Influence.* New York: Free Press.

BEER, S. H. (1956) "Pressure Groups and Parties in Britain," *American Political Science Review,* Vol. 50, No. 1 (March): 1-23.

——— (1957) "Representation of Interests in British Government: Historical Background," *American Political Science Review,* Vol. 51, No. 3 (September): 613-650.

BELL, D. (1960) *The End of Ideology.* Glencoe, Ill.: Free Press.

BENTLEY, A. (1908) *The Process of Government: A Study of Social Pressures.* Bloomington, Ind.: Principia Press.

BLOCK, W. J. (1960) *The Separation of the Farm Bureau and the Extension Service.* Urbana: Univ. of Illinois Press.

BOORSTIN, D. J. (1953) *The Genius of American Politics.* Chicago: Univ. of Chicago Press.

BURNS, J. M. (1953) Review of Latham (1952b) in *American Political Science Review,* Vol. 47, No. 1 (March): 236.

COSER, L. A. (1956) *The Functions of Social Conflict.* Glencoe, Ill.: Free Press.

DAHL, R. A. (1956) *A Preface to Democratic Theory.* Chicago: Univ. of Chicago Press.

——— (1958) "A Critique of the Ruling Elite Model," *American Political Science Review,* Vol. 52, No. 2 (June): 463-469.

——— (1959a) "Business and Politics: A Critical Appraisal of Political Science," *American Political Science Review,* Vol. 53, No. 1 (March): 1-34.

——— (1961a) *Who Governs?: Democracy and Power in an American City.* New Haven: Yale Univ. Press.

——— (1961b) "The Behavioral Approach in Political Science: Epitaph to a Monument to a Successful Protest," *American Political Science Review,* Vol. 55, No. 4 (December): 763-772.

——— (1967) "The City in the Future of Democracy," *American Political Science Review,* Vol. 61, No. 4 (December): 953-970.

——— (1970) *After the Revolution?: Authority in a Good Society.* New Haven: Yale Univ. Press.

DAHL, R. A., M. HAIRE, and P. F. LAZARSFELD (1959b) *Social Science Research on Business: Product and Potential.* New York: Columbia Univ. Press.

DAHL, R. A. and C. E. LINDBLOM (1953) *Politics, Economics and Welfare.* New York: Harper.

DAHL, R. A. and E. R. TUFTE (1973) *Size and Democracy.* Stanford: Stanford Univ. Press.

DEUTSCH, K. (1961) "Social Mobilization and Political Development," *American Political Science Review,* Vol. 55, No. 3 (September): 493-514.

DILLON, M. E. (1942) "Pressure Groups," *American Political Science Review,* Vol. 36, No. 3 (June): 471-481.

DOWLING, R. E. (1960) "Pressure Group Theory: Its Methodological Range," *American Political Science Review,* Vol. 54, No. 4 (December): 944-954.

DOWNS, A. (1957) *An Economic Theory of Democracy.* New York: Harper.

DUVERGER, M. (1951) *Les Partis Politiques.* Paris: Librairie Armand Colin.

EASTON, D. (1953) *The Political System: An Inquiry into the State of Political Science.* New York: Knopf.

ECKSTEIN, H. (1961) *Pressure Group Politics.* Stanford: Stanford Univ. Press.

EDELMAN, M. (1960) "Symbols and Political Quiescence," *American Political Science Review,* Vol. 54, No. 3 (September): 695-704.

EHRMANN, H. W. (1957) *Organized Business in France.* Princeton: Princeton Univ. Press.

――― ed. (1958) *Interest Groups on Four Continents.* Pittsburgh: Univ. of Pittsburgh Press.

ENGLER, R. (1961) *The Politics of Oil.* New York: Macmillan.

EULAU, H. (1962) Review of Dahl (1961a) in *American Political Science Review,* Vol. 56, No. 1 (February): 144-145.

FERGUSON, L. and R. SMUCKLER (1954) *Politics in the Press: An Analysis of Press Content in 1952 Senatorial Campaigns.* East Lansing: Governmental Research Bureau, Michigan State College.

FINER, H. (1945) "Towards a Democratic Theory," *American Political Science Review,* Vol. 39, No. 2 (April): 249-256.

FOSS, P. O. (1960) *Politics and Grass.* Seattle: Univ. of Washington Press.

FRIEDRICH, C. J. (1945) Review of Hayek (1944) in *American Political Science Review,* Vol. 39, No. 3 (June): 579.

GABLE, R. W. (1953) "NAM: Influential Lobby or Kiss of Death?" *Journal of Politics,* Vol. 15, No. 2 (May): 254-273.

GALBRAITH, J. K. (1952) *American Capitalism: The Concept of Countervailing Power.* Boston: Houghton Mifflin.

GARCEAU, O. (1951) "Research in the Political Process," *American Political Science Review,* Vol. 45, No. 1 (March): 69-85.

GARSON, G. D. (1974) "On the Origins of Interest-Group Theory: A Critique of a Process," *American Political Science Review,* Vol. 68, No. 4 (December): 1505-1519.

GOLEMBIEWSKI, R. T. (1960) " 'The Group Basis of Politics': Notes on Analysis and Development," *American Political Science Review,* Vol. 54, No. 4 (December): 962-971.

GORDON, R. A. (1945) *Business Leadership in the Large Corporation.* Berkeley: Univ. of California Press.

GRIFFITH, E. S. (1951) *Congress: Its Contemporary Role.* New York: New York Univ. Press.

GROSS, B. (1950) Review of Bentley (1908) in *American Political Science Review,* Vol. 44, No. 3 (September): 742-748.

HACKER, A. (1957) "Liberal Democracy and Social Control," *American Political Science Review,* Vol. 51, No. 4 (December): 1009-1026.

――― (1961) "The Elected and The Anointed: Two American Elites," *American Political Science Review,* Vol. 55, No. 3 (September): 539-549.

HALE, M. Q. (1960) "The Cosmology of Arthur F. Bentley," *American Political Science Review,* Vol. 54, No. 4 (December): 955-961.

HALLOWELL, J. H. (1944) "Politics and Ethics," *American Political Science Review,* Vol. 38, No. 4 (August): 639-655.

HARBRECHT, P. P. (1959) *Pension Funds and Economic Power.* New York: Twentieth Century Fund.

HARDIN, C. (1952) *The Politics of Agriculture: Soil Conservation and the Struggle for Power in Rural America.* Glencoe, Ill.: Free Press.

HARTZ, L. (1955) *The Liberal Tradition in America: An Interpretation of American Political Thought Since the Revolution.* New York: Harcourt, Brace.

HAVILAND, F. F., Jr. (1958) "Foreign Aid and the Policy Process: 1957" *American Political Science Review*, Vol. 52, No. 3 (September): 689-725.

HERRING, E. P. (1940) *The Politics of Democracy*. New York: W. W. Norton.

HERSON, L.J.R. (1961) "In the Footsteps of Community Power," *American Political Science Review*, Vol. 55, No. 4 (December): 817-830.

HILSMAN, R. (1958) "Congressional-Executive Relations and the Foreign Policy Consensus," *American Political Science Review*, Vol. 52, No. 3 (September): 725-744.

HUITT, R. K. (1954) "The Congressional Committee: A Case Study," *American Political Science Review*, Vol. 48, No. 2 (June): 340-365.

HUNTER, F. (1953) *Community Power Structure: A Study of Decision-Makers*. Chapel Hill: Univ. of North Carolina Press.

——— (1959) *Top Leadership USA*. Chapel Hill: Univ. of North Carolina Press.

KARIEL, H. S. (1961) *The Decline of American Pluralism*. Stanford: Stanford Univ. Press.

KAUFMAN, H. (1956) "Emerging Conflicts in the Doctrines of Public Administration," *American Political Science Review*, Vol. 50, No. 4 (December): 1057-1073.

KEEFE, W. J. (1954) "Parties, Partisanship, and Public Policy in the Pennsylvania Legislature," *American Political Science Review*, Vol. 48, No. 2 (June): 450-464.

KNAPPEN, M. (1950) "Shipping Quotas and the Military Assistance Program," *American Political Science Review*, Vol. 44, No. 4 (December): 933-941.

KUHN, T. (1970) *The Structure of Scientific Revolutions, Second Edition*. Chicago: Univ. of Chicago Press.

LAPALOMBARA, J. (1960) "The Utility and Limitations of Interest Group Theory in Non-American Field Situations," *Journal of Politics*, Vol. 22, No. 1 (February): 29-49.

LASSWELL, H. D. and A. KAPLAN (1950) *Power and Society: A Framework for Political Inquiry*. New Haven: Yale Univ. Press.

LATHAM, E. (1952a) "The Group Basis of Politics: Notes for a Theory," *American Political Science Review*, Vol. 46, No. 2 (June): 376-397.

——— (1952b) *The Group Basis of Politics: A Study in Basing-Point Legislation*. Ithaca: Cornell Univ. Press.

LEDERER, E. (1940) *State of the Masses: The Threat of the Classless Society*. New York: W. W. Norton.

LEISERSON, A. (1951) Review of Truman (1951) in *American Political Science Review*, Vol. 45, No. 4 (December): 1192-1193.

LIPPMAN, W. (1955) *Essays in the Public Philosophy*. Boston: Little, Brown.

LIPSET, S. M. (1960) *Political Man*. Garden City, N.Y.: Doubleday.

McCONNELL, G. (1958) "The Spirit of Private Government," *American Political Science Review*, Vol. 52, No. 3 (September): 754-770.

MacDONALD, H. M. (1956) Review of Mills (1956) in *American Political Science Review*, Vol. 50, No. 4 (December): 1168.

MacIVER, R. M. (1947) *The Web of Government*. New York: Macmillan.

McLEAN, J. (1945) "Areas for Postwar Research," *American Political Science Review*, Vol. 39, No. 4 (August): 741-757.

MacMAHON, A. (1948) "Conflict, Consensus, Confirmed Trends, and Open Choices," *American Political Science Review*, Vol. 42, No. 1 (February): 1-15.

MASON, A. T. (1950) "Business Organized as Power: The New Imperium in Imperio," *American Political Science Review*, Vol. 44, No. 2 (June): 323-342.

MATTHEWS, D. (1959) "The Folkways of the U.S. Senate: Conformity to Group Norms and Legislative Effectiveness," *American Political Science Review,* Vol. 53, No. 4 (December): 1064-1089.

—— (1960) *U.S. Senators and Their World.* Vintage.

MILBRATH, L. W. (1958) "The Political Party Activity of Washington Lobbyists," *Journal of Politics,* Vol. 20, No. 2 (May): 339-352.

MILLS, C. W. (1956) *The Power Elite.* New York: Oxford Univ. Press.

MORGAN, D. (1957) "A Postscript to Professor Dahl's 'Preface'," *American Political Science Review,* Vol. 51, No. 4 (December): 1040-1052.

MORGENTHAU, H. J. (1952) Review of Lasswell and Kaplan (1950), *American Political Science Review,* Vol. 46, No. 1 (March): 232-233.

NISBET, R. A. (1953) *The Quest for Community: A Study in the Ethics of Order and Freedom.* New York: Oxford Univ. Press.

ODEGARD, P. H. (1958) "A Group Basis of Politics: A New Name for an Old Myth," *Western Political Quarterly,* Vol. 11, No. 3 (September): 689-702.

PARSONS, T. (1951) *The Social System.* Glencoe, Ill.: Free Press.

PATEMAN, C. (1970) *Participation and Democratic Theory.* Cambridge, England: Cambridge Univ. Press.

POLSBY, N. W. (1960) "How to Study Community Power: The Pluralist Alternative," *Journal of Politics,* Vol. 22, No. 3 (August): 474-484.

President's Commission on National Goals (1960) *Goals for Americans.* Englewood Cliffs, N.J.: Prentice-Hall.

RANNEY, A. (1954) *The Doctrine of Responsible Party Government: Its Origins and Present State.* Urbana: Univ. of Illinois Press.

REDFORD, E. (1952) *Administration of National Economic Control.* New York: Macmillan.

—— (1954) "The Protection of the Public Interest With Special Reference to Administrative Regulation," *American Political Science Review,* Vol. 48, No. 4 (December): 1103-1113.

ROELOFS, H. M. (1957) *The Tension of Citizenship: Private Man and Public Duty.* New York: Rinehart.

ROTHMAN, S. (1960) "Systematic Political Theory: Observations of the Group Approach," *American Political Science Review,* Vol. 54, No. 1 (February): 15-33.

SAYRE, W. S. and H. KAUFMAN (1960) *Governing New York City: Politics in the Metropolis.* New York: Russell Sage.

SCHATTSCHNEIDER, E. E. (1942) *Party Government.* New York: Farrar and Rinehard.

—— (1957) "Intensity, Visibility, Direction and Scope," *American Political Science Review,* Vol. 51, No. 4 (December): 933-942.

SCHRIFTGIESSER, K. (1951) *The Lobbyists.* Boston: Little, Brown.

SCHUBERT, G. A., Jr. (1957) " 'The Public Interest' in Administrative Decision-Making," *American Political Science Review,* Vol. 51, No. 2 (June): 346-368.

—— (1960) *The Public Interest: A Critique and The Theory of a Political Concept.* Glencoe, Ill.: Free Press.

SCOBLE, H. (1959) Review of Hunter (1959) in *American Political Science Review,* Vol. 53, No. 4 (December): 1131-1132.

SHOTT, J. (1950) *The Railroad Monopoly: An Instrument of Banker Control of the American Economy.* Washington, D.C.: Public Affairs Institute.

SOMIT, A. and J. TANENHAUS (1967) *The Development of Political Science.* Boston: Allyn and Bacon.

SOROKIN, P. (1956) *Fads and Foibles in Modern Sociology.* Chicago: Henry Regnery.

SPENGLER, J. J. (1950) "Generalists vs. Specialists in Social Science: An Economist's View," *American Political Science Review,* Vol. 44, No. 2 (June): 358-379.

SPITZ, D. (1958) *Democracy and the Challenge of Power.* New York: Columbia Univ. Press.

STEWART, J. D. (1958) *British Pressure Groups: Their Role in Relation to the House of Commons.* New York: Oxford.

STOCKING, G. W. (1954) *Basing Point Pricing and Regional Development: A Case Study of the Iron and Steel Industry.* Chapel Hill: Univ. of North Carolina Press.

STRONG, D. (1954) Review of Hunter (1953) in *American Political Science Review,* Vol. 48, No. 1 (March): 235-237.

TRUMAN, D. B. (1951) *The Governmental Process.* New York: Knopf.

——— (1959) Review of Ehrmann (1958) in *Journal of Politics,* Vol. 21, No. 4 (November): 726-728.

——— (1960) "On the Invention of Systems," *American Political Science Review,* Vol. 54, No. 2 (June): 494-495.

TURNER, J. (1951) "Responsible Parties: A Dissent from the Floor," *American Political Science Review,* Vol. 45, No. 1 (March): 143-152.

WAHLKE, J. C., W. BUCHANAN, H. EULAU, and L. C. FERGUSON (1960) "American State Legislators' Role Orientations Toward Pressure Groups," *Journal of Politics,* Vol. 22, No. 2 (May): 203-227.

WALDO, D. (1952) "Development of Theory of Democratic Administration," *American Political Science Review,* Vol. 46, No. 1 (March): 81-103.

WENGERT, N. (1955) *Natural Resources and the Political Struggle.* Garden City, N.Y.: Doubleday.

WHYTE, W. F. (1943) "A Challenge to Political Scientists," *American Political Science Review,* Vol. 36, No. 4 (August): 692-697.

WILSON, H. H. (1961) *Pressure Group, The Campaign for Commercial Television in England.* New Brunswick, N.J.: Rutgers Univ. Press.

WOODWARD, J. and E. ROPER (1950) "Political Activity of American Citizens," *American Political Science Review,* Vol. 44, No. 4 (December): 872-885.

WORMUTH, F. D. (1961) "The Politics of George Catlin," *Western Political Quarterly,* Vol. 14, No. 3 (September): 807-811.

WRIGHT, C. R. and H. H. HYMAN (1958) "Voluntary Association Membership of American Adults," *American Sociological Review,* Vol. 23, No. 3 (June): 284-294.

WRIGHT, Q. (1950) "Political Science and World Stabilization," *American Political Science Review,* Vol. 44, No. 1 (March): 1-13.

ZELLER, B. (1950) Review of Bailey (1950) in *American Political Science Review,* Vol. 44, No. 2 (June): 468-470.

Chapter 4

From Research "Theory" to Research "Area": The Disintegration of the Group Approach to Political Science in the 1960s

To leave orderly theory where chaotic complexity had reigned supreme is a seeming drive of the human mind from which political science has not been immune. Aspiration to systematic theory has provided the common theme around which political science has evolved. If this process has been marked by greater aspiration than theory, one may advance two causal reasons. First, one may argue that the subject matter of the discipline is inappropriate to theory in the scientific sense. Men and women are too irrational, too spontaneous, display too much "free will" if you like, to be reduced to patterned lines of analysis and neat statistical sequences. Second, one may reason that the problem lies not so much with the subject as with the theorists. Political science may have fallen into patterns of analytic development that are themselves irrational and unscientific.

The former view, that human nature dictates the study of politics be an art rather than a science, is similar to that of Woodrow Wilson. "Know your people and you can lead them; study your people and you may know them," Wilson wrote. "But study them, not as congeries of interests, but as a body of human souls, the least as significant as the greatest—not as you would calculate forces, but as you would comprehend life" (Wilson, 1911: 11). Thus, at Wilson's Princeton, the department is "Politics," not "Political Science."

The second view would contend that the scientific study of politics *is* possible, that the lack of success to date is due to failure of imagination, not intrinsic limits. Why is the subject of power different from that encountered in the "hard" sciences? Are social interactions said to be more complex? Then what of the countless combinations of chemistry and the ever-escalating myriad of subatomic particles? Does the human mind introduce too much of an element of unpredictability? Then what of the subtle interrelationships of instinct and organism in biological science? Like all negative propositions, it can never be proved that a science of human behavior is impossible. Moreover, the patterns and recurrent themes that may be observed in social life, even if their notation does not add up to scientific theory, continually hint that a sharper eye may discern a hidden, underlying world of order.

Then, too, political scientists do not set for themselves the task of rendering the study of politics a science in the near future. Rather, the goal is set to lay a scientific foundation: a vocabulary, a set of hypotheses that provide a starting point for analyzing a world of meaning in which everything is related to everything else. Insights may be formulated in probabilistic terms, not as immutable laws. Research may concentrate on refuting rather than establishing. The immediate goal is, above all, to delineate the general terms within which analysis is to proceed; these set the constraints that would discipline a field of study.

The group approach to politics has been perhaps the most influential of the proposed general frameworks for analysis. By 1961, with the publication of Robert A. Dahl's classic study, *Who Governs?: Democracy and Power in an American City,* group theory and its pluralist variant were widely accepted orientations in political science. Numerous criticisms had been lodged against it (see Rothman, 1960; Dowling, 1960; Hale, 1960), but, if only by default, the group approach was still at a peak of influence. If the criticisms that had been made were profound (that it was not a scientific theory, that it was conservative in ideology, that it provided a poor starting point for analysis because it misestimated the importance of interest groups), they were not yet effective. The germ of doubt had been introduced, but the patient did not yet perceive any ill health.

In this essay, the deterioration of group theory from a state of confident assertion to one of circumscribed concern is traced. In the decade and a half following the publication of *Who Governs?*, the group approach, including pluralism, was transformed from a proposed general theory of politics to a specialized area of political study—the study of the relation of group interests to government affairs. Of course, certain hypothesis remained identified with the group approach (e.g., the hypothesis that overlapping group memberships were a critical basis of political stability), but what was lost was a sense that such hypotheses fitted together to form a convincing general theory. The exciting prospect that political science could be united around this system of ideas, placing the discipline on a new, more scientific foundation, was lost as well.

Pluralist theory itself was a more sophisticated variant of group theory, presented as a more convincing vision of political order. Its focus on the fragmentation of government structure rather than on the social division of labor underlying group formation, and on political entrepreneurship rather than interest-group power, avoided many of the criticisms lodged against earlier group theories, such as David Truman's *The Governmental Process* (1951). The criticisms of Rothman and others, mentioned above, were directed more against Truman's group theory than against Dahl's pluralism, for example.

Pluralism was nonetheless a variant of group theory. Its emphasis on "multiple centers of power" (Dahl, 1967a: 24) broadened the focus from private sector to public sector group interests, emphasizing the latter, but change in this direction was underway among group theorists well before the reassertion of "pluralist" theory. Moreover, by viewing the electoral process as the heart of democratic practice, and by viewing the winning of elections as determined by the "heterogeneous combination of groups" (Dahl, 1967a: 456), Dahl's pluralist theory was an explicit group theory of politics, but one which deemphasized the role of private sector lobbies.

In both group theory and its pluralist variant, American politics was defended, at least implicitly, as a benign system in which no one group could dominate. Both emphasized the eufunctions of fragmentation, the legitimacy of the contest of interests, the multiplicity and wide distribution of political resources, and the pervasiveness of the bargaining process. Consequently, both held little prospect for comprehensive, planned change or for responsible political parties and other forms of ideological purity. In terms of political science, both embraced the decision-making approach and, more broadly, represented an empirical and pragmatic orientation to the study of politics that fueled bitter debates between normative theorists and traditional institutionalists on the one hand, and the newer empirical theorists and behaviorists on the other.

This, then, was the setting at the time Dahl's *Who Governs?* appeared. Group theories of politics, including pluralism, were widely accepted, but criticisms were becoming common as well. What is the process by which a widely accepted framework in political science subsides amid challenge on many fronts? Was this decline due to a failure of imagination or to the intrinsic intractability of the subject matter causing the proliferation of newer frameworks, each to prove unworkable in turn? It is to this question that we now turn in an analysis of the splintering of group theory in the decade and a half since Dahl's famous work.

1962: A Cross Section
of Views on Group Theory

Analysis may be started by asking what appraisal was given to group theory by American political scientists after the appearance of *Who Governs?* By taking the following year, 1962, as a benchmark, one is able to appreciate in cross section the range of approaches of writers on group process. It is not true, for example, that even at its height of influence Truman's group theory or Dahl's pluralism "dominated" the discipline. Rather, from the start, reactions to the group approach reflected the critical nature of the intellectual enterprise and the vulnerability of the group approach itself.

Not all appraisals were critical, of course. In particular, authors of case studies were often very *uncritical* in accepting group theory as a patina giving an academic gloss on what were, in fact, highly untheoretical and descriptive works. Aaron Wildavsky's study of the Dixon-Yates power controversy was of this sort, for example (Wildavsky, 1962). Wildavsky found that group conflict, which eventuated in a public power victory, contrary to the desires of the Eisenhower administration, generated results preferable to those of central planning from Washington. Such studies buttressed the group approach in an eclectic way, but no particular case study ever approached the influence upon the discipline of Dahl's New Haven study.

Also, among more theoretical works independently appraising group theory, some were favorable. Bernard Crick, for example, arrived at a fundamentally pluralist position in his *In Defence of Politics* (1962). Crick's work extolled the virtue of politics in the sense of multiple conflict, compromise, and interaction. Likewise it rejected "apolitical" and "antipolitical" orientations that held the politics of compromise in low regard: ideologists, nationalists, conservatives, and radicals of various stripes all wishing to remove "politics" from "administration." Like Dahl, Crick argued that an underlying consensus on a public interest was not a cornerstone of democracy (Crick, 1962: 24, 181). Rather, political conflict was portrayed by Crick as a value in itself. If Crick saw no possibility of reducing the study of politics to a science, he concurred with the general description of American politics being put forward by the group theorists.

Rather than find order in either legal lines of accountability or in some form of control by an extralegal power elite, Crick had argued, in essence, for an appreciation of the transcendent order to be found in seemingly unruly interest conflict. This view, so supportive of pluralist theory, was articulated more explicitly in another influential book of this period: Paul Diesing's *Reason in Society: Five Types of Decisions and Their Social Conditions* (1962).

Diesing argued that different types of decisions required different forms of rationality. Technical rationality involves the continual solution of technical problems to achieve order as utility. Economic rationality involves the continual comparison of values to achieve order as efficiency. Legal rationality involves the continual application of rules and precedents to achieve order as law. Social rationality involves the continual resolution of conflicts to achieve order as integration. Finally, political rationality involves premising decision on the understanding that different kinds of order require different kinds of reason. Beyond this, however, Diesing argued that social and political rationality were the types most in neglect in the world today. What was not sufficiently appreciated was the order that emerges from conflict, the social benefits of which cannot be valued in terms technical utility, economic efficiency, or legal legitimacy. On technical, economic, or legal grounds it might seem more reasonable to minimize participation by interests and citizens in public decisions, but an entirely different light is shed, Diesing contended, when public decisions are considered from the viewpoint of social rationality. The role of the political decision maker is to be sensitive to this, understanding when decisions may be left to technical experts, or to the economic marketplace, or to the courts, but also understanding when social rationality requires a solution that only can emerge from pluralist conflict of interests.

Diesing's analysis, of course, prefigured the later, better-known work of Charles E. Lindblom, extolling the merits of incrementalist bargaining as a basis for decision and rejecting more centralist planning strategies. It harmonized with other contemporary defenses of group theory (e.g., see Loveday and Campbell, 1962). But it was also inconsistent with an even larger number of studies of a very diverse nature.

In the case of some studies, the inconsistency was subtle. Such was the case with the emerging body of literature based on economic and game theories of politics. Superficially, this research supported group theories of politics. James Buchanan and Gordon Tullock, for example, defended the pressure group system of checks and balances against traditional majoritarian conceptions of democracy in their book, *The Calculus of Consent: Logical Foundations of Constitutional Democracy* (1962). Likewise, William Riker's game-theoretic work, *The Theory of Political Coalitions* (1962), drew explicit analogies between game-theory models and American interest-group politics. But while both seemed to overlap with the concerns of the group theorists, both also assumed a different model of the political actor.

Economic and game theories of politics ultimately rested on the assumption of rational individuals maximizing utility. They were, in the nineteenth century sense, liberal theories. Group theory, in the nineteenth century sense, was a conservative theory assuming irrational citizens whose activities are benign only when mediated through a constraining network of units that perform a socializing and restraining function. "A restless and immoderate people," Dahl (1956: 151) had termed Americans. Such individuals could not be expected to meet the assumptions of voter rationality and participatory democracy contained in classical democratic theory. One of the central thrusts of group theory, including pluralism, had been redefine democracy along group lines precisely to avoid the rationalist assumptions now reappearing in economic and game theories of politics.

Considerable research supported the group-theoretic view of individuals and organizations. Lane's study of public opinion (1962), for example, documented widespread voter irrationality (intolerance, authoritarianism, and shallowness of political opinions). Presthus (1962) likewise analyzed large organizations, emphasizing their function (only partially successful) in standardizing and disciplining their members. Nonetheless, other public opinion research, notably the highly influential work of V. O. Key, did not support group-theory expectations. Key had found little consensus on general principles of democracy, in spite of group-theory predication of politics on public acceptance of the "rules of the game." At the same time, though group theorists downgraded the public interest concept as a criterion for policy-making, Key found consensus of opinion on some specific policy areas (Key, 1961; see review by James Prothro, 1962). Finding consensus on particular policies but not on democratic principles was, of course, the opposite of what might be expected on the basis of group theory.

The whole question of rational opinions in relation to one's interest was problematic for group theory. If interests were to be defined as those expressed by the actor, then, as Vernon

Van Dyke pointed out, this leaves "no room for the scholar or any detached observer to say that the actor goes against his own interests or that he should pursue an interest other than the one he in fact pursues" (Van Dyke, 1962: 574). If one accepts that an interest implies a goal, then the detached observer can make some judgment about whether the goal is being pursued rationally. The actor himself may even be persuaded to change his actions on the basis of such a judgment. But, this implies that the actor might feel that the activity of the interest group was not in his best interests, after all. And this in turn means, Van Dyke concluded, "that there are difficulties in a conception that identifies interests with the current attitudes of those pursuing them," as in the writing of Bentley, Truman, and other group theorists (Van Dyke, 1962: 576). That is, Van Dyke's essay in the *American Political Science Review* not only suggested a major problem in the group theorists' rejection of a public interest concept in favor of simple acceptance of current interest attitudes, but it also opened the door to the notion of objective versus subjective interests.

Interpreting politics in terms of objective interests had been, of course, identified with Marxist and other class analyses. It immediately led back to a discussion of objective social outcomes and particularly the stratification thereof. The unequal distribution of benefits in society might be interpreted as more indicative of American politics than the fact of widely dispersed political conflict. How, indeed, could one explain the relatively low level of "pluralism" of social outcomes in a system marked by a "pluralism" of political process?

Peter Bachrach explained this discrepancy in terms of the concept of "nondecisions" in pluralist politics. This thesis was to emerge as a major basis of challenge to group theory. With Morton Baratz, Bachrach contended that the pluralists dealt with only part of the "Two Faces of Power" (Bachrach and Baratz, 1962b). Overt governmental decisions, often evidencing the fragmentation of power emphasized by group theorists, was indeed one "face" of American politics. But the other, more subtle and far more pervasively important "face" of power was said to have been neglected. This other aspect was related to what Schattschneider had called the "mobilization of bias."

The group theorists had implied that all political acts were effected through organization, including, as the pluralists wished to emphasize, the quasi-personal organization centered on political entrepreneurs. Truman, in particular, had gone quite far in this direction, emphasizing the role of such entrepreneurs and political elites in protecting democracy from demagogues the masses might support (Bachrach, 1962a). Bachrach argued that the other "face" of power justified an opposite inference.

The distribution of social outcomes was, Bachrach said, less effected by overt decisions, even those at elite levels, than by the mobilization of cultural biases through "nondecisions." A nondecision was a potential one never reaching the overt agenda of politics because it was dismissed out of hand as illegitimate, "utopian," or unfeasible. Bachrach argued that overt political decisions in the United States took place within a circumscribed realm. Studies of government decisions, all taking place within narrow limits, might indeed reveal a pluralist pattern. But what was more significant was the nature of these limits themselves. The pattern of decision-making on regulating the steel industry, for example, said less about the nature of American politics than the out-of-hand dismissal ("nondecision") of nationalization as an alternative. (That nationalization of steel *could* have been a plausible alternative, see Means, 1962.)

The difference between the pattern of overt decisions compared to nondecisions could account for the seemingly anomalous findings mentioned earlier: that overt political processes were found to be pluralist, yet the distribution of social benefits was highly stratified. That is, as Giovanni Sartori was also contending in *Democratic Theory* (1962), Dahl and the pluralists erred in thinking that studies such as *Who Governs?* proved the absence of a "power elite." Elite influence could be far more complex, subtle, and elusive.

In sum, group theory might tempt the researcher to believe that the group forms found in overt decision-making processes were the key causal elements in politics. Roy Macridis criticized

group theory on this ground (Macridis, 1961: 33-35), and on
the ground that it veiled a hidden normative theory—the theory
that group process is an intrinsic good and its effects beneficial.
In terms of empirical theory, of course, many polities rejected
these premises (e.g., see Weiner, 1962). Though participation
in group process was held to be a form of representation, cooption and redirection away from participants' objective interests
were commonly the outcome, even for highly educated political
actors (see Schilling, 1962, and Lapp, 1965, on scientists; see
Zeigler, 1961, on small businessmen). And, as Macridis, Van
Dyke, and others had indicated, the very concepts of interest
and interest group remained unclear. Thus, combined with
the research of Key and Bachrach discussed above, there were
already in 1962 numerous bases to take exception to the group
theory and pluralist approach to the study of political science.

1963-1966: From "Nondecision" Theory
to the Walker-Dahl Debate

Over the next few years, the discussion of group theory in political science literature, while always evolving in an eclectic and
disjointed manner, drifted toward intensifying criticism of
group theory and pluralism. This drift was signalled by the
explicit formulation of the "nondecision-making" concept
as an analytic framework around which critics of the group
approach might rally (see Bachrach and Baratz, 1963).

Bachrach's framework received additional impetus by its
association with the somewhat similar concept of "politics
as symbolic action" put forward a year later by Murray Edelman.
In *The Symbolic Uses of Politics* (1964), Edelman argued that
the ostensible ends of government decisions such as those studied
by the pluralists frequently might be found different from
the true ends. That is, Edelman suggested that much of what
government does (passage of laws, establishment of bureaus,
and issuing of public pronouncements) functions not so much
to effect changes in the socioeconomic environment as to reassure and render quiescent potential insurgencies. Moreover,

the political wants and knowledge of the public, he said, were determined largely by the actions of the leadership stratum of society. Later research gave some credence to this position (see Cornwell, 1965). Edelman's concept of symbolic manipulation of public opinion was but a step away from the concept of mobilization of bias and nondecision-making. Both were opposed to pluralist assumptions about political process.

As the work of Bachrach and Edelman appeared, establishing an alternative to group-theory analyses of American politics, writers in the group-theory tradition were directing their attacks on stratification theory (Hunter, Mills) popularized in 1950s' sociology. In part, publishers' time lag accounts for this disjuncture in political discourse, but the phenomenon of differing "sides" in the debate over group theory talking past each other was a recurrent one. Nelson Polsby, extending Dahl's New Haven research, again formulated the pluralist critique of stratification theory in *Community Power and Political Theory* (1963). Its demonstration that New Haven was not characterized by a cohesive upper-class in overt conflict with a lower class or in a position of direct domination of political and civic leaders was an attack on a straw man. This was so even for stratification (elite) theory, let alone the more subtle criticisms of pluralism by Bachrach and others. As Thomas Dye observed of Aaron Wildavsky's rather similar demonstration (in 1964) of pluralism in Oberlin, Ohio, the "definition of elitism is so restrictive and his definition of pluralism so inclusive that he is foreordained to conclude that any set of power relationships he discovered in Oberlin were pluralist" (Dye, 1965: 173). Both Polsby and Dye cast stratification theory as tantamount to belief that politics is controlled by upper-class conspiracies. In expending great energy on rebutting this point, debate was sidetracked from the real issues confronting those who would use group theory as a basis for political science interpretations of government.

This period was marked by a plethora of specific studies taking one side or the other in the elitist-pluralist debate. If Polsby showed pluralism upheld in New Haven politics, Thometz (1963) demonstrated a pattern of business dominance in Dallas. If Grossman (1965) found group theory useful in understanding

the activities of lawyers, Kimbrough (1964) uncovered a mono-
polistic, business-dominated pattern among certain educators.
If Lindblom extolled the virtues of incrementalism compared
to central planning (Braybrooke and Lindblom, 1963; Lindblom, 1965), Reagan (1963) attacked pluralism as an ideological
smokescreen for what was in fact a managed economy. Others
tried to steer a middle path between the elitists and pluralists
(see Williams and Adrian, 1963; Agger, Goldrich, and Swanson,
1964).

Perhaps the most influential "middle road" formulation
was that put forward by Theodore Lowi. Lowi argued that
decision-making patterns varied according to the subject matter
of the issue. Three types of decisions was distinguished: distributive, regulative, and redistributive. Regulatory politics,
in which a government decision clearly benefits one party and
equally clearly disadvantages another, occurs in a pluralist
group-conflict context. The nature of the decision usually
elicits interest articulation and organization. Distributive
politics is a contrasting form in which benefits are conferred
on one party without obvious and direct disadvantage to another. Here patronage and pork barrel politics is the rule,
opening the door to corporatist collusion between government
and private interests rather different from the benign image
of American politics put forward by the group theorists. Finally,
Lowi defined redistributive politics as the politics of decisions
in which broad classes are advantaged or disadvantaged. This
type of decision, perhaps corresponding to what C. Wright
Mills had called "big decisions," could be analyzed in class
rather than group terms, allowing a far more radical interpretation than that of group theory (Lowi, 1964a).

Lowi viewed his work as representative of a general shift
away from pluralism and group theory. Alluding to Herring's
work on group theory in the 1930s and 1940s and to the revival
of group theory after World War II, Lowi wrote, "At that time
the prevailing theoretical notion had come to be 'pluralism,'
and the method was crude behavioralism and the use of elaborate
case-studies, observations and descriptions of political decisions
or activities. For many, the 'group approach' became observation

for its own sake. . . . In the 1950's theory began slowly to shift from 'group laissez-faire' toward the political system—toward more universal concepts and hypotheses that might do justice to masses and institutions as well as groups . . ." (Lowi, 1964b: 599). Pluralism had extended group theory in this direction, but Lowi's analysis went beyond the group approach entirely, allowing partial corporatist and class interpretations of American political events.

The inclination to "broaden" group theory to the point of disintegration was widely apparent in the discipline. Truman himself had already disavowed the group approach as a general theory in political science, preferring instead to view it simply as a misnomer for an area of research—not a predictive theory, but only a body of literature, largely descriptive, dealing with the relation of groups to the political process (Truman, 1960: 494-495). This modest view of the import of group theory now became more general. For example, in his standard text on interest groups, Harmon Zeigler noted that the "intention of group theory has been misinterpreted on occasion as the establishment of a broad-gauge theory of the political process . . ." (Zeigler, 1964: iii). Zeigler proposed group theory be regarded instead merely as the view that public policy is formed by competing interests including not only groups, but officials' conceptions of the "public interest," and the political culture of institutions or governmental jurisdictions. As Zeigler's reviewer in the *American Political Science Review* observed, the modesty of this view of group theory was a "theoretical retreat rather than advance" (Flinn, 1965: 174).

Lewis Froman made much the same point as Zeigler in noting the polarization of group theory into very abstract theoretical frameworks on the one hand, and very empirical cases on the other (Froman, 1966: 952). Like Zeigler, Froman urged the raising of the study of group process to the level of general theory. This would be, however, a general theory of groups, not a group-based general theory of politics. Thus, for example, Froman proposed such propositions as the following: (1) the more numerous elected state officials, the stronger interest-group power; and (2) the longer the state constitution, the stronger interest-group power. Such propositions, however interesting, cast the group approach not as a theory of American politics, but as a specialized area of study that might, when developed and integrated with numerous other such areas, provide the basis for a new theory of American politics.

This retreat to middle-range theory was entirely reasonable given the mounting criticisms at that time of the more general version of group theory. At the level of conceptualization, the "interest" concept continued to be condemned as hopelessly ambiguous—interests defined by subjective perception? by identified common values? on the basis of group behavior? (see Krislov, 1963: 842). The redefinition of democracy away from classical standards of rational participation and accountability in the work of Truman (1951), Dahl (1956), Herring (1965), and other group theorists was condemned for removing the very criteria by which democracies might be evaluated, reducing democratic theory to a mere codification of the common features of societies proclaimed democratic (Davis, 1964: 46). The emphasis on politics as the system of peaceful battles between competing private interests was rejected as resting on "antipolitical" assumptions about the impossibility of politics as struggle toward a more humane, rationally organized society (Bay, 1965: 44).

At the empirical level, other cornerstones of group theory were crumbling. Verba (1965a: 495) found that overlapping group memberships were not a major stabilizing factor, diminishing conflict, as suggested by the group theorists. McCloskey (1964: 381-382) found low development of democratic consensus, reinforcing Key's research, contrary to group theory expectations. Indeed, the early 1960s saw a revival of academic concern for the undemocratic susceptibilities of the masses (Bell, 1963; Broyles, 1964; Truman, 1959; Bachrach's commentary on Truman, 1962). Also, Luttbeg and Zeigler (1966: 664, 666) found interest organizations unrepresentative of their members, bringing into question the legitimacy of basing democracy on "virtual" representation through groups and institutions.

At the same time, Mancur Olson was arguing that the group process lacked even the *potential* to become representative.

In his highly influential *The Logic of Collective Action* (1965), Olson argued that it was unreasonable to expect individuals to sacrifice individual values (time, money) attending to their group membership when they would reap the collective benefits of the group's activity in any event. Lobbies were inevitably so characterized. They dispensed collective benefits to members and nonmembers alike. Why should a consumer, for example, join a consumers' group when he or she would benefit from any legislation passed, regardless? Strong groups, Olson contended, based membership on individual benefits, not collective benefits. Specifically, economic organizations (businesses, unions) would inevitably overshadow organizations dependent on altruistic appeals to the worth of collective benefits. Politics based on group process would always underrepresent collective interests in this sense.

Even in the realm of economic groups, representative balance did not seem to prevail. E. E. Schattschneider (1960: 30-36) had written about the class bias of the structure of organized interests, but group theorists and pluralists had suggested that groups provided a sort of "virtual representation." However, not only had Luttbeg and Zeigler demonstrated that unrepresentativeness of groups vis-à-vis their members, but other research (Holtzman, 1966: 6-7) showed intervention by organized groups on behalf of the unorganized tended to be haphazard and uncertain. Even labor was still a marginal group in terms of organizational political power (Holtzman, 1966: 25). Such findings blended with a revived interest in elitist interpretations of the politics of Western parliamentary democracies (Porter, 1965; Bottomore, 1966), and did not support the "virtual representation" theory at all.

That interest groups were not as powerful as hitherto thought became a widely accepted idea, further eroding the group approach and, by implication, pluralism. Milbrath's (1963) study of Washington lobbyists detailed their role as a professionalized and delimited one concerned their role as a professionalized and delimited one concerned with orchestrating a communications process under difficult circumstances. The elite-theory image of the behind-the-scenes puppeteer was rejected in this research, of course, but it was likewise out of harmony with group-theory focus on interest groups as the key forces of politics. Milbrath's research, moreover, was corroborated by that of Patterson (1963) and of Bauer, Pool, and Dexter (1963), all of whom cast interest groups as adjuncts to legislators already predisposed toward their cause.

A corollary of this realization was a revived interest in other bases of decision-making than simply the pressures of various interests. Miller and Stokes, for instance, demonstrated the independent importance of the legislator's own attitudes in arriving at a decision, quite apart from perceived constituency attitudes and interests (Miller and Stokes, 1963). Similar conclusions were reached by Tillett (1963) and Smith (1964: 609-610), both of whom saw their work as rebutting the group theory of politics.

For many, decision-making seemed based on far more diffuse factors than interest pressures. Some emphasized the role of public opinion (e.g., McAdams, 1964), but the most popular "new" thrust centered on the concept of "political culture." Political culture seemed to embody a sense of the subtleness of the decision process, preserving an important role for the decision maker's "own attitudes" while emphasizing the indirect and socializing forces of the decision maker's milieu without reducing this to a Bentleyan physics of group pressures. Dahl himself had given increased weight to culture as a political determinant and subsequent researchers studying interest groups (e.g., LaPalombara, 1964) also emphasized the need to transcend the culturebound categories of analysis favored by American political scientists.

Lucian Pye and Sidney Verba's *Political Culture and Political Development* (1965) provided a general statement of the view of politics that emphasized political culture rather than current interest forces as the basis of politics. If this was not quite the idealist theory of historical causation then being revived by the functionalists (see Mitchell, 1963) and their disciples (see Lipset, 1963), it was close to it. Like functionalism, the political culture approach stood in opposition to the materialist premises of *both* elite and group theories of politics.

The political culture approach was also associated with developmentalism, an alternative orientation toward analysis associated with the SSRC Committee on Comparative Politics and their sponsored studies (e.g., Almond and Verba, 1963). As Truman observed, the work of the Social Science Research Council committee and its associates generated "a renewed emphasis on theory of all kinds," not harmony or theoretical consensus (Truman, 1965: 870). Much of this work (e.g., Almond and Powell, 1966) drew on the input-output categories of systems analysis (see Easton, 1965a, 1965b). Often, as with Almond (1966: 876), systems analysis extended to functionalism, in spite of ideological opposition to that approach by scholars of the left (e.g., see Horowitz, 1963). Systems analysis also took an influential communications theory variant (Deutsch, 1963). Finally, these various approaches were interwoven with behaviorism that, in turn, often rejected an institutional focus in favor of analysis of individuals and roles (see Ranney, 1962; Eulau, 1963). Thus, the debate over pluralism and group theory took place in a setting often overshadowed by a variety of more abstract frameworks of analysis that were frequently inconsistent in focus or assumptions with the group approach.

The Walker-Dahl Debate

In this period, the most important manifestation of that debate was an exchange between Robert Dahl and Jack Walker in the pages of the *American Political Science Review*. In this debate, Walker attacked pluralist theory on both normative and descriptive grounds. In normative terms, the pluralist and group approach was held to have changed the meaning of democracy in a fundamentally conservative direction. Like Bachrach, Walker emphasized Truman's article (1959) calling for elite consensus as the safeguard of democracy against demagogues of the right and left. Like other group-theoretic literature, this rejected classical democratic emphasis on responsible, participant citizens in favor of responsive, pluralist groups and institutions as the basis of democratic practice. Stability and efficiency, Walker stated, had displaced participation and accountability as the prime goals of democracy. This was tantamount to inviting political scientists to become "sophisticated apologists for the existing political order" (Walker, 1966: 289).

In responding to this aspect of Walker's critique of pluralism, Dahl sought refuge in two points. First, he denied that there was a "school" of theory such as Walker described, other than in the lowest-common-denominator sense that the authors described all shared a belief in the desirability of representative government (Dahl, 1966: 298). This reply, while correct, also served (as Truman's earlier disavowal of the group approach as general theory had earlier) to underscore the incapacity of pluralism to constitute a convincing, coherent, and viable system of analysis that might be the basis for an accepted political science paradigm.

Second, Dahl noted that pluralist theory was "mainly if not wholly intended" as descriptive work without normative import (Dahl, 1966: 298). While we cannot know the subjective dispositions of pluralist scholars, this reply was also quite reasonable provided one emphasized the word "intended." Intentionality, however, was beside the point of Walker's criticism, which was that pluralism, intentionally or not, carried conservative norms. Certainly, the pluralists did not in general perceive themselves to be conservative. On the other hand, group theorists had long since redefined democracy to emphasize procedural (e.g., group process, consensus on "rules of the game") rather than substantive (e.g., citizens' rational participation, opinion representation) criteria. Equally certainly, scholars to the "left" of the pluralists were outraged by the ideological tone of the pluralist writers, however much Dahl and others might insist they meant no normative implication one way or the other. Ultimately, Dahl's reply on this ground was a weak one, depending on the belief in "value-free" science. In the context of the increasingly tumultuous 1960s, this concept had lost much of whatever force it might once have had.

This was related to Walker's criticism of pluralism on descriptive grounds. By emphasizing elite consensus and interest-group process, Walker said, political scientists, following the group approach, have chosen to concentrate on "competition among rival leaders and the clever maneuvering of political entrepreneurs" (Walker, 1966: 293). In fact, however, the most dramatic variance in political variables might well have more to do with social movements and collective behavior than with normal group process. To this argument Dahl replied that social movements were more properly the subjects of historians because the examples were mainly historical, and besides, political scientists had, indeed, studied social movements (Dahl, 1966: 304-305)! Here, however, Dahl could cite only a fifteen year old study by V. O. Key, research on America's right wing, and a few studies of the labor movement. Actually, the study of social movements had been undertaken primarily by sociologists for reasons having little to do with historicity. Again, Dahl's reply was a weak one, pointing up the relatively narrow band of interest of the group theorists. This band focused on group process amid postwar tranquility; it lacked the broader concerns with social change of the Marxists or, for that matter, the developmentalists. If one viewed social movements not as curious historical artifacts, but rather as a critical aspect of the sociopolitical change process, then students of the variance in political phenomena should have done a great deal more. Certainly the general focus of the pluralists on normal group process, wherein any active and legitimate group could get its fair share of the pie (see Dahl, 1956: 150), was out of touch with those oriented toward the civil rights and antiwar movements that swept across academia at this time.

But if in these debates the defense of pluralism was a weak one, so Walker's attack was an example of overkill. Through numerous exaggerations, Walker caricatured the position of Dahl and other pluralists in ways Dahl could easily rebut. These errors of argumentation served to blunt severely the impact of Walker's arguments, distracting attention to lesser issues. Nonetheless, the normative and descriptive deficiencies of the group approach became increasingly apparent in the 1960s for the reasons Walker had cited.

The 1967-1970 Period and the Revival of
Critical Social Theory

The social turmoil of the late 1960s and early 1970s did not mean, of course, the disappearance of group theory and pluralism. Such theories have been around at least since John Locke (see Marini, 1969) and can be expected to survive well into the future. The importance of this orientation continued to be taught to new generations of students in pluralist-oriented textbooks in political science (Dahl, 1967a; Mahood, 1967; Wootton, 1969) and sociology (Rose, 1967). Moreover, it was an easily documented fact that numerous political settings were, in fact, characterized by fragmentation of power among diverse and shifting interests (see Watson, Downing and Spiegel, 1967; Prewitt and Eulau, 1969: 440; Eidenberg and Morey, 1969; Adams, 1970; Soule and Clarke, 1970; and Black, 1970). More specifically, many instances could be cited to show business was not the preeminent power so often described by critics of pluralism (see Galambos, 1966; Heidenheimer and Langdon, 1968; Hall, 1969; and Epstein, 1969). Criticisms of pluralism on normative grounds were tempered by the irrelevance of many critiques to pluralist description of the political process (on this point, see Medding, 1969). Also, of course, the very fact that the group approach had been so important in postwar American political science assured that many scholars would continue to genuflect to group theory as a prelude to ignoring it in ensuing descriptive studies of groups (see Goodman, 1967). Finally, group theory endured in subfields of the discipline where it was novel. Such was the case with the group approach to Soviet studies, for example (see Schwartz and Keech, 1968), where the group approach was employed so loosely it ceased to be a theory of democratic politics at all! (As Inkeles argued, this was possible because the definition of democracy as it pertained to the citizen's role, and as used by scholars who had abandoned classical democratic standards, did not in fact differentiate citizen roles in nondemocratic countries compared to democratic. It was this point Bachrach, Walker, and others had used as the center of their normative criticism of group theory. See Inkeles, 1969: 1123.)

In addition to these factors favoring the persistence of pluralism and group theory, a few social trends of the day also favored the continued importance of these ideas. The judicialization of many social issues, for example, was associated with broadened standing to sue and a further opening of the political process to various social interests (see Vose, 1966). Even more important, a crisis in liberal thought was leading to a reappraisal of decentralization as a possibly superior philosophical alternative to New Deal centralism (e.g., on decentralism in liberal economic theory see Heller, 1966).

Often, however, the group theory of politics was transmuted into the political theory of groups. That is, group research was presented not as a basis for understanding general principles of politics, but rather as a way to construct hypotheses about a specialized segment of the polity—interest group behavior. Froman and Zeigler both continued their previously discussed work of this type, for example. Interest group strength was correlated with longer state constitutions, easier amendment processes, and more elected officials (Froman, 1966: 961). Strength was also linked to cultural traditions of nonpartisanship, open primaries, and high participation (Zeigler, 1969a: 139). Other correlates of group strength were length of experience of the target official (Teune, 1967: 503); gubernatorial support and a cooperative interest-group strategy (Longley, 1967: 658); weak traditions of central authority combined with a well developed middle and upper-class whose values include responsibility for public service (Glaser and Sills, 1966); having a headquarters in Washington, D.C., and not being committed to only one strategy of influence (Dexter, 1969); and economic development and its effect on the status system (Nie, Powell, and Prewitt, 1969: 808-809).

Uncovering the correlates of interest group strength, however, was far from the original concern of group theory. The correlative approach, essentially descriptive, sought to reveal why interest groups were more important in some settings than others. There was no conclusion that interest groups were more important across-the-board than other political forces. Indeed, a growing body of literature pointed to the limits of interest group power.

In *Congress and Lobbies: Image and Reality* (1966), Scott and Hunt had shown congressmen perceived interest group power to be low, though their sample was not adequate to arrive at firm conclusions. However, a better study by Zeigler and Beer (1969b) showed essentially the same thing: legislators disliked pressure tactics and perceived lobbyists in terms of a relatively weak, information-providing role. While legislators sometimes thought groups opposed to them to be powerful, the groups with which they worked were felt to have only marginal importance. Comparative studies of interest group process, moreover, repeatedly showed the preeminence of government over interest group activity (Clark, 1967; Stern, 1970; Lieber, 1970).

Choice and Exchange Theories of Politics

If interest groups themselves seemed to be less important than hitherto thought, however, some of the more general concepts of the group approach fared better. This was particularly true of the marketplace image of conflicting interests yielding a social optimum. As in Lindblom's earlier work, writing in this vein tread an uncertain line between normative theory and empirical description. Exchange theory and public-goods theory, which arose to take up the banner of marketplace and economic analogies to politics, were usually not group theories since they typically based decision on individual rather than collective choice. Nonetheless, by extolling the virtues of decentralized "muddling through" and leaving decisions to the market, they filled a void that was appearing as group theory faltered. Both were perceived as conservative ideologies by scholars of the Left.

Most books on exchange theory utilized the economists' kit of terms (e.g., utility, supply and demand, and preference curves) in conjunction with an assumption of political man as a rational, utility-maximizing decision maker (e.g., see Curry and Wadf, 1968). The exchange theory of groups portrayed group leaders as entrepreneurs selling the benefits of group affiliation for a price (Salisbury, 1969: 1). Political organizations were quasi-firms, producing and exchanging legitimacy (a quasi-good) in a broader political exchange environment (see Ilchman and Uphoff, 1969). The clear normative implication of this perspective supported more government reliance on the economic marketplace and other more esoteric mechanisms whereby individual choice could be the basis of aggregate decision (see Tullock, 1970; Coleman, 1970; and for critical review, see Barry, 1970).

Exchange and public choice theory, while bearing similarities to the group approach, were quite dissimilar in terms of impact on the discipline. While they were to grow to be significant minority perspectives in American political science, they drew intense support only from a relative few. As proposed paradigms for political analysis, they were less than appealing. In normative terms, exchange and public choice theories were far more explicitly conservative than group theory. Their view of the marketplace as a benign, perhaps optimum decision-making mechanism was akin to the position of the right wing Austrian school of economics that had enjoyed a postwar resurgence (but not in political science). In descriptive terms, their reversion to individualistic and rationalist assumptions of politics was flatly inconsistent with the group approach. If the group approach was past its peak of influence, it had nonetheless succeeded in helping popularize quite contrary assumptions about politics.

More important than these problems of exchange and public choice theories was an aspect they shared with the group approach: a value system that seemed supportive of the status quo in a time of social upheaval. In his presidential address to the 1969 meeting of the American Political Science convention, David Easton acknowledged "The New Revolution in Political Science" brought about in reflection of the civil rights, antiwar, and other protest movements of the 1960s. "We have learned a great deal about this system," Easton wrote, "but all within a value framework that accepts ongoing practices as essentially satisfactory. . . . Today the hazards of neglecting our normative presuppositions are all too apparent." Easton then went on to ask, "How can we account for the failure of current pluralist interpretations of democracy to identify, understand, and anticipate the kinds of domestic needs and wants that began to express themselves as political demands during the 1960's?" (Easton, 1969: 1057). As issues of social relevance and social change arose, dissatisfaction grew with pluralism, group theory, and other approaches that focused attention on equilibrating normal process judged implicitly by values of stability and conservatism.

Theories of Political Change

Concern for a more critical approach to political science manifested itself on a number of fronts. One was the emergence of a literature on social protest movements. Here the work of Michael Lipsky was most influential. Lipsky, a sympathetic observer of a wave of New York City rent strikes, portrayed protest as a political resource aimed at influencing the reference group of decision makers by impact on the media (Lipsky, 1968; Lipsky, 1970). Critiquing pluralist writers like Dahl (Lipsky, 1968: 1147-1148), Lipsky concluded that it was misleading to convey the impression that any group could gain its fair share or make itself heard effectively in American politics. In part, as Edelman had emphasized, the eventual outcome was apt to be symbolic reward without significant substantive impact. In larger measure, however, groups based on the poor lacked the skills and resources necessary to be effective in any event (see also Parenti, 1970; Wolman and Thomas, 1970). This pessimistic view regarding the limits of protest suggested for some the need to create new vehicles for the representation of the poor. Here the "new Left" slogan of "participatory democracy" was heard. In political science the groundwork for this was laid by the tendency of voting studies to reassert voter rationality (Key, 1966; Shapiro, 1969) in contrast to the image of the emotional and irrational citizen predominant in political science since a wave of pessimistic "realism" had swept the discipline after World War I.

The concern for extending democracy became a common theme in the late 1960s; the call for participation was not confined to the discipline's Left. Robert Pranger, for example, in *The Eclipse of Citizenship: Power and Participation in Contemporary Politics* (1968), critiqued American democratic practice for neglecting civic experience and for leaving a gap between authority and anarchy (Pranger, 1968: 102). To fill this gap, more participatory institutions were needed. Even the writings of Robert Dahl, representing the pluralist school, displayed a renewed concern for the creation of more democratic political settings than then existed (Dahl, 1967b). Congress itself was induced to add the famous "maximum feasible participation" clause to the Economic Opportunity Act (1964), precipitating much published condemnation of government sponsored mobilization of the poor (see Moynihan, 1969), but little actual insurgency in spite of participatory rhetoric (see Kramer, 1969).

More radical scholars began to popularize theories of extreme decentralization (Kotler, 1969) and economic democracy (Blumberg, 1969). These carried participatory democracy much further, envisioning new systems of semiautonomous neighborhood government, and workers' control of private enterprise. The concept of the neighborhood corporation, the self-managing firm, and other self-governing units had a long tradition going back to guild socialism and other radical offshoots of pluralism as raised by Harold Laski after World War I. If democracy were to be based on group process, the argument went, democracy would have a hollow ring so long as its operating units were not themselves internally democratic.

Revival of Elite Theory

Aside from writing on social movements and participatory democracy, the emergence of a more critical orientation in political science was marked by a resurrection of stratification research and elite theory. Unlike the continuing journalistic exposés of the dangers of business power (Deakin, 1966; Pearson and Anderson, 1969), or research showing the corporatist (as opposed to pluralist group conflict) nature of business-government-labor relations (see Kohlmeier, 1969; Radosh, 1969), the new stratification research was self-consciously put forward as a radical alternative to group theory and pluralism.

Works such as G. William Domhoff's *Who Rules America?* (1967) brought stratification research and elite theory back into serious debate in political science. More moderate authors also had countenanced class analysis and other nongroup interpretations of democratic politics (see Lenski, 1966). Others had argued that the choice between pluralism and elite theory rested essentially on ideological, not empirical considerations (Connolly, 1967). Whether one believed in the "iron law of oligarchy" or participatory democratic radicalism was said to depend upon an open choice between views of human nature (Parry, 1969). But the new stratification research embraced class analysis openly and sought to rebut the group approach in terms of empirical description, not on normative or ideological terms alone. Pluralism was held to be factually in error, regardless of one's ideology or assumptions about human nature.

The disjunction between pluralist theory and political fact in the 1960s was widely noted, even by scholars like Easton, cited earlier. Claude Burtenshaw summarized this realization in a critique of pluralism that appeared in the *Western Political Quarterly* (Burtenshaw, 1968: 586-587):

> Substantial areas of twelve great cities lay in ruins. The damage ran into billions of dollars. There is open advocacy of revolution and of guerrilla war in the cities. How could this happen in a society of slack resources, in which any active and legitimate group can make itself heard effectively? . . . There must have been something fundamentally wrong with the theory of pluralist democracy or the analysis would not have gone so wide of the mark.

What was wrong, Burtenshaw argued, was pluralism's concept of the state as a neutral arbiter. Instead, the fact was that the state was the instrument whereby a favored group or groups could "bend others to its will, through the taxing power, the enactment of criminal law, or the other means of compulsion which the state affords " (Burtenshaw, 1968: 586).

Rather than mediate a pluralistic struggle of groups and public entrepreneurs under accepted and neutral rules of the game, more critical research in the United States (Ross, 1970) and abroad (Lijphart, 1968) pointed to the political preeminence of elite accommodation. To the extent fragmentation of power and decentralization of policy-making did exist in the United States, other research found this "pluralism" not democracy, but corruption (Gardiner, 1970) and structural incapacity to deal with mounting social problems in the comprehensive way needed (Beam, 1970; Gawthrop, 1971).

Indeed, it easily could be argued that pluralism was a major cause of social crisis. The liberal approach to interest groups it embodied was a rationale for delegation of public power to private groups relying for accountability on very little in the way of clear and detailed legislative or executive mandate. As Theodore Lowi pointed out in a highly influential article and subsequent book, public policy predicated on interest-group liberalism "pretends through 'pluralism,' 'countervailing power,' 'creative federalism,' 'partnership,' and 'participatory democracy,' that the unsentimental business of coercion is not involved and that the unsentimental decisions of how to apply coercion need not really be made at all" (Lowi, 1967: 18). In *The End of Liberalism* (1969), Lowi concluded that this version of pluralism, in seeking to end the crisis of public authority through delegation of decision-making to various groups, would in the end exacerbate it.

The perception of social crisis and the need to do something about it was the core of the slogan of "relevance" that became a catchword at this time. The Caucus for a New Political Science, uniting a loose confederation of more critically oriented political scientists, shared little else except a common distaste for the conservative value system (see Baskin, 1970: 95) of the group approach and a common commitment to reuniting political theory with praxis (see Surkin and Wolfe, 1970).

The very concern for reuniting theory and practice bore implications contrary to the group approach and its several variants (e.g., Dahl's pluralism, Almond's systems theory). Democratic action implied democratic ideals that would constitute the standards for evaluating practice. But as Sheldon Wolin pointed out in an influential essay, the basic thrust of such contemporary approaches was to deflate democratic theory. That is, if democratic ideals were held to have been "unreasonably high" in classical conceptions of democracy, then the solution was to lower standards to correspond to and describe actual practice. This emasculated the normative power of the concept of democracy and stripped it of its radical implications. In the course of social turmoil in the 1960s, however, classical democratic ideals were being reasserted in slogans like "participatory democracy" and "black power in community control." Discerning the tendency of such real-world events to undermine theories embracing a low and merely descriptive notion of democracy, Wolin asked rhetorically if these theories were not "beginning to falter as (they) speed over a real world that is increasingly discordant and is beginning to voice demands and hopes that are 'unreasonably high'?" (Wolin, 1969: 1082).

The appeal of the critical social theory that began to be popularized in political science in the late 1960s was that, unlike group theory and pluralism, it seemed to account for the crises of that decade. Its portrayal of elitist practice under a veil of democratic ideology seemed to explain why, a century after emancipation, black people still constituted an underclass in American society. It seemed to lend understanding to why, after a president felt constrained by public opinion to campaign on a platform of peace, he was then able to involve the country in the most unpopular war in the nation's history. This was a theory for a period of discontent, as the group approach had been one for a period of wartime unity and ensuing tranquility.

The new elite theories of politics varied greatly in their relative emphasis on whether an elite dominated politics directly or through more subtle means. The former emphasis was represented in the writings of G. William Domhoff, a psychologist working in the tradition of C. Wright Mills. Domhoff's *Who Rules America?* (1967) simplified and updated Mills' *The Power Elite* (1956). In this work, Domhoff correlated a social upperclass (documented from *Social Registers* and data on wealth) with what he termed "the governing class" (those occupying a disproportionate number of elite governmental, corporate, and policy-making positions). Both could be shown related to the relatively highly differentiated stratification of social and economic benefits in the United States.

A later work by Domhoff, *The Higher Circles: The Governing Class in America* (1970), extended this analysis. In addition to providing additional data of the sort contained in *Who Rules America?*, Domhoff sought to address the question of the mechanism by which a documentable upper-class translated its interests into the equally documentable unequal distribution of wealth and benefits. It was this invisible connection that had been the weakest part of the earlier book. Pluralist writers, engaged in decision-making studies, could argue that the social backgrounds of policy makers were irrelevant. The diversity and conflict of interests within the upper-class and "business establishment" could be seen as sufficiently great so that virtually all points of view were represented. If there was some class bias in the composition of government or in the leadership of corporations and media-related business, this in no way proved there was "domination" by any particular point of view. To know that, the pluralists said, one had to examine the concrete details that, the pluralist said, one had to examine the concrete details of particular decisions—a process that yielded findings of pluralism, not elitism.

Domhoff's counter to this argument was to contend that the connection between the upper-class and social outcomes could be revealed by a different sort of study of the policy-making process. In examining national social-welfare policy or foreign policy, for example, Domhoff could show the possible importance of certain policy institutions such as the Brookings Institution and the Council on Foreign Relations. These policy bodies, in turn, could be shown to be headed by boards of trustees who were members of the upper-class. In addition, Domhoff emphasized the role of social clubs (e.g., the Metropolitan, the Links) as milieus for discussion of major national issues by members of the social upper-class.

Prestigious policy associations and elite men's clubs were, however, a slender foundation upon which to build contemporary elite theory. Bauer, Pool and Dexter, for example, had already found the Council on Foreign Relations to be only marginally important in foreign policy formation (Bauer, Pool and Dexter, 1963). Domhoff's discussion of the social network of men's clubs, resorts, schools, and other elite facilities, while interesting, failed to provide evidence that any significant policy formation transpired in these settings. While some other studies in this period also reflected the "direct dominance" version of elite theory (see Tabb, 1970), most chose to emphasize more subtle and indirect connections between socioeconomic elites and political outcomes.

One such work was Ralph Miliband's *The State in Capitalist Society: An Analysis of the Western System of Power* (1969). Miliband, a leading British socialist theoreticiam, documented many of the same facts about the relation of government to the class system as had Domhoff. Unlike Domhoff, however, Miliband emphasized the indirect forms of hegemony of the economic elite, not direct domination. After a lengthy discussion of various processes whereby elite interests and values are perpetuated (e.g., through the media, schools, and universities), Miliband wrote, indicating the general nature of his argument, "There is one last aspect of the process of legitimation to which reference must be made, and which is of crucial importance, since it underlies all others. This is the degree to which capitalism as an economic and social system tends to produce, in itself, by its very existence, the conditions of its legitimation in the subordinate classes, and in other classes as well" (Miliband, 1969: 261-262).

In critical social theory the most important aspects of politics lay in its functions regarding cultural legitimation. If repression and manipulation were important, it was as an auxiliary means of control, becoming critical only when periods of profound social crisis stripped from capitalism its veneer of legitimacy and democracy to reveal underneath its ultimate value: protection of the profit system at any cost.

Thus, Miliband argued, pluralists like Dahl were "profoundly misleading" in taking America's democratic ideology largely at face value simply on the ground that the routine politics of normal times was not characterized chiefly by conspiratorial manipulation or repression, at least not in settings like New Haven in the 1950s. The crucial fact about normal politics was, as Dahl acknowledged in passing, that, even then, government officials avoided policies that might incite business fury (Dahl, 1961: 84). "In the light of the real economic power which business enjoys, and of the prevailing culture which legitimates this power, the question whether top executives or middle ones actually run for election and serve in local or state government appears grotesquely irrelevant" (Miliband, 1969: 173). Instead, what was relevant was the deference paid to the legitimacy of the capitalist system, and the consequences for this on the stratification of benefits in society. Ultimately, Miliband noted, had not business elites exercised so much influence the cities would not be locked in a crisis of poverty, both private and public. "The answer to pluralist theories of local power is provided by the critics themselves," Miliband concluded (Miliband, 1969: 175).

Miliband's work was, in many ways, simply a more concrete and forceful articulation of Bottomore's *Elites and Society* (1964) and other works of British radicalism (e.g., the *New Left Review*) that had had an influence on younger scholars and on the student movement for some time. But Miliband's work, like Domhoff's less sophisticated volumes, provided a more systematic, documented model of democratic politics than had hitherto existed. Both were explicit in rejecting pluralism and the group approach, and both provided a focus for the rise of more critical approaches to the study of American political science.

In addition to English influences, critical theory was furthered by the introduction of perspectives of the Frankfurt school, as in Norman Birnbaum's *The Crisis of Industrial Society* (1969). Like Miliband, Birnbaum rejected both the group approach and the "direct domination" school of elite theory. Likewise, Birnbaum also emphasized the crucial importance of legitimation processes as a key to understanding the politics of industrial capitalism. Pluralists, he said, misunderstood the nature of legitimation, interpreting it in terms of "group consensus." Genuine consensus coalesces spontaneously from below, however, whereas the American seeming "consensus" reflected values emanating from above. In industrial society, it was political culture, not conspiracy or repression, that served as the essential vehicle of domination by privileged interests over the mass of citizens.

The issue of false consensus and indirect domination by socioeconomic elites was, of course, a more pointed and radical rephrasing of Bachrach's concept of "nondecision-making." Nondecision-making took a pattern having a cumulative effect on the social stratification system, rather than a random one, because of the factors of legitimation and political culture discussed by Miliband and Birnbaum.

Here, defenders of the group approach took issue. Richard Merelman, for example, attacked the concept of "false consensus" (Merelman, 1968: 466). It was, he said, a nonfalsifiable and, therefore, unscientific notion that could be used ideologically to "explain" almost any social or governmental outcome. To distinguish genuine from false consensus, one would have to become embroiled in epistemological philosophizing about the origins of popular beliefs and dispositions. To contemplate the study of false consensus would be to consider in depth psychological analysis of opinion formation on a mass basis, itself a preposterous notion. Ultimately, even that approach, could it be undertaken, would founder on situational relativism —the unknowability of what an only partially rational actor would have done in a context other than the one that prevailed.

Merelman's critique, like a quite similar, subsequent defense of pluralism against "nondecision-making" by Wolfinger (1971), was methodologically true, but contained a non sequitur of analysis. The false consensus and elite cultural hegemony discussed by Miliband, Birnbaum, Bachrach, and other critical social theorists could not be distinguished, it is true, from pluralist consensus and acceptance of the "rules of the game" emphasized by Dahl, Truman, and group theorists. Or, more properly, the distinction could not be made by analyzing contemporary American politics.

Nonetheless, the distinction was real. Merelman erred in reasoning that because false consensus was not demonstrable through the techniques of political science research methodology, therefore, it was of no consequence. By seeking to reduce the purview of political science to the observable, Merelman, Wolfinger, and other pluralists took an extreme behavioralist stand, at best difficult to defend and at worst, silly. False consensus, critical social theorists understood, was demonstrable only through revolution, not through social science. The falsity of prevailing popular beliefs would be manifest in the rapid change of public opinion when, in the overthrow of capitalism, new and more radical alternatives would be perceived, manipulative role socialization to capitalist needs would be shed, and what had yesterday seemed illegitimate would now be made possible and right.

Critical social theory in the late 1960s was thus marked by a rejection of behavioralism (see Wormuth, 1967) and the rise of a more phenomenological approach to politics (Schutz, 1967; Schutz, 1970; Natanson, ed., 1973). Contrary to the group approach, the literature of critical social theory located the heart of political choice at the elite rather than interest group level. It phrased analysis in terms of questions of conditioning of beliefs, not direct and conscious decision-making choices. It focused on the role of ideology in fostering elite power (see Thoenes, 1966; Sartori, 1969), a concern almost alien to a group approach that had been based on assumptions of pragmatism and the "end of ideology."

The concern of critical social theory with the system of cultural and political legitimation, finally, was reinforced by findings of "mainstream" political scientists seeking to explain the basis of pluralist consensus. As Lipsitz noted in a much discussed critique of the work of Sidney Verba, an associate of Gabriel Almond, this research exposed the value premises of conventional interpretations of American politics in a way favorable to those disposed toward more critical social theory.

Verba, in the wake of the assassination of President Kennedy, had written on the religious-like role of central political symbols in social control (Verba, 1965b). Lipsitz, like Edelman and many other critical theorists, found this emphasis on the control function of political symbolism persuasive. "But accepting the potential insightfulness of Verba's analysis," Lipsitz asked (1968: 528), "where does it lead us?" It led to the notion of the political leader as a monarch-priest, building authority on attitudes of awe and reverence ingrained since citizens' childhood (see Easton and Hess, 1962). With this, Lipsitz could concur. It was in the normative appraisal of this description that issue was taken. Where the tone of Verba's analysis accepted the religious-like function of elite symbols as a natural part of the political process of legitimation and consensus-formation, Lipsitz found in the same facts the danger of undemocratic manipulation of political life in a way entirely inconsistent with traditional values of active citizensip in a republican state.

In general, the emerging critical approach to political science emphasized the subtle manner in which various aspects of reality, those that would undermine elite position, became subdued in a political culture that served to reinforce elite interests (see Kariel, 1969). This perspective blended with research showing the role of political elites as active mobilizers rather than passive reflectors of interest group pressures (see Holtzman, 1970: 289). But critical social theory went beyond this to attack the fundamental premises of group theory. It did not merely deny that interest groups were the key to decision processes in government. More, it denied that the overt political decision-making process itself was the central element of political life. As this perspective was popularized, the group approach was viewed as not so much wrong in its empirical findings, but wrong in the very questions it posed.

_____

References appear at the end of Chapter 5.

Chapter 5

**From Research "Theory" to
Research "Area": The
Disintegration of the Group
Approach to Political
Science in the 1970s**

No social theory ever becomes widespread without its containing an important element of truth and, for the same reason, important social theories never truly "disappear." Rather, as in the case of the group approach to political science, the elements in them that seem true are reformulated and incorporated into newer social theories. While such a process connotes evolution, in American political science the term "evolution" would suggest a linearity, dialectic, or other pattern of development that is not discernible. What has occurred in the area of group studies in the 1970s is a splintering and fragmentation of approach. The disintegration of the group approach transformed what had been a research theory with a claim to providing a unifying disciplinary paradigm into a mere research area in a discipline adrift with dozens of rudimentary competing "frameworks," none able to rise to the level of professional acceptance of that which had been displaced.

Surveying the group approach to political science after 1970, one is led to ask, "What's left?" Certainly the group approach, while in drastic eclipse, is far from moribund. This is particularly so in the comparative area that, having come to the group orientation later, may be expected to lose interest later as well. Thus, for example, the early 1970s saw a flutter of group analyses of Soviet politics (Skilling and Griffiths, eds., 1971; Frolic, 1972; Kelley, 1972), building on the work of Schwartz and Keech (1968). Here the group approach seemed useful as a theoretical umbrella for discussing the slow increase in "interest group power" in the USSR, by which was meant an ill-defined factionalization of the Communist Party, sometimes on the basis of generic interests.

The comparative survey of interest groups also found expression in 1974 in a special issue of the *Annals of the American Academy of Political and Social Science*. Here the group approach was simply a matter of description with no pretense to constituting a theory of politics. The institutionalization of groups was discussed with regard to Switzerland (Sidjanski, 1974) and the Netherlands (Daalder and Irwin, 1974); class and socioeconomic bases of organizations were analyzed in Italy (Sani, 1974); and racial divisions and the role of groups in *apartheid* were examined in South Africa (Pretorius and Vosloo, 1974). In these studies and in others (e.g., Roberts' 1972 study of pressure groups in Britain), comparative scholarship, apart from purposes of sheer documentation, served mainly to present a view of pressure groups as benign and accepted components of virtually all political systems.

Only rarely was the group approach integrated with the comparativists' existing theories, such as theories of political development. Almond, Verba, and others connected with the influential comparative politics group of the Social Science Research Council (SSRC) had, of course, emphasized the role of groups in interest aggregation and articulation, two basic process functions fundamental to political modernization. But these statements were of such a broad nature that they amounted to little more than acknowledgment of the tendency of modernization to be accompanied by functional specialization and differentiation. The SSRC approach did not, for example, empirically predict or normatively prescribe any mode or sequence of interest-group processes, whether of pluralism or corporatism.

If the comparative study of interest groups harbored a central academic thesis, it was simply that the functional organization that accompanied the division of labor in modernizing societies was a necessary, but not sufficient, determinant of liberal democracy. Thus, Tarrow found, for example, that the professional organization of French peasants improved their level of political information and encouraged their participation in politics (e.g., running for office; see Tarrow, 1971: 355). Similarly, Agpalo traced the increasing legitimization of liberal democracy in the Philippines to the rise of new men of wealth capable of challenging the position of old families, combined with increased farmer participation and the rise of poor people's interest organizations (Agpalo, 1972). Closer to home, Laumann's study of Detroit showed that among America's dominant religious grouping, the Protestants, occupational organization provided the basis for social networks cutting across ethnoreligious solidarities (Laumann, 1973). Because in most definitions democracy is defined as requiring freedom of group formation ("freedom of assembly"; see Plano and Greenberg, 1967: 6), such studies merely tended to give historical dimensionality to a definitional component of the implicit dependent variable. That is, if such studies were to be treated as using the group approach as a general theory of politics, which would be a misinterpretation of the authors' intentions, one would be "explaining" democracy on the basis of the historical presence of a definitional component of democracy. The explanation would be circular.

When, in the 1970s, academics rose to defend the group approach to politics and pluralist theories, the defense was based not on such methodologies being predictive political theories, but rather on two wholly different grounds: that much of contemporary American politics was pluralist, and that this was all to the good. In this vein, for example, Robert Fluno defended pluralism in a 1971 presidential address to the Pacific Northwest Political Science Association, stating, "so long as pluralism is so frustrating and so embarrassingly selfish, men will be angered by it. Pluralism implies a muddling through. As a process of collective policy-making it is too intellectually unattractive, too incredibly clumsy, for those of us who prize

order in a world so depressingly chaotic. . . . But the gamble
that concentration is better than pluralism is simply that: a
gamble, perhaps the most ancient and risky of political gambles"
(Fluno, 1971: 563-564).

This defense of the group approach fit in with studies that
showed that in some issues all interests "got a share" of the
outcome (e.g., in the bracero program; see Craig, 1971). The
success of certain minority interests in effecting American
government (e.g., Zionists; see Huff, 1972), and optimism
associated with the recent rise of public interest organizations
(see Lutrin and Settle, 1975) and their newly improved legal
standing (see Orren, 1976), also seemed to reinforce the pluralist
viewpoint.

Then, too, the aftermath of the antiwar, civil rights, and
new Left movements in the 1960s had undermined traditional
liberal faith in federal centralism and legitimated many types
of "grass roots" participation that earlier had not seemed attrac-
tive to liberals (e.g., revenue sharing, education vouchers,
and community control of schools). Private sector voluntarism
became a national movement with government blessing and
attendant academic interest (see Smith and Freedman, 1972).
Increased socially concerned corporate activities were widely
touted as counters to the negative images of industry put forth
by critics of pluralism and others (see Cohn, 1971).

Even if the normative bias toward lauding various tendencies
toward political fragmentation was rejected, however, numerous
studies continued to demonstrate that in this or that particular
setting, group pressures were indeed important. Francis, for
example, showed that in American state politics, group pressures
were strong in issues of labor, liquor, business, agriculture,
water, gambling, welfare, and education, but less so in civil
rights and taxation questions (Francis, 1971: 712). In states
with a weak executive, such as Texas, groups were found to
be important in policy formation also (Nimmo and Oden,
1971; Anderson, Murray, and Farley, 1971). The same seemed
to be true where, as in Nebraska, political parties were weak
(Kolasa, 1971: 77). Groups astute enough to participate in

state politics often found their lobbying rewarding (Burman, 1973: 113), though many groups neglected their opportunities. At the national level, too, Presthus (1974a) found groups playing a sometimes critical role in crystallizing public policy. In some countries, such as Britain, that role seemed to be increasing (Benewick, 1974). In the United States, the growing sophistication of lobbies in letter, telephone, and telegram campaigns, not to mention advertising, business-supported policy institutes, and traditional lobbying, also suggested an increasing interest-group role in the future (see Bacheller, 1977).

That some studies showed interest groups to be important in particular settings, or certain government decisions to be marked by political fragmentation and pluralism, though, was insufficient to defend the group approach as a general political theory. In the 1970s, criticism of the descriptiveness, value premises, and other assumptions of the group-theoretic and pluralist models of politics became commonplace. Anti-pluralist criticism was no longer confined to the Left.

If some studies showed group theory description of the politcal process borne out, many did not. Lander (1971), for example, showed that in formation of President Johnson's "War on Poverty" program, groups such as blacks, youth, and the elderly were not well organized and played too limited a role to explain this decision area on the basis of group theory. Similarly, the Ralph Nader series of exposés of federal regulatory agencies (e.g., Turner, 1970; Fellmeth, 1970) showed corporatist accommodation, not competitive pluralism, to be the dominant mode of government decision-making in various policy areas. Even at the state level, 1960s' reforms such as increased legislative staff, annual sessions, higher salaries, and modernized committee structure tended to diminish the power of private pressure groups (Robinson, ed., 1973).

Often, pluralism was seen as a smokescreen for a realpolitik of elite accommodation. In Europe, Eisfeld (1972) found in pluralist traits of limited representativeness of groups and inequality of resources the basis for the case for socialist reorganization of society. In the United States, the same criticism of pluralism was apt to lead scholars to advocate further liberal reforms. Davidson (1974), for example, found Congressional committees were marked by the underrepresentation of generalized public interests. As a solution he advocated not socialism, but rather Congressional committee reform to regulate "natural" pluralist unrepresentativeness by systematic introduction of counter-vailing forces. Theodore Lowi (1974), finding interest-group liberalism founded on organization as distortion of representa-tiveness, on artificial majorities, and on the tendency of collective action to neglect diffuse but important public goods, urged that the embrace of spontaneous pluralism be broken by rein-troduction of traditional concepts of disinterested regulation. The rise of economic inflation in the 1970s underlined the inequitableness of the group representative bias of American politics. Indeed, Killick (1975: 425) cogently argued that Ameri-can acceptance of unfettered pluralism was a major facilitant of inflation, the inconveniences of which were diffused across a consuming public less organized than the well-equipped interests who stood to gain from inflationary government policies.

Louis Gawthrop, in *Administrative Politics and Social Change* (1971), had argued along much the same lines. The fragmentation embodied in pluralist politics, he said, prevented the comprehensive responses to mounting social problems brought about in part by the very incrementalism of pluralist group process. Incrementalism, however, found defense in the 1970s in the rise of public choice theory. Public choice theory, by orienting analytic assumptions toward marketplace and marginalist economics, inevitably entailed a view of politics as incrementalism. Because clothed in the seemingly sceintific garments of marginalist economics, however, public choice theory and its near relatives (e.g., exchange theory, and Downsian analyses) were able to reformulate incrementalism in a way that successfully avoided some of the criticism to which group approach was then being subjected.

The public choice theorists, such as Niskanen (1971), extended the public goods perspective of scholars like Tullock (1970), and the marketplace analogies of Downs (1957), into a more detailed discussion of government decision-making. Bureaucrats, Niskanen argued, were monopolists maximizing their budgets through dominance over the information process, wresting from their legislative sponsors an undue average cost for the public product and authority to overproduce public services far more than marginal costing criteria would justify. Niskanen's budget-maximization thrust differed from the vote-maximization assumptions of followers of Downs (see Bartlett, 1973) or the vaguer political "profit" maximization criteria of Frohlich, Oppenheimer, and Young (1971), but like them and like other examples of exchange theory and public goods theory discussed earlier, this approach supported the incrementalist view of politics as a process of aggregation of many decisions in a political marketplace. And, like them, its conservative (pro-market determination of priorities) and individualist/rational assumptions about political process assured that it, too, would receive similar criticism.

Criticism of public choice incrementalism proceeded from numerous grounds. First, the concept of maximization motivation that all variants posited, required a quantification of governmentally relevant variables that had already brought program planning and budgeting into disrepute (see Schick, 1973). Even if accepted, maximization motivation assumed an objectionable emphasis on individualist rationality. As Rae acknowledged in an essay attempting to apply another quantitative-rational methodology (game theory) to politics, "through manipulation, neurosis, ignorance, or 'false consciousness,' the members of a domain may not, in a given policy choice, know their own interests and may therefore plump for self-damaging outcomes" (Rae, 1971: 118). Second, authors like Niskanen could be questioned on the grounds that government tends to under- rather than overproduce goods and services of a collective nature. This, of course, had been the argument of Galbraith (1958) and Olson (1965), but now it became a point of specific attack on public choice theory such as that represented by the Ostroms (Ostrom and Ostrom, 1971; see critique, Sproule-Jones, 1973). Third, as Schulman noted

(Schulman, 1975: 1370), public choice theory, like pluralism and other forms of incrementalism, frequently amplified social problems through a series of marginal decisions that in the aggregate were dysfunctional to the social welfare.

The analogy between economic and political decision-making was never an exact one to say the least (see Baldwin, 1971). Without a clear equivalent to profit-maximization, with a far more factionalized decision-making body than that of the firm, characterized by political actors with quasi-rational and diverse motives not describable as "maximization" along any single dimension, and with an often unmeasurable "product," the economic tools of public choice theory were not calculated to win reacceptance of pluralist incrementalism among large numbers of American political scientists. Rather, public goods, exchange, and public choice theories provided for a relatively conservative minority in the profession a seemingly more scientific and certainly more policy-relevant tent in which to camp than had the now tired vehicles of group theory and pluralism.

In the 1970s, then, group theory was advancing on only a few fronts such as comparative studies of interest groups and public choice theories of politics. Because even here basic criticisms abounded, when one turned to consider other areas of the discipline, the disintegration of the group approach was evident.

A process of disintegration, by definition involving a splintering into a large number of parts, is inherently difficult to describe in detail. The attempt to do so results in tedious lists of splinter effects, the recounting of which is apt to seem confusing and unnecessarily obscure in relation to general themes of one's analysis. Therefore, after presenting a brief sampling of such splinter developments, the remainder of the present essay will be devoted to examining further development of critical social theory in the mid-1970s as the theme uniting the largest number of publications bearing on pluralism and other group theories of politics.

Splinter effects usually took up arguments already discussed with regard to works critical of the group approach as presented

in the 1960s. Group theory was attacked for its base on actors
motivated through calculations of self-interest, for instance,
again raising the objection to group theory's neglect of ideological and other normative bases of political action (Cochran,
1973: 766). Not only was ideology asserted to be more important
than group theorists suggested, authors such as Putnam (1971:
680) cogently argued that ideological politics was also normatively preferable to incrementalism, even in terms of maximization of policy effectiveness. The permissive attitudes of group
theorists regarding interest groups did not, it was said, realistically assess the dysfunctional nature of the group influence
process on government policy (see Lieber, 1972). As attention
was increasingly focused on the negative consequences of both
corporate and social protest activities, liberal (e.g., Cochran,
1973) and conservative (e.g., Belz, 1974) commentators found
themselves reasserting constitutionalism and other public-
interest conceptions as part of a critique of pure tolerance of
group process. In general it was argued that the empiricism
of the group approach was simplistic and that the advance of
political science as a discipline depended precisely on the re-
legitimization of various dimensions of normative theory,
including theories of the public interest (see Garson, 1974).

In the 1970s, various intellectual currents were pushing
social science to a more critical orientation toward the American
system. Although academic critiques of pluralism and group
theory had by then become commonplace (e.g., Baskin, 1971),
the extension and institutionalization of the consumer movement provided a more visible public symbol of the renewed
antipathy toward those most prevalent of interest groups,
business pressures. The many works associated with Ralph
Nader (see Fallows, 1971; Green, Fallows, and Zwick, 1972)
helped spread even in academia a profound malaise over any
such sanguine acceptance of group-politics-as-usual often
found in pluralist writings. Then, too, this viewpoint drew
on a more generalized sort of radicalism popularized in the
previous decade among students now becoming the professors
and policy analysts of the 1970s. The government-like but
undemocratic nature of corporate power was condemned by

political scientists (Vogel, 1975), echoing McConnell's earlier warnings about "private government" (McConnell, 1958, 1967). Even the few ventures of business into the realm of social action and altruism came under sharp attack as camouflage for racist or self-serving ends (Orren, 1974). Reformers proposed that Congress fund "public lobbyists" to counter business pressures (Lipsen and Lesher, 1977). And, of course, the scandals of the Watergate era provided the perfect opportunity for elite stratification theorists to reiterate their view that politics was as far removed from pluralist theory as the practice of the Nixon administration was from its public pronouncements (see Domhoff, 1974).

In spite of research showing that wealth did not, in general, dominate campaigns and elections (see review by Adamany, 1977), there was a growing interest in studies that showed an indirect connection between business and politics. The concepts of "private government" and of "nongovernmental public policy" (Nadel, 1975: 33) again raised the issue of the subtle effects of corporate policy practices. This area had been central to Bachrach's "nondecision-making" critique of group theory. Now, however, policy research in a variety of areas documented how government inaction combined with capitalist economics to reinforce a highly structured stratification system (on health policy, see Alford, 1972; on education, see Jencks, 1972, and Katzman, 1971; on housing, see Aaron, 1972).

On the one hand, critical research on the output side of policy process showed a harmonization of governmental and business perspectives at elite levels that could be seen as reflective of convergence of social background factors (e.g., Dye and Pickering, 1974). On the other hand, the very reemergence of interest in class analysis of American politics (see Form and Huber, 1971; Hamilton, 1972; Huber and Form, 1973), went hand in hand with new attention to social movements directed against class elites.

The renewed research on social movements and on public-interest groups was based, of course, on the proliferation and front-page headlines of such groups in the late 1960s and early

1970s. Partisans of such causes often saw politics as elitist, or at least not as equitable as the tone of group theory seemed to promise. But the very emergence of social movements and public-interest associations breathed a new pluralism into American politics that, ironically, easily might be cited as further evidence for the correctness of group theories of politics!

Research on social movements and protest groups, however, indicated that such pressures could not be expected to alter American power structure appreciably. In spite of numerous organizing manuals containing enthusiastic how-to-do-it advice (Kahn, 1970; Nader and Ross, 1971; Walzer, 1971; Alinsky, 1971; Simpson, 1972) actual protest experience led more to frustration than to a sense of political efficacy. As James Q. Wilson observed in *Political Organizations* (1973), the syndrome of low-income family disintegration, and lack of organizational skills and resources hardly promised a firm foundation for the effort to organize the poor. As Lipsky had earlier suggested (Lipsky, 1968), the success of protest organizations depended critically on the support of sympathetic third parties (see also Gelb and Sardell, 1975), another fundamental problem of lower class protest groups. Though officials might be the subject of direct appeal at times (as opposed to indirect appeals, such as through the media), militancy seemed to be negatively related to enhancing policy responsiveness (see Schumaker, 1975: 519). Protest frequently failed because the disenfranchised overrated their political influence (Boschken, 1975: 70-71). Such movements required a long period of consciousness-raising and agenda-building (Cobb, Ross, and Ross, 1976), not providing early gratification of needs, yet necessitating skills rarely found to an adequate extent among the poor.

All of this was not to deny that the social movements and public-interest organizations of the 1960s and 1970s lacked the potential to render the American system substantially more pluralistic. The civil rights movement succeeded in institutionalizing many of its perspectives in legislation, regulatory decisions, and court rulings. The public-interest organizations became a regular feature of the Washington scene, based not

on the disenfranchised but on a seemingly solid base of middle-
and upper-class altruism. Without entering into the murky
debate over whether the political accomplishments of such
interest groups have been more symbolic than tangible, it may
be noted safely that the immediate effect of the social ferment
of the late 1960s and early 1970s, coincident with its later stages
when the level of frustration was higher, was a rising interest
in employing government to aid in the organization of groups
otherwise resource poor and difficult to mobilize.

"Participatory democracy" and "community control" were,
of course, the catchwords of this interest, particularly on the
political left (see Kramer, 1972). These slogans found heterogeneous support from blacks (Fainstein and Fainstein, 1976),
the young (an international phenomenon, see Inglehart, 1971;
Marsh, 1975), and interests seeking to assert domestic priorities
over foreign affairs (Rosenfeld, 1974). In terms of more remote
causes, the interest in participatory democracy may be associated
with the decline of American political parties and traditional
forms of interest aggregation (Abramson, 1976), and with
a new belief in the power of information in an age of mass media
(Henderson, 1974).

Participatory democracy was a common meeting ground
for group theorists and their critics on the left. For the critics,
it represented the reintroduction into political discourse of
explicitly normative terminology. As Scaff observed, "As
a concept it is capable of reestablishing the fundamental idea
that politics is concerned with communication and justice
as well as competition and influence" (Scaff, 1975: 462). Participatory democracy also fit in nicely with advocacy planning
and other radical conceptions of professional roles (Mazziotti,
1974). Group theorists, on the other hand, also often favored
participatory representation on community boards and government committees (see Dion, 1971-1972). New Haven politics
under Mayor Lee, made the model of pluralist practice in Dahl's
famous study, was marked by successful poverty-program
efforts at citizen involvement and community participation
(Murphy, 1971). To a considerable extent, the more participation, the more pluralist theory was justified.

The meeting of group theorists and their critics on the movement for expanded participatory roles was superficial at best,
however. Pluralists like Dahl recognized that a true movement
for making American political institutions optimum for participatory democracy would require a political and perhaps
demographic decentralization of the most drastic sort (see
Dahl and Tufte, 1973). In reality, citizen participation was
likely to become yet another public management tool for conflict
adjustment (see Irland, 1975). Moreover, given the historic
pattern of political participation (Verba and Nie, 1972: 12-
13), and the tendency of elites to share the same issue perceptions
and priorities as upper-class participators (Rusk, 1976: 583),
participatory democracy was likely to be no more successful
than earlier reform movements (civic education, responsible
parties) had been in seeking to transform the nature of the
relation of the mass of citizens to the state (Adamany, 1972:
1325). As Schattschneider had written in 1960, "The flaw in
the pluralist heaven is that the heavenly chorus sings with a
strong upper-class accent" (Schattschneider, 1960: 35).

For many observers, the upshot of the new interest in citizen
participation was simply to legitimize further the role of the
administrator, acting on a subjective concept of public interest,
actively to mobilize and educate a supportive constituency
(Etzioni, 1975). Some wished to institutionalize the representation of diverse viewpoints directly in the bureaucracy (e.g.,
George, 1972). Others simply projected an interpretation of
politics that, by emphasizing the role of the bureaucratic actor,
was quite at variance with the participatory ideals of the critics
or even the group-process views of the pluralists. Though the
pluralists had emphasized political entrepreneurship far more
than earlier group theorists, now views of politics became
popular that went far beyond this. A particularly popular example was Graham Allison's *The Essence of Decision* (1971).
Allison cogently argued that the group-theoretic model of
politics (bureaucratic politics of bargaining among players)
was, by itself, no more accurate than rational models (e.g.,
systems theoretic) of decision-making. Both needed to be joined
to each other and to a third model, that of "organizational

process," emphasizing the importance of bureaucratic practices and standard operating procedures in policy formation.

Allison's perspective could, of course, be interpreted as a further broadening of pluralist theory to include yet additional types of competing influences. But the emphasis on nongroup bases of political decision (professional rationality, bureaucratic standards and norms) by Allison removed his theory of American political process far indeed from the group-theory base of pluralism. To interpret such theories as a more inclusive pluralist theory is to broaden pluralism to mean almost anything.

In fact, ideas such as Allison's related far more closely to that venerable companion and intellectual nemesis of pluralism, corporatism. And in convergence with corporatist ideas, discussion is returned to the central themes of contemporary social theory. In his recent essay, "A World of Becoming: From Pluralism to Corporatism," Norman Keehn argued that if pluralism had ever been a true description of the American polity, that truth was rapidly becoming eroded by the very tendency of group process to undermine traditional sovereignty. Technology, he wrote, tends toward the obliteration of the distinction between "public" and "private." Government acquires property rights and intrudes everywhere upon management prerogatives, while at the same time public functions are devolved to private interests on a massive scale (Keehn, 1976: 38). In this situation government ceases to be the referee of group process. It becomes, instead, the mobilizer of groups toward desired ends it chooses.

If this is "still the century of corporatism" as Schmitter has also suggested (Schmitter, 1974), it is, perhaps, because corporatism serves quite modern purposes. It addresses the rise of large-scale economic interests in a way far more sophisticated than traditional, formal theories of sovereignty and authority. This had also been a major factor in the rise of group theory as it displaced nineteenth-century jurisprudential approaches to political science. But where group theory excelled in describing the new realities of private power, it contained no real theory of government, corporatism is manifested in the elite accommodaworkings of a free economic marketplace. Indeed, group theory assumed that incrementalism forestalled comprehensive (compromise-minimizing) directed change. Corporatism not only explained the rise of private interests, but also advanced a theory of their coordination for public purposes.

Though American politics are not corporatist in the sense of formally reorganizing government operations along functional jurisdictions or routinizing the direct and formal representation of corporate and institutional delegates in the agencies of government, corporatism is manifested in the elite accomodation of public and private sector interests on regulatory agencies, advisory committees, and congressional committees; interchange of personnel between the two sectors; similarity of social backgrounds; and, above all, mutual elite acceptance of the fundamental premises of the prevailing economic system. Many other indications of informal corporatism could be cited, such as the rise of government-industrial complexes in defense, urban renewal, and transportation. Observing these phenomena, elite accommodation rather than group competition might be thought the dominant characteristic of the American political system and the necessary cornerstone of useful theories about it.

Robert Presthus's work on the politics of elite accommodation was perhaps best known of those presenting a critical alternative to group theories of politics in the 1970s (see Presthus, 1973). In *Elites and the Policy Process* (1974b), Presthus presented empirical data on American and Canadian interest-group directors, legislators, and senior bureaucrats, showing similarities of background and a "consociational" pattern in which lobbyists rarely believed they had competitors or enemies opposing their efforts at public-private elite accommodation within the specialized functional arenas in which they operated.

The literature on "consociational democracy" and elite accommodation had been discussed by Lijphart (1968) with regard to the Netherlands, but Presthus' work served to translate a similar concept into American terms. The key to consociational accommodation, as Apter wrote (1977: 321), is elite bargaining. By emphasizing "bargaining," as Apter does, it is possible to see the consociational model as a variant of pluralism. By emphasizing "elite" and "accommodation," however, one is carried over the dim boundary separating group and interest competition analyses from corporatist and other elite theories of politics.

"Consociational democracy," "elite accomodation," "neo-corporatism," and "corporatism" were, in the 1970s, increasingly recognized as labels for states contrasting to pluralism and toward which may modernizing societies were already well advanced. This was particularly so with regard to analyses of Latin American politics, where the continued importance of the traditional bases of the fascist version of corporatism were most obvious: strong military, church influence, large propertied and business interests, and government-dominated labor movements made corporatism seem, in Newton's words, a "natural development" in Spanish America (Newton, 1974). The modernizing authoritarianism of the Peruvian junta, for example, was explicitly corporatist (see Malloy, 1974). Similarly, as Schmitter noted of Brazilian politics, actual interest patterns did not seem to conform to classic group models of political process. While interest groups proliferated with modernization as predicted by group theory, groups did not become independently influential apart from their coopted role as auxiliaries of state policy operating in a neocorporatist manner (Schmitter, 1971).

In terms of American politics, Milbrath (1963) and Dexter (1969) had shown a pattern neither of pluralist theory competition and countervailing powers, nor of elite theory political subjection to economic pressure, but rather of "a network of accommodation and mutual assistance" (Vogler, 1974: 271). Citing this pattern of elite accommodation, Vogler faulted pluralist theory on two counts: its neglect of "the collusion of seemingly disparate groups" and its assumption that "competing groups will prevent any one interest from dominating a particular policy subsystem" and "that most policy areas involve opposing groups that serve to check the demands of others" (Vogler, 1974: 279). The actual pattern, he argued, was one of collusion within norms of mutual noninterference.

Evidence in support of the "elite accommodation" view was easy to come by. In education, Wirt and Kirst (1972) documented the dominance of bureaucratic experts whose power was legitimized by an ideology of lay participation never implemented in practice. In the health area, Strickland (1972) found decision-making to be of the accommodating "old boy" style, a style supported by legislators who opposed lobbyists' involving the wider public even when they were so disposed. And in addition to the elite accommodation aspect of corporatism, new government programs such as manpower administration showed the spread of another corporatist element, the delegation of public authority to "private government" (see Kobrak, 1973).

In the 1970s, as the debate between pluralist and other group theorists on the one hand, and elite and stratification theorists on the other, receded into the realm of academic history, it was replaced by another. The emerging debate is between those who have revised pluralism to the extent that it ceases to be a group theory of politics, but is instead a theory of "consociational democracy" or "elite accomodation;" and critical social theorists who have revised elite theory to the extent that it is no longer an economic theory of politics, but is instead based on concepts such as "neocorporatism" and "elite cultural hegemony."

One of the most interesting exponents of the postpluralist view is Daniel Bell. In *The Coming of Post-Industrial Society* (1973), Bell agreed that the emerging American political order could be seen as corporatist to the extent that power was increasingly organized along functional-institutional "situses" (economic, governmental, academic, social service, and military). Bell did not, however, agree that functional organization of power would lead to corporatist style accommodation. Elite accomodation would be by function, not between functions. Politics would not be between a class of corporate "ins" and the mass of dispossessed "outs". Rather, politics would center on interfunctional rivalries regarding national allocative priorities. "My argument," he wrote, "is that the major interest conflicts will be between the situs groups and that the attachments to these situses might be sufficiently strong to prevent the organization of the new, professional groups into a coherent class in society" (Bell, 1973: xvii).

Later in *The Coming of Post-Industrial Society,* however, Bell so revised the view just quoted that he virtually contradicted himself. "The politics of the future—at least for those who operate within society—," he wrote, "will not be quarrels between functional economic-interest groups for distributive shares of the national product, but the concerns of communal society, particularly the inclusion of disadvantaged groups. They will turn on issues of instilling a responsible social ethos in our leaders, the demand for more amenities, for greater beauty and a better quality of life in the arrangement of our cities, a more differentiated and intellectual educational system, and an improvement in the character of our culture" (Bell, 1973: 367).

This lofty view suggested a politics cutting across functional lines and centering on noneconomic issues, non interfunctional rivalry based on self interested desires for aggrandizement relative to other situses. This view also suggested that that politics was spontaneous in development and benign in nature. Critical social theorists viewed the same drive to achieve cross-functional accommodation on a politics deemphasizing economic issues as elitist in origin and purpose.

Some critical theorists, such as Duverger (1974), continued to view democratic politics as merely a modern context for the traditional conflict of an economic oligarchy with popular will. A more subtle interpretation was more influential, however. Two strands were important: radical criticism growing out of the influence of praxis theory and of the Frankfurt school, sometimes in conjunction with phenomenology; and liberal criticism growing out of Bachrach's "nondecision-making" concept and Edelman's theories about "symbolic action."

Anthony Giddens has usefully summarized the similarity and contrast between Bell's postpluralist position and critical theory of the sort represented by the Frankfurt school of social philosophy. The similarity lies in the correspondence between Bell's vision of the rise of an all-pervasive technocratic ethos, and the prediction by authors such as Marcuse and Habermas that policy-making will be increasingly legitimated by an ostensibly "neutral" technocratic mode, in fact serving elite ideological purposes (see Giddens, 1973: 258). Also, both are similar in their rejection of the Marxist notion that the revolutionary promise of the working class has been forestalled by the tendency of imperialism to "buy off" worker insurgency and displace class conflict onto the confrontation of advanced with less developed countries. Instead, both view technology and rising productivity as the paramount basis for a far more sophisticated system of social control. The essential difference with Bell centered on the insistence by most members of the Frankfurt school that the emerging world order, technocratic or even corporatist as it might be, still was premised on the priorities of capitalism. That is, Bell, like Burnham three decades earlier (Burnham, 1941), profoundly misestimated the capacity of capitalism to thrive under increasingly corporatist and tech-nocratic conditions (for a discussion of the Frankfurt school on this point, see Harrington, 1976: 216-223).

This capacity, Habermas wrote, depended upon meeting the increased needs for delegitimization of authority correspond-ing to the increased functions of the state in contemporary demo-cracies (Habermas, 1973, in Connerton, ed., 1976: 376). Offe, another of the Frankfurt school writers, described the necessary state response as requiring "that both the limits defining the range of action of the political system, as well as those defining the prospects for the political articulation of needs, were com-mensurate with economically drawn class lines . . . the pluralistic system of organized interests excludes from the processes con-cerned with consensus formation all articulations of demands that are general in nature and not associated with any status group; that are incapable of conflict because they have no functional significance for the utilization of capital and labor power; and that represent utopian projections beyond the historically specific system insofar as they do not unconditionally abide by the pragmatic rules of judicious bargaining" (Offe, 1972, in Connerton, ed., 1976: 395, 404). That is, legitimation and social control depend upon the ability to define what is perceived as the parameters of a viable political agenda.

The reader will recognize, of course, that this concept, if stripped from its place in radical discussions of the adaptability of capitalism in specific, is the central theme of the liberal tradition of critical theory represented by Bachrach and Edelman. Bachrach's "nondecision-making" concept referred to a process of mobilization of bias in a political culture whereby potential policies inconsistent with basic system interests were deligitimated as "utopian," "subversive," "unrealistic," "immoral," or were repressed or ignored. This perspective, similar to Marcuse's concept of "repressive tolerance," assumed that, given the political culture and its biases, free speech and popular elections in fact operated systematically to legitimate elite interests. As Wolfinger (1971) pointed out, this contention is almost impossible to operationalize, a charge later repeated by Debnam (1975: 895).

The reply of Bachrach and his colleague Morton Baratz to this charge asserted that "In a reasonably stable polity, power is mainly exercised not by those who make decisions nor by those who decide agendas, but by persons and groups who direct their energy toward shaping or reinforcing predominant norms, precedents, myths, institutions, and procedures that undergird and characterize the political process" (Bachrach and Baratz, 1975: 900-901). Decision-making studies, pluralism, and group theory, in general, assumed that the political cultural system was a "given," setting the parameters for analysis. Critical social theorists, in contrast, regarded political culture and the pattern of political decision-making as mutually reinforcing manifestations of societal power structure.

The elusiveness of the nondecision-making concept has often been exaggerated. In Bachrach's definition of the term, nondecision-making is an overt or covert *act* that can, in principle, be observed. Its impact also may be studied empirically. Nondecision-making acts include cooption of opponents, public denial of legitimacy to demands for change, and deflection of challenges by referring grievances to study commissions (Bachrach and Baratz, 1975: 902). Most forms of what Edelman terms "symbolic action" would also be included.

Symbolic action, by which government employs cultural catchwords and symbolic acts of state (e.g., creation of new programs, new legislation, appointment of new officials, and reorganization of administration) to reassure citizens that "things are being done," when in fact the actions may have little prospect of remedying the grievances toward which they are ostensibly addressed, is easily noted in authoritarian polities (see Mueller, 1973). However, the same sort of ideological control is exerted in western democracies as well, Edelman has argued. Consensus and feelings of political efficacy, so emphasized in group theorists' interpretations of American politics, may be equally significant as evidence of mass quiescence (Weissberg, 1975: 487). In *Politics as Symbolic Action,* (1971) Edelman summarized his view that "Government plays an especially salient function in the shaping of cognitions about political issues. On many of the most controversial ones the impact of governmental actions upon mass beliefs and perceptions is, in fact, the major, or the only, consequence of political activity" (Edelman, 1971: 174).

Whether discussing "neocorporatism" and "elite cultural hegemony" in the radical version, or "nondecision-making" and "symbolic action" in the liberal version, critical social theory pointed in the direction of increased concern for the study of political socialization, role adjustment, and reference models. By this point in the confused line of intellectual history we have been tracing, the issues of group theory seemed almost irrelevant. In emphasizing the role of lobbies as key influence-wielders, it seemed factually incorrect. In employing decision-making studies as a central methodology, it seemed to bias discussion away from the more subtle issues of consciousness formation that had become central by the 1970s. In posing a pluralist description of American politics, it conflicted with emergent corporatism. In prescribing incrementalism, it constituted an ideological obstacle to all efforts toward directed comprehensive change at a time in history when the need for change had reached crisis proportions. In short, the world of group theory seemed increasingly anachronistic in the new political discourse of the 1970s.

Summary

At the outset of this essay the question was raised of what has happened to group theories of politics in the last two decades. How is it that students of political science have received such a meager inheritance from a drive toward systematic theory that consumed the most intense energies of the political science profession over a quarter century? In his recent essay, "What's Wrong With Political Science," Michael Nelson, an editor of the *Washington Monthly*, attributed much of the blame to the behaviorist propensities of Merriam and others who controlled Social Science Research Council monies for so long. Under their aegis, political science was led toward arcane studies divorced from reality. "It got to the point," Nelson wrote, "where one could pick up the current issue of the *American Political Science Review* and come away blissfully ignorant of all the burning political questions of the day" (Nelson, 1977: 16-17). To underline his point, an official of the American Political Science Association was quoted to the effect that, "If a political scientist comes to Washington and waves his sheepskin, he'll get his ass kicked. People in government, in business, in the media, and so on have no expectations of us at all. In fact some employers have to be convinced that a political scientist isn't overly handicapped by what he learned in graduate school" (Nelson, 1977: 13).

Certainly the behavioral revolution of the 1970s did not do for political science what Keynesianism had done for economics a decade earlier. The current massive resurgence of "policy studies" in political science must be interpreted in large measure as a disciplinary acknowledgment that behavioralism did not provide an adequate basis for approaching political issues of consequence to those outside the rarified atmosphere of the empirical theorists which behavioralism had spawned. Behaviorally oriented theories such as systems analysis are now in a state of severe eclipse amid widespread criticism (see McGlen and Rabushka, 1971; Fowler, 1972; Reading, 1972; Weltman, 1972; Holt and Turner, 1975; Sorzano, 1975).

Group theory was not at the heart of the behavioral revolution, but it was contemporary with it, and there was an enthusiastic optimism that group-theoretic hypotheses (e.g., on the stabilizing effect of crosscutting group memberships) could be investigated behaviorally and that, taken together, such theorems could be fitted together to form a convincing systematic theory. Pluralism was a more sophisticated version of group theory, emphasizing political entrepreneurship and political culture, but here also the claim to provide a framework for systematic political theory was based on undue optimism.

In 1962, a year after Dahl's *Who Governs?* presented the classic case for pluralist analysis of American politics, group theory came under serious challenge even as it was being consolidated. Balancing the consolidators (Crick on the appreciation of the transcendent qualities of politics, and Diesing on social and political rationality) were authors representing important new schools of thought standing in subtle or open opposition to group approaches. The most important of the subtle challenges was found in the emerging literature on economic theories of politics, such as Buchanan and Tullock's *Calculus of Consent* (1962). These theories, harbingers of the rise of public choice theory as a rallying point for a new, conservative approach to political questions, were based on a neo-utilitarian rationalism foreign to the assumptions of group theory. The most important direct challenge to group theory in 1962 was Bachrach and Baratz's thesis on "nondecision-making." By concentrating on overt decisional studies, Bachrach and Baratz asserted, the group theorists neglected the far more important effect of political culture and socialization in screening the working agenda of "pragmatic" politics.

Between 1963 and 1965 the debate between the pluralists and their direct challengers intensified. Bachrach and Baratz (1963) reiterated their analysis in more precise fashion. Edelman's writings, emphasizing "symbolic action," added fuel to the same fire, critiquing conventional approaches to political science for neglect of the subtle manner in which elites influence opinion formation. The group approach also was undermined by numerous studies empirically refuting various group-theory hypotheses: Verba (1965a) on overlapping group memberships *not* being important in political stability, McCloskey (1964) on low acceptance of "rules of the game," Luttbeg and Zeigler (1966) on groups being unrepresentative of their members, and Milbrath (1963) on the relatively limited role of interest lobbies. While pluralists expended their intellectual energy on attacking a caricature of elite-stratification theory of the previous decade, influential theories were advanced to account for these findings discrepant with pluralist theory. Olson (1965) used a form of economic-utility theory to explain the unre-presentativeness of group formation documented by writers like Holtzman (1966). Pye and Verba (1965) revived interest in political culture as a concept explaining why decision-making operated in a more subtle manner than decision-making studies usually suggested. Walker (1966) suggested that sociological theories of social movements might explain more about political change than the study of normal interest articulation so empha-sized by group theorists.

The late 1960s brought a social ferment that carried over into political science in the form of a revival of critical social theory. As social turmoil increased, even behavioralists like David Easton (1969: 1057) were moved to ask where pluralism had gone wrong. A new literature on social protest emerged (see Lipsky, 1968, 1970), along with a reassertion of classical democratic norms that had been abandoned by the group the-orists (see Pranger, 1968; Kotler, 1969). Elite-stratification theory enjoyed a strong resurgence (see Domhoff, 1967, 1970) as did more conservative theories of law whose advocates found in pluralism the seeds of the crisis of public authority (see Lowi, 1967, 1969). The Caucus for a New Political Science arose as a vehicle for political scientists sharing little else except a common, left-of-center distaste for group theory, and a com-mitment to more relevant political science that would reunite theory and praxis. English (Miliband, 1969) and German (Birnbaum, 1969) radical influence introduced a more sophisti-cated variety of critical social theory constituting a fundamental attack on group theory. Competing interests were not merely denied to be the critical factors in understanding government; it was denied that the overt decision-making process itself was the central element of political life. In this, the theory represented a radicalization of the views of Bachrach and Edelman.

By the 1970s, group theory, including pluralism, was well along its process of disintegration. The splintering of group approaches to politics left scattered manifestations of influence in Soviet studies, theories of comparative development, and in various case studies of successful interest associations. Liberal criticisms of the group approach (cf. Lowi, Bachrach, Edelman, Nader, Gawthrop) were diverse, but telling in their aggregate effect. Theories of politics as elite accommodation, whether to be understood as consociational democracy or as neocorporatism, became popular. Along with a revival of interest in the concepts of elite accommodation and corporatism came a revived concern for "private government" and the impact of social class. And radical social theorists (the Frankfurt school and praxis theorists, among others) provided a new, more subtle framework for the critique of capitalist representative democracies, emphasizing the cultural hegemony of ruling elites. But whether in liberal or radical perspective, group theory was viewed as incorrect in both descriptive and normative implication.

If anything characterized the new perspectives that arose in criticism of and competition with the group theory tradition of political science, it was *not* a fervor for developing the study of politics into a science. The exception to this statement was public choice theory, where the "science" of economics was taken as a direct and immediate model, replete with references to marginal costs and utility curves. Such rationalist utilitarianism, however, was conservative in normative implication, and ill-calculated to garner half the support for being the discipline's consensual, scientific paradigm that group theory had at its peak. In a discipline adrift in a massive upsurge of pragmatic policy studies, area studies, and the like, liberal and radical critical-social theory emerged, if only by default, as the central theoretical alternative to previous methodologies. But the central drift of critical social theory was as much an attack on scientism as on group theory. With more or less explicitly phenomenological overtones, the shallowness of previous methodologies (government decision-making cases, survey research on public satisfaction with government outputs, and voting studies) was laid to a superficial behaviorism, serving as a scientific and neutral legitimator of an existing reality beneath which lay, repressed and latent, wholly different social orders. The debate over whether the scientific study of politics was possible, mentioned at the outset of this essay, here was transmuted into the question of whether it was even desirable. Thus, the passing of group theory was indicative of an epistemological crisis in political science a half century in the making. Wilson's 1911 contrast, between political science as the study of human souls and the calculation of political forces, found modern manifestation in the contrast between the concern of critical social theorists for the formation of political consciousness, in the deepest sense, and the emphasis by public choice theorists and policy analysts on the calculation of observable utilities. Between the study of souls and the calculation of forces lay a gulf into which group theory fell, unsuited to satisfy either.

REFERENCES

AARON, H. J. (1972) *Shelter and Subsidies: Who Benefits from Federal Housing Policies?* Washington, D.C.: Brookings.

ABRAMSON, P. R. (1976) "Generational Change and the Decline of Party Identification in America, 1952-1974," *American Political Science Review,* Vol. 70, No. 2 (June): 469-478.

ADAMANY, D. (1972) "The Political Science of E. E. Schattschneider: A Review Essay," *American Political Science Review,* Vol. 66, No. 4 (December): 1321-1335.

——— (1977) "Money, Politics, and Democracy: A Review Essay," *American Political Science Review,* Vol. 71, No. 1 (March): 289-304.

ADAMS, J. L. (1970) *The Growing Church Lobby in Washington.* Grand Rapids, Mich.: Eerdman's.

AGGER, R., D. GOLDRICH, and B. SWANSON (1964) *The Rulers and the Ruled: Political Power and Impotence in American Communities.* New York: Wiley.

AGPALO, R. E. (1972) *The Political Elite and the People.* Manila: College of Public Administration, Univ. of the Philippines.

ALFORD, R. R. (1972) "The Political Economy of Health Care: Dynamics Without Change," *Politics and Society,* Vol. 2, No. 2 (Winter): 127-164.

ALINSKY, S. D. (1971) *Rules for Radicals: A Pragmatic Primer for Realistic Radicals.* New York: Random House.

ALLISON, G. T. (1971) *Essence of Decision: Explaining the Cuban Missile Crisis.* Boston: Little, Brown.

ALMOND, G. (1966) "Political Theory and Political Science," *American Political Science Review,* Vol. 60, No. 4 (December): 869-879.

ALMOND, G. and G. B. POWELL, Jr. (1966) *Comparative Politics: A Developmental Approach.* Boston: Little, Brown.

ALMOND, G. and S. VERBA (1963) *The Civic Culture: Political Attitudes and Democracy in Five Nations.* Princeton, N.J.: Princeton Univ. Press.

ANDERSON, J., R. MURRAY, and E. FARLEY (1971) *Texas Politics: An Introduction.* New York: Harper and Row.

APTER, D. E. (1977) *Introduction to Political Analysis.* Cambridge, Mass.: Winthrop.

BACHELLER, J. M. (1977) "Lobbyists and the Legislative Process: The Impact of Environmental Constraints," *American Political Science Review,* Vol. 71, No. 1 (March): 252-264.

BACHRACH, P. (1962a) "Elite Consensus and Democracy," *Journal of Politics,* Vol. 24, No. 3 (August): 439-452.

BACHRACH, P. and M. BARATZ (1962b) "Two Faces of Power," *American Political Science Review,* Vol. 56, No. 4 (December): 947-952.

——— (1963) "Decisions and Nondecisions: An Analytical Framework," *American Political Science Review,* Vol. 57, No. 3 (September): 632-642.

——— (1975) "Power and Its Two Faces Revisited: A Reply to Geoffrey Debnam," *American Political Science Review,* Vol. 69, No. 3 (September): 900-904.

BALDWIN, D. A. (1971) "Money and Power," *Journal of Politics,* Vol. 33, No. 3 (August): 578-614.

BARRY, B. (1970) *Sociologists, Economists, and Democracy.* London: Collier-Macmillan.

BARTLETT, R. (1973) *Economic Foundations of Political Power.* New York: Free Press.

BASKIN, D. (1970) "American Pluralism: Theory, Practice, and Ideology," *Journal of Politics,* Vol. 32, No. 1 (February): 71-95.

——— (1971) *American Pluralist Democracy: A Critique.* New York: Van Nostrand.

BAUER, R., I. de SOLA POOL, and L. A. DEXTER (1963) *American Business and Public Policy.* New York: Atherton.

BAY, C. (1965) "Politics and Pseudopolitics: A Critical Evaluation of Some Behavioral Literature," *American Political Science Review,* Vol. 59, No. 1 (March): 39-51.

BEAM, G. D. (1970) *Usual Politics: A Critique and Some Suggestions for an Alternative.* New York: Holt, Rinehart & Winston.

BELL, D., ed. (1963) *The Radical Right.* New York: Doubleday.

——— (1976) *The Coming of Post-Industrial Society: A Venture in Social Forecasting.* New York: Basic Books.

BELZ, H. (1974) "New Left Reverberations in the Academy: The Antipluralist Critique of Constitutionalism," *Review of Politics,* Vol. 36, No. 2 (April): 265-283.

BENEWICK, R. (1974) "British Pressure Group Politics: The National Council for Civil Liberties," *Annals of the American Academy of Political and Social Sciences,* Vol. 413 (May): 145-157.

BIRNBAUM, N. (1969) *The Crisis of Industrial Society.* New York: Oxford.

BLACK, G. S. (1970) "A Theory of Professionalization in Politics," *American Political Science Review,* Vol. 64, No. 3 (September): 865-878.

BLUMBERG, P. (1969) *Industrial Democracy: The Sociology of Participation.* New York: Schocken.

BOSCHKEN, H. L. (1975) "The Logic of Protest Action," *Western Political Quarterly,* Vol. 28, No. 1 (March): 59-71.

BOTTOMORE, T. B. (1964) *Elites and Society.* New York: Basic Books.

——— (1966) *Classes and Society.* New York: Basic Books.

BRAYBROOKE, D. and C. E. LINDBLOM (1963) *A Strategy of Decision.* New York: Free Press.

BROYLES, J. A. (1964) *The John Birch Society: Anatomy of a Protest.* Boston: Beacon.

BUCHANAN, J. M. and G. TULLOCK (1962) *The Calculus of Consent: Logical Foundations of Constitutional Democracy.* Ann Arbor: Univ. of Michigan Press.

BURMAN, I. D. (1973) *Lobbying at the Illinois Constitutional Convention.* Urbana: Univ. of Illinois Press.

BURNHAM, J. (1966) *The Managerial Revolution.* Bloomington: Indiana Univ. Press.

BURTENSHAW, C. J. (1968) "The Political Theory of Pluralist Democracy," *Western Political Quarterly,* Vol. 21, No. 4 (December): 577-587.

CLARK, J. M. (1967) *Teachers and Politics in France: A Pressure Group Study of the Fédération de l'Education Nationale.* Syracuse, N.Y.: Syracuse Univ. Press.

COBB, R. W., J.-K. ROSS, and M. H. ROSS (1976) "Agenda Building as a Comparative Political Process," *American Political Science Review,* Vol. 70, No. 1 (March): 126-138.

COCHRAN, C. E. (1973) "The Politics of Interest: Philosophy and the Limitations of the Science of Politics," *American Journal of Political Science,* Vol. 17, No. 4 (November): 745-766.

COHN, J. (1971) *The Conscience of the Corporations: Business and Urban Affairs 1967-1970.* Baltimore: Johns Hopkins Univ. Press.

COLEMAN, J. S. (1970) "Political Money," *American Political Science Review,* Vol. 64, No. 4 (December): 1074-1087.

CONNERTON, P., ed. (1976) *Critical Sociology.* Baltimore: Penguin.

CONNOLLY, W. E. (1967) *Political Science and Ideology.* New York: Atherton.

CORNWELL, E. C., Jr. (1965) *Presidential Leadership of Public Opinion.* Bloomington: Indiana Univ. Press.

CRAIG, R. B. (1971) *The Bracero Program: Interest Groups and Foreign Policy.* Austin: Univ. of Texas Press.

CRICK, B. (1962) *In Defence of Politics.* Chicago: Univ. of Chicago Press.

CURRY, R. L., Jr., and L. L. WADF (1968) *A Theory of Political Exchange: Economic Reasoning in Political Analysis.* Englewood Cliffs, N.J.: Prentice-Hall.

DAALDER, H. and G. A. IRWIN (1974) "Interests and Institutions in the Netherlands: An Assessment by the People and by Parliament," *Annals of the American Academy of Political and Social Science,* Vol. 413 (May): 58-71.

DAHL, R. A. (1956) *A Preface to Democratic Theory.* Chicago: Univ. of Chicago Press.

——— (1961) *Who Governs?: Democracy and Power in an American City.* New Haven: Yale Univ. Press.

——— (1966) "Further Reflections on 'The Elitist Theory of Democracy,' " *American Political Science Review,* Vol. 60, No. 2 (June): 296-305.

——— (1967a) *Pluralist Democracy in the United States: Conflict and Consent.* Chicago: Rand McNally.

——— (1967b) "The City in the Future of Democracy," *American Political Science Review,* Vol. 61, No. 4 (December): 953-970.

DAHL, R. A. and E. R. TUFTE (1973) *Size and Democracy.* Stanford, Cal.: Stanford Univ. Press.

DAVIDSON, R. H. (1974) "Representation and Congressional Committees," *Annals of the American Academy of Political and Social Science*, Vol. 411 (January): 48-62.

DAVIS, L. (1964) "The Cost of Realism: Contemporary Restatements of Democracy," *Western Political Quarterly*, Vol. 17, No. 1 (March): 37-46.

DEAKIN, J. (1966) *The Lobbyists*. Washington, D.C.: Public Affairs Press.

DEBNAM, G. (1975) "Nondecisions and Power: The Two Faces of Bachrach and Baratz," *American Political Science Review*, Vol. 69, No. 3 (September): 889-899.

DEUTSCH, K. W. (1963) *The Nerves of Government: Models of Political Communications Control*. New York: Free Press.

DEXTER, L. A. (1969) *How Organizations Are Represented in Washington*. Indianapolis: Bobbs-Merrill.

DIESING, P. (1962) *Reason in Society: Five Types of Decisions and Their Social Conditions*. Urbana: Univ. of Illinois Press.

DION, L. (1971-1972) *Société et Politique: La Vie des Groupes* (2 vols.) Quebec: Les Presses de l'Université de Laval.

DOMHOFF, G. W. (1967) *Who Rules America?* Englewood Cliffs, N.J.: Prentice-Hall.

——— (1970) *The Higher Circles: The Governing Class in America*. New York: Random House.

——— (1974) "Watergate: Conflict and Antagonisms Within the Power Elite," *Theory and Society*, Vol. 1, No. 1 (Winter): 99-102.

DOWLING, R. E. (1960) "Pressure Group Theory: Its Methodological Range," *American Political Science Review*, Vol. 54, No. 4 (December): 944-954.

DOWNS, A. (1957) *An Economic Theory of Democracy*. New York: Harper and Row.

DUVERGER, M. (1974) *Modern Democracies: Economic Power vs. Political Power*. Hinsdale, Ill.: Dryden Press.

DYE, T. R. (1965) Review of Wildavsky (1964) in *American Political Science Review*, Vol. 59, No. 1 (March): 173.

DYE, T. R. and J. W. PICKERING (1974) "Governmental and Corporate Elites and Convergence and Differentiation," *Journal of Politics*, Vol. 36, No. 4 (November): 900-925.

EASTON, D. (1965a) *A Framework for Political Analysis*. Englewood Cliffs, N.J.: Prentice-Hall.

——— (1965b) *A Systems Analysis of Political Life*. New York: Wiley.

——— (1969) "The New Revolution in Political Science," *American Political Science Review*, Vol. 63, No. 4 (December): 1051-1061.

EASTON, D. and R. D. HESS (1962) "The Child's Political World," *Midwest Journal of Political Science*, Vol. 6 (August): 231-239.

EDELMAN, M. (1964) *The Symbolic Uses of Politics*. Urbana: Univ. of Illinois Press.

——— (1971) *Politics as Symbolic Action: Mass Arousal and Quiescence*. Chicago: Markham.

EIDENBERG, E. and R. D. MOREY (1969) *An Act of Congress: The Legislative Process and the Making of Education Policy*. New York: Norton.

EISFELD, R. (1972) *Pluralismus zwischen Liberalismus und Sozialismus*. Stuttgart: Verlag w. Kohlhammer.

EPSTEIN, E. M. (1969) *The Corporation in American Politics*. Englewood Cliffs, N.J.: Prentice-Hall.

ETZIONI, A. (1975) "Alternative Conceptions of Accountability: The Example of Health Administration," *Public Administration Review*, Vol. 35, No. 3 (May/June): 279-286.

EULAU, H. (1963) *The Behavioral Persuasion in Politics*. New York: Random House.
FAINSTEIN, N. I. and S. S. FAINSTEIN (1976) "The Future of Community Control," *American Political Science Review*, Vol. 70, No. 3 (September): 905-923.
FALLOWS, J. W. (1971) *The Water Lords*. New York: Grossman.
FELLMETH, R. (1970) *The Interstate Commerce Omission*. New York: Grossman.
FLINN, T. A. (1965) Review of ZEIGLER (1964) in *American Political Science Review*, Vol. 59, No. 1 (March): 173-174.
FLUNO, R. Y. (1971) "The Floundering Leviathan: Pluralism in Age of Ungovernability," *Western Political Quarterly*, Vol. 24, No. 3 (September): 560-566.
FORM, W. H. and J. HUBER (1971) "Income, Race and the Ideology of Political Efficacy," *Journal of Politics*, Vol. 33, No. 3 (August): 659-688.
FOWLER, R. B. (1972) "Easton I and Easton II," *Western Political Quarterly*, Vol. 25, No. 4 (December): 726-737.
FRANCIS, W. L. (1971) "A Profile of Legislator Perceptions in Interest Group Behavior Relating to Legislative Issues in the States," *Western Political Quarterly*, Vol. 24, No. 4 (December): 702-712.
FROHLICH, N., J. A. OPPENHEIMER, and O. R. YOUNG (1971) *Political Leadership and Collective Goods*. Princeton, N.J.: Princeton Univ. Press.
FROLIC, B. M. (1972) "Decision-Making in Soviet Cities," *American Political Science Review*, Vol. 66, No. 1 (March): 38-52.
FROMAN, L. A. (1966) "Some Effects of Interest Group Strength in State Politics," *American Political Science Review*, Vol. 60, No. 4 (December): 952-962.
GALAMBOS, L. (1966) *Competition and Cooperation: The Emergence of a National Trade Association*. Baltimore: Johns Hopkins Univ. Press.
GALBRAITH, J. K. (1958) *The Affluent Society*. Boston: Houghton Mifflin.
GARDINER, J. H. (1970) *The Politics of Corruption: Organized Crime in an American City*. New York: Russell Sage.
GARSON, G. D. (1974) "On the Origins of Interest Group Theory: A Critique of a Process," *American Political Science Review*, Vol. 68, No. 4 (December): 1505-1519.
GAWTHROP, L. C. (1971) *Administrative Politics and Social Change:* New York: St. Martin's.
GELB, J. and A. SARDELL (1975) "Organizing the Poor: A Brief Analysis of the Politics of the Welfare Rights Movement," *Policy Studies Journal*, Vol. 3, No. 4 (Summer): 346-353.
GEORGE, A. L. (1972) "The Case for Multiple Advocacy in Making Foreign Policy," *American Political Science Review*, Vol. 66, No. 3 (September): 751-795.
GIDDENS, A. (1973) *The Class Structure of the Advanced Societies*. New York: Harper and Row.
GLASER, W. A. and D. L. SILLS, eds. (1966) "Introduction" to *The Government of Associations*. Totowa, N.J.: Bedminster.
GOODMAN, J. S. (1967) *The Democrats and Labor in Rhode Island, 1952-1962: Changes in the Old Alliance*. Providence, R.I.: Brown Univ. Press.
GREEN, M., J. M. FALLOWS, and D. R. ZWICK (1972) *Who Runs Congress?* New York: Bantam.
GROSSMAN, J. (1965) *Lawyers and Judges: The ABA and the Politics of Judicial Selection*. New York: Wiley.
HALE, M. Q. (1960) "The Cosmology of Arthur F. Bentley," *American Political Science Review*, Vol. 54, No. 4 (December): 955-961.
HALL, D. R. (1969) *Cooperative Lobbying: The Power of Pressure*. Tucson: Univ. of Arizona Press.

HAMILTON, R. F. (1972) *Class and Politics in the United States.* New York: Wiley.

HARRINGTON, M. (1976) *The Twilight of Capitalism.* New York: Simon and Schuster.

HEIDENHEIMER, A. J. and F. C. LANGDON (1968) *Business Associations and the Financing of Political Parties.* The Hague: Martinus Nijhoff.

HELLER, W. W. (1966) *New Dimensions of Political Economy.* Cambridge, Mass.: Harvard Univ. Press.

HENDERSON, H. (1974) "Information and the New Movements for Citizen Participation," *Annals of the American Academy of Political and Social Science,* Vol. 412 (March): 34-43.

HERRING, E. P. (1965) *The Politics of Democracy: American Politics in Action.* New York: Norton.

HOLT, R. T. and J. E. TURNER (1975) "Crises and Sequences in Collective Theory Development," *American Political Science Review,* Vol.412 No. 3 (September): 979-994.

HOLTZMAN, A. (1966) *Interest Groups and Lobbying.* New York: Macmillan.

——— (1970) *Legislative Liaison: Executive Leadership in Congress.* Chicago: Rand McNally.

HOROWITZ, I. L. (1963) "Sociology and Politics: The Myth of Functionalism Revisited," *Journal of Politics,* Vol. 25, No. 2 (May): 248-264.

HUBER, J. and W. H. FORM (1973) *Income and Ideology: An Analysis of the American Political Formula.* New York: Free Press.

HUFF, E. D. (1972) "A Study of a Successful Interest Group, the American Zionist Movement," *Western Political Quarterly,* Vol. 25, No. 1 (March): 109-124.

HUNTER, F. (1953) *Community Power Structure.* Chapel Hill: Univ. of North Carolina Press.

ILCHMAN, W. F. and N. T. UPHOFF (1969) *The Political Economy of Change.* Berkeley: Univ. of California Press.

INGLEHART, R. (1971) "The Silent Revolution in Europe: Intergenerational Change in Post-Industrial Societies," *American Political Science Review,* Vol. 65, No. 4 (December): 991-1017.

INKELES, A. (1969) "Participant Citizenship in Six Developing Countries," *American Political Science Review,* Vol. 63, No. 4 (December): 1120-1141.

IRLAND, L. C. (1975) "Citizen Participation: A Tool for Conflict Management on the Public Lands," *Public Administration Review,* Vol. 35, No. 3 (May/June): 263-269.

JENCKS, C. (1972) *Inequality: A Reassessment of the Effect of Family and Schooling in America.* New York: Basic Books.

KAHN, S. (1970) *How People Get Power: Organizing Oppressed Communities for Action.* New York: McGraw Hill.

KARIEL, H. S. (1969) *Open Systems: Arenas for Political Action.* Itasca, Ill.: Peacock.

KATZMAN, M. T. (1971) *The Political Economy of Urban Schools.* Cambridge, Mass.: Harvard Univ. Press.

KEEHN, N. H. (1976) "A World of Becoming: From Pluralism to Corporatism," *Polity,* Vol. 9, No. 1 (Fall): 19-39.

KELLEY, D. R. (1972) "Interest Groups in the USSR: The Impact of Political Sensitivity on Group Influences," *Journal of Politics,* Vol. 34, No. 3 (August): 860-888.

KEY, V. O. (1961) *Public Opinion and American Democracy.* New York: Knopf.

——— (1966) *The Responsible Electorate.* Cambridge, Mass.: Harvard Univ. Press.

KILLICK, T. (1975) "Inflation, Interest Groups, and Political Response," *Polity,* Vol. 7, No. 4 (Summer): 418-426.

KIMBROUGH, R. (1964) *Political Power and Educational Decision-Making.* Chicago: Rand McNally.

KOBRAK, P. (1973) *Private Assumption of Public Responsibility: The Role of American Business in Urban Manpower Programs.* New York: Praeger.

KOHLMEIER, L. M. (1969) *The Regulators: Watchdog Agencies and the Public Interest.* New York: Harper and Row.

KOLASA, B. D. (1971) "Lobbying in the Nonpartisan Environment: The Case of Nebraska," *Western Political Quarterly,* Vol. 24, No. 1 (March): 65-78.

KOTLER, M. (1969) *Neighborhood Government: The Local Foundations of Political Life.* Indianapolis: Bobbs-Merrill.

KRAMER, D. C. (1972) *Participatory Democracy: Developing Ideals of the Political Left.* Cambridge, Mass.: Schenkman.

KRAMER, R. M. (1969) *Participation of the Poor: Comparative Community Case Studies in the War on Poverty.* Englewood Cliffs, N.J.: Prentice-Hall.

KRISLOV, S. (1963) "What is an Interest?: The Rival Answers of Bentley, Pound, and MacIver," *Western Political Quarterly,* Vol. 16, No. 4 (December): 830-843.

LANDER, B. G. (1971) "Group Theory and Individuals: The Origin of Poverty as a Political Issue in 1964," *Western Political Quarterly,* Vol. 24, No. 3 (September): 514-526.

LANE, R. (1962) *Political Ideology: Why the American Common Man Believes What He Does.* New York: Free Press.

LAPALOMBARA, J. (1964) *Interest Groups in Italian Politics.* Princeton: Princeton Univ. Press.

LAPP, R. E. (1965) *The New Priesthood: The Scientific Elite and the Uses of Power.* New York: Harper and Row.

LAUMANN, E. O. (1973) *Bonds of Pluralism: The Form and Substance of Urban Social Network.* New York: Wiley.

LENSKI, G. E. (1966) *Power and Privilege: A Theory of Social Stratification.* New York: McGraw Hill.

LIEBER, R. J. (1970) *British Politics and European Unity: Parties, Elites and Pressure Groups.* Berkeley: Univ. of California Press.

——— (1972) "Interest Groups and Political Integration: British Entry into Europe," *American Political Science Review,* Vol. 66, No. 1 (March): 53-67.

LIJPHART, A. (1968) *The Politics of Accommodation: Pluralism and Democracy in the Netherlands.* Berkeley: Univ. of California Press.

LINDBLOM, C. E. (1965) *The Intelligence of Democracy: Decision-Making Through Mutual Adjustment.* New York: Free Press.

LIPSEN, C. B. and S. LESHER (1977) *Vested Interest: A Lobbyist's Account of Washington Power and How It Really Works.* Garden City, N.Y.: Doubleday.

LIPSET, S. M. (1963) *The First New Nation.* New York: Basic Books.

LIPSITZ, L. (1968) "If, As Verba Says, the State Functions as a Religion, What Are We to Do Then to Save Our Souls?" *American Political Science Review,* Vol. 62, No. 2 (June): 527-535.

LIPSKY, M. (1968) "Protest as a Political Resource," *American Political Science Review,* Vol. 62, No. 4 (December): 1144-1158.

——— (1970) *Protest in City Politics: Rent Strikes, Housing, and the Power of the Poor.* Chicago: Rand McNally.

LONGLEY, L. D. (1967) "Interest Group Interaction in a Legislative System," *Journal of Politics,* Vol. 29, No. 3 (August): 637-658.

LOVEDAY, P. and J. CAMPBELL (1962) *Groups in Theory and Practice.* Melbourne: Cheshire.

LOWI, T. (1964a) "American Business, Public Policy, Case-Studies, and Political Theory," *World Politics,* Vol. 16 (July): 677-715.

——— (1964b) "American Government, 1933-1963: Fission and Confusion in Theory and Research," *American Political Science Review,* Vol. 58, No. 3 (September): 589-599.

——— (1967) "The Public Philosophy: Interest Group Liberalism," *American Political Science Review,* Vol. 61, No. 1 (March): 5-24.

——— (1969) *The End of Liberalism: Ideology, Policy, and the Crisis of Public Authority.* New York: Norton.

——— (1974) "Interest Groups and the Consent to Govern: Getting the People Out, for What?" *Annals of the American Academy of Political and Social Science,* Vol. 413 (May): 86-100.

LUTRIN, C. E. and A. K. SETTLE (1975) "The Public and Ecology: The Rule of Initiatives in California's Environmental Politics," *Western Political Quarterly,* Vol. 28 No. 2 (June): 352-371.

LUTTBEG, N. R. and H. ZEIGLER (1966) "Attitude Consensus and Conflict in an Interest Group: An Assessment of Cohesion," *American Political Science Review,* Vol. 60, No. 3 (September): 655-666.

McADAMS, A. K. (1964) *Power and Politics in Labor Legislation.* New York: Columbia Univ. Press.

McCLOSKEY, H. (1964) "Consensus and Ideology in American Politics," *American Political Science Review,* Vol. 58, No. 2 (June): 361-382.

McCONNELL, G. (1958) "The Spirit of Private Government," *American Political Science Review,* Vol. 52, No. 3 (September): 754-770.

——— (1967) *Private Power and American Democracy.* New York: Knopf.

McGLEN, N. E. and A. RABUSHKA (1971) "Polemics on Functional Analysis: Variations on a Belabored Theme," *Midwest Journal of Political Science,* Vol. 15, No. 1 (February): 133-143.

MACRIDIS, R. C. (1961) "Interest Groups in Comparative Analysis," *Journal of Politics,* Vol. 23, No. 1 (February): 25-45.

MAHOOD, H. R., ed. (1967) *Pressure Groups in American Politics.* New York: Scribners.

MALLOY, J. M. (1974) "Authoritarianism, Corporatism, and Mobilization in Peru," *Review of Politics,* Vol. 36, No. 1 (January): 52-84.

MARINI, F. (1969) "John Locke and the Revision of Classical Democratic Theory," *Western Political Quarterly,* Vol. 22, No. 1 (March): 5-18.

MARSH, A. (1975) "The 'Silent Revolution,' Value Priorities and the Quality of Life in Britain," *American Political Science Review,* Vol. 69, No. 1 (March): 21-30.

MAZZIOTTI, D. F. (1974) "The Underlying Assumptions of Advocacy Planning: Pluralism and Reform," *Journal of the American Institute of Planners,* Vol. 40, No. 1 (January): 38-47.

MEANS, G. (1962) *Pricing Power and the Public Interest, A Study Based on Steel.* New York: Harper.

MEDDING, P. Y. (1969) " 'Elitist' Democracy: An Unsuccessful Critique of a Misunderstood Theory," *Journal of Politics,* Vol. 31, No. 3 (August): 641-654.

MERELMAN, R. M. (1968) "On the Neo-Elitist Critique of Community Power," *American Political Science Review,* Vol. 62, No. 2 (June): 451-460.

MILBRATH, L. W. (1963) *The Washington Lobbyists.* Chicago: Rand McNally.
MILIBAND, R. (1969) *The State in Capitalist Society: An Analysis of the Western System of Power.* New York: Basic Books.
MILLER, W. E. and D. E. STOKES (1963) "Constituency Influence in Congress," *American Political Science Review,* Vol. 57, No. 1 (February): 45-56.
MILLS, C. W. (1956) *The Power Elite.* New York: Oxford Univ. Press.
MITCHELL, W. C. (1963) *The American Polity.* New York: Free Press.
MOYNIHAN, D. P. (1969) *Maximum Feasible Misunderstanding: Community Action in the War on Poverty.* New York: Free Press.
MUELLER, C. (1973) *The Politics of Communication: A Study in the Political Sociology of Language, Socialization, and Legitimation.* New York: Oxford.
MURPHY, R. D. (1971) *Political Entrepreneurs and Urban Poverty.* Lexington, Mass.: Lexington Books.
NADEL, M. V. (1975) "The Hidden Dimensions of Public Policy: Private Governments and the Policy-Making Process," *Journal of Politics,* Vol. 37, No. 1 (February): 2-34.
NADER, R. and D. ROSS (1971) *Action for Change: A Student's Manual for Public Interest Organizing.* New York: Grossman.
NATANSON, M., ed. (1973) *Phenomenology and the Social Sciences.* Evanston, Ill.: Northwestern Univ. Press.
NELSON, M. (1977) "What's Wrong with Political Science," *Washington Monthly,* Vol. 9, No. 7 (September): 13-20.
NEWTON, R. C. (1974) "Natural Corporatism and the Passing of Populism in Spanish America," *Review of Politics,* Vol. 36, No. 1 (January): 34-51.
NIE, N. H., G. B. POWELL, and K. PREWITT (1969) "Social Structure and Political Participation: Developmental Relationships, II," *American Political Science Review,* Vol. 63, No. 3 (September): 808-832.
NIMMO, D. and W. E. ODEN (1971) *The Texas Political System.* Englewood Cliffs, N.J.: Prentice-Hall.
NISKANEN, W. A. (1971) *Bureaucracy and Representative Government.* Chicago: Aldine-Atherton.
OLSON, M. (1965) *The Logic of Collective Action: Public Goods and the Theory of Groups.* Cambridge, Mass.: Harvard Univ. Press.
ORREN, K. (1974) *Corporate Power and Social Change: The Politics of the Life Insurance Industry.* Baltimore: Johns Hopkins Univ. Press.
——— (1976) "Standing to Sue: Interest Group Conflict in the Federal Courts," *American Political Science Review,* Vol. 70, No. 3 (September): 723-741.
OSTROM, V. and E. OSTROM (1971) "Public Choice: A Different Approach to the Study of Public Administration," *Public Administration Review,* Vol. 31, No. 2 (March/April): 203-216.
PARENTI, M. (1970) "Power and Pluralism: A View from the Bottom," *Journal of Politics,* Vol. 32, No. 3 (August): 501-530.
PARRY, G. (1969) *Political Elites.* New York: Praeger.
PATTERSON, S. C. (1963) "The Role of the Lobbyist: The Case of Oklahoma," *Journal of Politics,* Vol. 25, No. 1 (February): 72-92.
PEARSON, D. and J. ANDERSON (1969) *The Case Against Congress.* New York: Pocket Books.
PLANO, J. C. and M. GREENBERG (1967) *The American Political Dictionary, Second Edition.* New York: Holt, Rinehart and Winston.

POLSBY, N. (1963) *Community Power and Political Theory.* New Haven: Yale Univ. Press.

PORTER, J. (1965) *The Vertical Mosaic: An Analysis of Social Class and Power in Canada.* Toronto: Univ. of Toronto Press.

PRANGER, R. J. (1968) *The Eclipse of Citizenship: Power and Participation in Contemporary Politics.* New York: Holt, Rinehart and Winston.

PRESTHUS, R. (1962) *The Organizational Society.* New York: Knopf.

——— (1973) *Elite Accommodation in Canadian Politics.* New York: Cambridge Univ. Press.

——— (1974a) "Interest Group Lobbying in Canada and the United States," *Annals of the American Academy of Political and Social Science,* Vol. 413 (May): 44-57.

——— (1974b) *Elites in the Policy Process.* New York: Cambridge Univ. Press.

PRETORIUS, L. and W. B. VOSLOO (1974) "Interest Groups in the Republic of South Africa," *Annals of the American Academy of Political and Social Science,* Vol. 413 (May): 72-85.

PREWITT, K. and H. EULAU (1969) "Political Matrix and Political Representation: Prolegomenon to a New Departure from an Old Problem," *American Political Science Review,* Vol. 63, No. 2 (June): 427-441.

PROTHRO, J. W. (1962) Review of Key (1961) in *Journal of Politics,* Vol. 24, No. 4 (November): 788-790.

PUTNAM, R. D. (1971) "Studying Elite Political Culture: The Case of 'Ideology'," *American Political Science Review,* Vol. 65, No. 3 (September): 651-681.

PYE, L. W. and S. VERBA, eds. (1965) *Political Culture and Political Development: Studies in Political Development.* Princeton: Princeton Univ. Press.

RADOSH, R. (1969) *American Labor and United States Foreign Policy.* New York: Vintage.

RAE, D. W. (1971) "Political Democracy as a Property of Political Institutions," *American Political Science Review,* Vol. 65, No. 1 (March): 111-119.

RANNEY, A., ed. (1962) *Essays on the Behavioral Study of Politics.* Urbana: Univ. of Illinois Press.

READING, R. R. (1972) "Is Easton's Systems-Persistence Framework Useful? A Research Note," *Journal of Politics,* Vol. 34, No. 1 (February): 258-267.

REAGAN, M. (1963) *The Managed Economy.* New York: Oxford Univ. Press.

RIKER, W. S. (1962) *The Theory of Political Coalitions.* New Haven: Yale Univ. Press.

ROBERTS, G. K. (1972) *Political Parties and Pressure Groups in Britain.* New York: St. Martin's.

ROBINSON, J. A., ed. (1973) *State Legislative Innovation.* New York: Praeger.

ROSE, A. M. (1967) *The Power Structure: Political Process in American Society.* New York: Oxford Univ. Press.

ROSENFELD, S. S. (1974) "Pluralism and Policy," *Foreign Affairs,* Vol. 52, No. 2 (January): 263-272.

ROSS, R. L. (1970) "Relations Among National Interest Groups," *Journal of Politics,* Vol. 32, No. 1 (February): 96-114.

ROTHMAN, S. (1960) "Systematic Political Theory: Observations on the Group Approach," *American Political Science Review,* Vol. 54, No. 1 (February): 15-33.

RUSK, J. G. (1976) "Political Participation in America: A Review Essay," *American Political Science Review,* Vol. 70, No. 2 (June): 583-591.

SALISBURY, R. H. (1969) "An Exchange Theory of Interest Groups," *Midwest Journal of Political Science,* Vol. 13, No. 1 (February): 1-32.

SANI, G. (1974) "Determinants of Party Preference in Italy: Toward the Integration of Complementary Models," *American Journal of Political Science,* Vol. 18, No. 2 (May): 315-329.

SARTORI, G. (1962) *Democratic Theory.* Detroit: Wayne State Univ. Press.

——— (1969) "Politics, Ideology, and Belief Systems," *American Political Science Review,* Vol. 63, No. 2 (June): 398-411.

SCAFF, L. A. (1975) "Two Concepts of Political Participation," *Western Political Quarterly,* Vol. 28, No. 3 (September): 447-462.

SCHATTSCHNEIDER, E. E. (1960) *The Semi-Sovereign People.* New York: Holt, Rinehart and Winston.

SCHICK, A. (1973) "A Death in the Bureaucracy: The Demise of Federal PPB," *Public Administration Review,* Vol. 33, No. 2 (March/April): 146-156.

SCHILLING, W. R. (1962) "Scientists, Foreign Policy, and Politics," *American Political Science Review,* Vol. 56, No. 2 (June): 287-300.

SCHMITTER, P. C. (1971) *Interest Conflict and Political Change in Brazil.* Stanford, Cal.: Stanford Univ. Press.

——— (1974) "Still the Century of Corporatism?" *Review of Politics,* Vol. 36, No. 1 (January): 86-131.

SCHULMAN, P. R. (1975) "Non-incremental Policy-Making: Notes Toward an Alternative Paradigm," *American Political Science Review,* Vol. 69, No. 4 (December): 1354-1370.

SCHUMAKER, P. D. (1975) "Policy Responsiveness to Protest-Group Demands," *Journal of Politics,* Vol. 37, No. 2 (May): 488-521.

SCHUTZ, A. (1967) *The Phenomenology of the Social World.* Evanston, Ill.: Northwestern Univ. Press.

——— (1970) *Reflections on the Problem of Relevance.* New Haven: Yale Univ. Press.

SCHWARTZ, J. J. and W. R. KEECH (1968) "Group Influence and the Policy Process in the Soviet Union," *American Political Science Review,* Vol. 62, No. 3 (September): 840-851.

SCOTT, A. M. and M. A. HUNT (1966) *Congress and Lobbies: Image and Reality.* Chapel Hill: Univ. of North Carolina Press.

SHAPIRO, M. J. (1969) "Rational Political Man: A Synthesis of Economic and Social-Psychological Perspectives," *American Political Science Review,* Vol. 63, No. 4 (December): 1106-1119.

SIDJANSKI, S. (1974) "Interest Groups in Switzerland," *Annals of the American Academy of Political and Social Science,* Vol. 413 (May): 101-123.

SIMPSON, D. (1972) *Winning Elections: A Handbook on Participatory Politics.* Chicago: Swallow Press.

SKILLING, G. and F. GRIFFITHS, eds. (1971) *Interest Groups in Soviet Politics.* Princeton: Princeton Univ. Press.

SMITH, C. and A. FREEDMAN (1972) *Voluntary Associations: Perspectives on the Literature.* Cambridge, Mass.: Harvard Univ. Press.

SMITH, D. G. (1964) "Pragmatism and the Group Theory of Politics," *American Political Science Review,* Vol. 58, No. 3 (September): 600-610.

SORZANO, J. S. (1975) "David Easton and the Invisible Hand," *American Political Science Review,* Vol. 69, No. 1 (March): 91-106.

SOULE, J. W. and J. W. CLARKE (1970) "Amateurs and Professionals: A Study of Delegates to the 1968 Democratic National Convention," *American Political Science Review,* Vol. 64, No. 3 (September): 888-898.

SPROULE-JONES, M. (1973) "Towards a Dynamic Analysis of Collective Action," *Western Political Quarterly,* Vol. 26, No. 3 (September): 414-426.

STERN, R. W. (1970) *The Process of Opposition in India.* Chicago: Univ. of Chicago Press.

STRICKLAND, S. P. (1972) *Politics, Science and Dread Disease: A Short History of United States Medical Research Policy.* Cambridge, Mass.: Harvard Univ. Press.

SURKIN, M. and A. WOLFE (1970) *An End to Political Science: The Caucus Papers.* New York: Basic Books.

TABB, W. K. (1970) *The Political Economy of the Black Ghetto.* New York: Norton.

TARROW, S. (1971) "The Urban-Rural Cleavage in Political Involvement: The Case of France," *American Political Science Review,* Vol. 65, No. 2 (June): 341-357.

TEUNE, H. (1967) "Legislative Attitude Toward Interest Groups," *Midwest Journal of Political Science,* Vol. 11, No. 4 (November): 489-504.

THOENES, P. (1966) *The Elite in the Welfare State.* New York: Free Press.

THOMETZ, C. E. (1963) *The Decision-Makers: The Power Structure of Dallas.* Dallas, Texas: Methodist Univ. Press.

TILLETT, P. (1963) *Doe Day: The Antlerless Deer Controversy in New Jersey.* New Brunswick, N.J.: Rutgers Univ. Press.

TRUMAN, D. (1951) *The Governmental Process.* New York: Knopf.

——— (1959) "The American System in Crisis," *Political Science Quarterly,* Vol. 74, No. 4 (December): 481-497.

——— (1960) "On the Invention of Systems," *American Political Science Review,* Vol. 54, No. 2 (June): 494-495.

——— (1965) "Disillusion and Regeneration: The Quest for a Discipline," *American Political Science Review,* Vol. 59, No. 4 (December): 865-873.

TULLOCK, G. (1970) *Private Wants, Public Means.* New York: Basic Books.

TURNER, J. S. (1970) *The Chemical Feast.* New York: Grossman.

VAN DYKE, V. (1962) "Values and Interests," *American Political Science Review,* Vol. 56, No. 3 (September): 567-576.

VERBA, S. (1965a) "Organizational Membership and Democratic Consensus," *Journal of Politics,* Vol. 27, No. 3 (August): 467-497.

——— (1965b) "The Kennedy Assassination and the Nature of Political Commitment," in *The Kennedy Assassination and the American Public* (B. S. Greenberg and E. B. Parker, eds.). Stanford, Cal.: Stanford Univ. Press.

VERBA, S. and N. H. NIE (1972) *Participation in America: Political Democracy and Social Equality.* New York: Harper and Row.

VOGEL, D. (1975) "The Corporation as Government: Challenges and Dilemmas," *Polity,* Vol. 8, No. 1 (Fall): 5-37.

VOGLER, D. J. (1974) *The Politics of Congress.* Boston: Allyn and Bacon.

VOSE, C. E. (1966) "Interest Groups, Judicial Review and Local Government," *Western Political Quarterly,* Vol. 19, No. 1 (March): 85-100.

WALKER, J. L. (1966) "A Critique of the Elitist Theory of Democracy," *American Political Science Review,* Vol. 60, No. 2 (June): 285-295.

WALZER, M. (1971) *Political Action: A Practical Guide to Movement Politics.* Chicago: Quadrangle.

WATSON, R. A., R. G. DOWNING, and F. C. SPIEGEL (1967) "Bar Politics, Judicial Selection, and the Representation of Social Interests," *American Political Science Review,* Vol. 61, No. 1 (March): 54-71.

WEINER, M. (1962) *The Politics of Scarcity: Public Pressure and Political Process in India.* Chicago: Univ. of Chicago Press.

WEISSBERG, R. (1975) "Political Efficacy and Political Illusion," *Journal of Politics*, Vol. 37, No. 3 (August): 469-487.
WELTMAN, J. J. (1972) "The Processes of Systemicist," *Journal of Politics*, Vol. 34, No. 3 (August): 592-611.
WILDAVSKY, A. (1962) *Dixon-Yates: A Study in Power Politics*. New Haven: Yale Univ. Press.
——— (1964) *Leadership in a Small Town*. Totowa, N.J.: Bedminster.
WILLIAMS, O. P. and C. R. ADRIAN (1963) *Four Cities: A Study in Comparative Policy-Making*. Philadelphia: Univ. of Pennsylvania Press.
WILSON, J. Q. (1973) *Political Organizations*. New York: Basic Books.
WILSON, W. (1911) "The Law and the Facts," *American Political Science Review*, Vol. 5, No. 1 (February): 1-11.
WIRT, F. and M. W. KIRST (1972) *The Political Web of American Schools*. Boston: Little, Brown.
WOLFINGER, R. E. (1971) "Nondecisions and the Study of Local Politics," *American Political Science Review*, Vol. 65, No. 4 (December): 1063-1079.
WOLIN, S. (1969) "Political Theory as a Vocation," *American Political Science Review*, Vol. 63, No. 4 (December): 1062-1082.
WOLMAN, H. L. and N. C. THOMAS (1970) "Black Interests, Black Groups and Black Influence in the Federal Policy Process: The Cases of Housing and Education," *Journal of Politics*, Vol. 32, No. 4 (November): 875-899.
WOOTTON, G. (1969) *Interest-Groups*. Englewood Cliffs, N.J.: Prentice-Hall.
WORMUTH, F. D. (1967) "Matched-Dependent Behavioralism: The Cargo Cult in Political Science," *Western Political Quarterly*, Vol. 20, No. 4 (December): 809-840.
ZEIGLER, H. (1961) *The Politics of Small Business*. Washington: Public Affairs Press.
——— (1964) *Interest Groups in American Society*. Englewood Cliffs, N.J.: Prentice-Hall.
——— (1969a) "The Effects of Lobbying: A Comparative Assessment," *Western Political Quarterly*, Vol. 22, No. 1 (March): 122-141.
——— and M. BEER (1969b) *Lobbying: Interaction and Influence in American State Legislatures*. Belmont, Cal.: Wadsworth.

Chapter 6

**Beyond Group Theories of Politics:
Notes on Political Economy**

With the disintegration of the group approach to political science in the 1970s came a proliferation of would-be alternative paradigms for analysis: public choice theory, phenomenology, and critical social theory being the most prominent new entries to a field including such aging frameworks as systems analysis, communications theory, and functionalism. None of these alternatives have been able to garner the wide support in the discipline that characterized group theory at its height of influence. The older contenders just mentioned are even more in eclipse than group theory itself, while public choice theory is too conservative and economistically simplistic, and phenomenology too philosophically abstruse to appeal to a discipline dominated by pragmatic liberalism. Critical social theory, if only by default, has emerged as the liveliest arena of contention. It has absorbed the greatest energies of American political science's "left" (e.g., the Caucus for a New Political Science, and the journal *Politics and Society*).

Adapted with permission from G. David Garson, Power and Politics in the United States *(Lexington, Mass.: Heath, 1977): Ch. 12.*

Like group theory, critical social theory is not a theory but rather an orientation toward theory. It subsumes three broad perspectives: (1) liberal critics of pluralism (e.g., Edelman, Bachrach, Lowi, Kariel); (2) Marxists and neo-Marxists of the "Frankfurt" and "praxis theory" schools (e.g., O'Connor, Greenberg, Domhoff, and Birnbaum); and (3) various independent radicals (e.g., Miliband, Giddens, Harrington, Dahrendorf). As with many schools of thought, proximity of concept is often inversely related to the social distance such authors may perceive between them. Nonetheless, in this essay I would like to put forward "political economy" as the core concept of critical social theory. It serves, I believe, to unite seemingly disparate analyses of American politics and constitutes the base of the "new political science" that emerged in the last decade. Though more complex and sophisticated theories of various stripes (e.g., Marxist) have developed in the broad domain labelled "political economy," the remainder of this essay is confined simply to drawing out its basic elements as points of contrast with group theories of politics.

At one time there was no such thing as political science, let alone a group approach to it. When John Burgess founded the first School of Political Science in 1880, he drew on scholars in history, government, law, and other disciplines. Some of these scholars had been educated in political economy, an eighteenth century craft concerned with explaining how government might increase the wealth of the nation. Later, this meaning was expanded to include the study of the relationship of economic forces to political and social forces in general. Political *science*, in contrast, directed attention to the study of law and, later, all aspects of power. As political science became an established part of academic structure, political economy faded away as a distinct approach to poltiics.

Like other viewpoints, political economy is not homogeneous. There are political economists of the right and of the left, advocates of public choice theories and other marketplace economics views, and advocates of critical social theory. To observe what political economists share in common, it is necessary to speak of basic "starting points" of political analysis. The distillation this involves is an injustice to the complexity of each author to be discussed and obscures the profound differences separating them. Yet the synthesis in indicative of the general direction of what is perhaps the largest (albeit, still minority) group of critical scholars seeking to transcend pluralist and other group theories of politics, which dominated American political science until recent years.

Political economy is a rather unpretentious approach to political science. It is neither a general theory of social action nor even a new or complex method of analysis. Often heavily historical, the insights political economy generates are often commonplace truths. No one set of political beliefs, conservative or radical, need result from a political-economic approach. But it *is* a distinct approach *not* compatible with either pluralism or, for that matter, the usual version of elite stratification theory. At its best, it harbors the potential to engender a lively debate that can fruitfully direct attention toward a different way of looking at American politics.

Works That Helped Shape Political Economy as an Approach to Analyzing Politics

John Stuart Mill's *Principles of Political Economy* appeared in 1848, the same year as Marx and Engels' *Communist Manifesto*. Though reflecting very different world views, some similarities remained in the way Mill and Marx looked at political life.

THE FUNCTION OF GOVERNMENT

Mill believed government's foremost functional tendency was its role as the protector of person and property. In particular, Mill noted that governments everywhere serve to protect the "productive classes" from the masses. Marx agreed with this, but said Mill was wrong in assuming all governments were the same. Rather, Marx held, governments differ according to the stage of production in society (feudal, capitalist, and so forth). In each stage, production creates its own legal relations, its own form of government, and its own culture.

Capitalism, for example, generates capitalist laws, capitalist government agencies, and capitalist literature and culture. Similarly, Marx predicted that socialist production would generate socialist laws, institutions and culture. That is, government functions to enhance the prevailing productive system. It does this by fostering a self-reinforcing system of laws, institutions, and culture.

These ideas are not new. The Federalists held similar beliefs. Madison's arguments against "faction" in *Federalist No. 10,* for example, alluded to the need to protect propertied interests from debtor factions that gained power in seven states prior to ratification of the Constitution. Nor is Marx's idea (of stages of government being correlated with stages of production) unique. In Robert Dahl's classic pluralist study, *Who Governs?,* New Haven politics, for instance, were traced from rule by the "patricians" (1784-1842, preindustrial), to rule by "entrepreneurs" (1842-1899, rise of industrialism), to rule by "ex-plebes" (since 1900, reflecting increased worker/ethnic power in later industrialism). The general concepts of the prime productive function of government and the relation of productive stages to government are only a starting point, which can lead to either pluralist or elite theory conclusions.

The ideas about the central economic functions of government are common to other political economists. One of the most influential was Charles A. Beard, the only individual ever to hold the presidency of both the American Political Science Association and the American Historical Association. His works, including *The Economic Basis of Politics* (1922), served as a guide for an entire generation of social scientists.

Beard cited Madison in support of the idea that government's prime function is the protection of the unequal faculties of individuals for acquiring property. Beard also believed that drastic changes in the economy would find reflection in changes in politics. This, too, was similar to Marx. But it can be interpreted more broadly. It is not just changes in the basic mode of production (such as feudalism changing to early industrialism) that are reflected in politics; it is any drastic change (such as the Depression, marking the shift from Hoover Republicanism to the political-economic program of the New Deal).

Mill, Marx and Beard were liberal or radical political economists. But even among more moderate contemporary social scientists employing a political-economic approach, similar themes usually emerge. For example, Talcott Parsons and Neil Smelser, writing in *Economy and Society* (1956), emphasize the role of government as the provider of capital. Government's role in increasing productivity through tax exemptions, subsidies, tariffs, and various forms of control over labor is seen as critical. At times, businesses with a particular vested interest may resist this encouragement to productivity, as in antitrust cases, but this reflects not "antibusiness" government action, but rather the opposite: the promotion of long term economic productivity.

Parsons and Smelser also emphasized the intricate interrelationship between government's economic role and political culture. They discussed how governments evoke cultural symbols as a crucial step in mobilizing support for the state. Edelman's *Politics as Symbolic Action* (1971) later made a similar argument in more pointed terms. Symbolic action was exemplified, for instance, in the Johnson and Nixon programs for "black capitalism." These sought to reassure black people that they were being included in economic growth. Great publicity was given to blacks acquiring the symbols of capitalist success (e.g., ownership of small firms), even though the "black capitalism" program held no serious prospect of significantly altering the structure of the American economy. More generally, the state fosters a self-reinforcing cultural system. Culture-perpetuating institutions are, in fact, the most important elements in social control.

Though this discussion emphasizes similarity rather than the substantial differences, it is still true that those who use a political-economic approach have more in common than is generally believed. These common themes may be developed in opposing ways, but they constitute, nonetheless, a useful starting point for most political economists. Of these starting points, three are listed here; others appear later in this essay:

(1) The normal function of government is to give primacy to the protection of property and the encouragement of economic productivity. Though other purposes may be given priority, in the long run it is these functions that override the others.

(2) Every system of production is self-reinforcing. Socialism elicits socialist culture, education, laws, organizations, and governmental forms, just as capitalism calls forth capitalist culture, education, laws, organizations, and forms of government that protect and nuture capitalist production.

(3) To maintain system stability, the state channels resources into activities that assert commitment to common cultural values. Symbolic action to maintain the legitimacy of the state is often manifested in "reform" legislation that reassures citizens without substantively altering basic government functions.

The Function of Expansion

John Stuart Mill, in *Principles of Political Economy,* emphasized the political importance of the increasing wealth of nations. It was increasing wealth that cemented the loyalty of the liberal citizen to the state. The politics of creating wealth is based on the ideology of success, not the more radical ideology of redistribution. Increased individual opportunity to succeed justifies giant business subsidies ranging from the "internal improvements" of the nineteenth century to the tax write offs of the 1970s. It justifies, Mill contended, the state's avoiding a redistributionist tax policy. "Overburdening" of "skill, industry and frugality" by taxing the wealthy would only inhibit economic expansion, dampen opportunity for success, and undermine the liberal state.

Marx was much more pessimistic, and wrongly so, about the possibilities for continued capitalist expansion. But he recognized the truth of Mill's point, for example, in his discussion of the English working class. The English subject, Marx noted, is not revolutionary because industrial expansion had brought cooption. Later, Marx and Engels castigated union interest in increased wages as merely "better pay for slaves," but the political effectiveness of economic expansion was evident in their own time.

Charles Beard, in *The Economic Basis of Politics* (1922), also discussed the importance of economic growth. The dominance of economic elites depended, he said, on their providing prosperity. The effectiveness of cultural, economic, and police controls over the citizenry cannot be long sustained in the absence of prosperity. Without it, the state must yield.

Parsons and Smelser, in *Economy and Society* (1956), put forward the following description of how lack of expansion is the critical component of institutional change. Change, they wrote, is cyclical:

(1) Dissatisfaction arises over the productive achievements of the economy.

(2) "Unjustified" negative emotional reactions and "unrealistic" aspirations are manifested by various groups.

(3) Cultural pressures channel discontent into patterns not inconsistent with widely shared values.

(4) Respected leaders advocate reforms, defining the alternatives.

(5) Attempts are made in and out of government to implement some of the proposed reforms.

(6) Innovations are accepted according to their impact on productivity and profit.

(7) Accepted innovations are institutionalized.

This cycle could be illustrated by the rise of the nineteenth century "robber barons." Reforms were advocated ranging from socialism to technocracy, but extreme movements were repressed by the state or were unable to surmount cultural barriers defining their goals as "un-American." Innovations were undertaken as corporate managers displaced the older generation of capitalist pioneers. Family control diminished. These changes led to higher profits (e.g., in Standard Oil), allowing further legitimization of the new forms of economic control.

Expansion is still a critical concept in contemporary Marxist explanations of American politics as well. Paul Baran and Paul Sweezy, for example, emphasize expansion in their book, *Monopoly Capital* (1966). They argue that American political stability does not rest on the competition of business, labor, and other interest groups. Rather, stability rests on the common interest of big business and labor in increased government expenditure. Far from constituting a tendency toward "socialism," government's rising share of the national product supports projects socially necessary to the continued well-being of the capitalist system. Corporate growth has facilitated government expansion. Economic growth necessitates government expenditures rising at an ever faster rate. The result is an economic crisis in government finance as the state tries to satisfy economic needs (for example, welfare costs of maintaining an increasingly large number of unemployed and other casualties of the economic system) without "overburdening" entrepreneurs with taxation. The solution to this crisis is elusive. Seeking it, recent governments have more and more emphasized the need of the state to intervene directly to promote economic expansion. The Republican Party has shed much of its reluctance to use Keynesian and even direct economic controls and public works when necessary, and the Democrats have come to emphasize expansion rather than redistribution. This modern convergence is a corollary of the crisis of government finance and, beyond that, reflects a response to the threat of political instability, that the end of the era of expansion would bring. We may now add a fourth item to the starting points in political economy:

(4) In addition to socialization to dominant values congenial to the economic system, and in addition to the symbolic activities of government, stability has been maintained by the joint interest of capital and labor in the progressive expansion of the economy and, with it, of the government sector.

CLASS AND INTEREST CONFLICT

The class and interest group basis of politics is laid by the primacy of the economic function of the state. Nonetheless, the liberal state is quite different from a class dictatorship. John Stuart Mill noted long ago the disastrous effect on public opinion of class legislation giving different rights to the rich than to the poor. An example is America's first military draft. This class legislation allowed the wealthy to buy their way out of military service, whereas the poor were conscripted involuntarily to serve as the fodder of the Civil War. The result was widespread hatred of the draft and of Lincoln, even in the North. It led to the worst rioting this country has ever experienced, necessitating the diversion of major military forces from battlefront positions. Similarly, differential legislation for blacks and whites underlay much of the social turmoil of the 1960s.

Mill knew that changes in class legislation would not alter the fundamental political-economic nature of the state. Abolition of overt class legislation might not even effect the distribution of benefits in society. Rather, abolition of such laws served a symbolic, moral function. Abolition fostered belief in the justice and legitimacy of the state.

Marx differed from Mill, who went too far in generalizing about the common belief of an entire nation in the legitimacy of the state. Marx believed it was too simple, for example, to talk about "the English people" as a whole. Most are aware that Marx preferred to discuss specific social classes rather than "peoples" at large. But it is often thought Marx simplified society into a dichotomy: owners versus workers. Actually, Marxist class analysis understands *these* categories as abstractions. That is, the broad categories based on the relation to the means of production (e.g., wage labor and capital) must be analyzed in terms of social patterns of exchange, division of labor, the setting of prices, and so on. Thus, the setting of prices determines what capital means concretely. What capital means helps determine the nature of social classes. Class formation in turn determines what is meant by "the English (or American) people." There is a great deal of room for different interpretations of the *concrete* class structure even if the *abstract* class structure of all capitalist societies can be reduced to capitalists versus workers.

Marx recognized that the division of labor gives rise to many roles, not just "owner" and "worker." But these roles are stratified into classes. Economic interdependence ties the classes together (for example, the Republican Party may campaign on the theme that aiding business aids workers), but this sort of "unity" masks underlying antagonisms.

Roles generate attitudinal role-sets (e.g., the development of military occupations fosters militaristic viewpoints, and the development of social work professionalism encourages belief in liberal reform; see Monsen and Cannon, 1965). Marx noted that the division of labor, which brought about great economic interdependence, also created classes of occupations holding differing perspectives. The integrative role of government is continually oriented toward obscuring such differences, but governmental reforms simply restructure (and often exacerbate) the underlying opposition of views. For example, urban renewal reform at first brought about a broad alliance of supportive interests (labor, social workers, and businesses), but as the reform proved to be symbolic rather than substantive in effect, this temporary unity fell apart, leaving more bitterness and disillusion than before.

Similarly, Charles Beard understood that the diversity of economic interests is the most common and enduring source of political conflict. While ethnicity, religion, and other social forces also generate conflict, they are of lesser importance in the long run. It is not an accident that the majority of Washington lobbies are of an economic character. Representative democracy, Beard wrote, does not eliminate economic interests. Like other governments, it enhances the interests who benefit from the prevailing political economic institutions. Government inculcates patriotism and civic participation, but the conflict of different classes of interests is not prevented.

But Beard differed from Marx in one important respect: he did not agree that ideas arose automatically and directly from economic conditions. Politics, the military, and intellectual life all retained an importance independent of economic production. To put this another way, the role-sets associated with occupational classes not in direct production (e.g., intellectuals, the clergy, the military, and social workers) also function as important elements in political conflict. These groupings are not simply "agents" of a business elite, as vulgar Marxism implies. Beard, like Parsons and Smelser, emphasized the independent role of the nonproductive classes.

More broadly, the class that benefits the most from a given political economy (the "elite") does not "dominate" society. While it may seek control in its interest, it is rarely a cohesive group in command of its history. If that were so, history would evolve far more slowly. Rather, unanticipated consequences of self-interested political actions are more the rule than the exception.

It is this point that is emphasized by contemporary Marxists like Baran and Sweezy. In *Monopoly Capital* (1966), these authors discuss how, as capitalism in American became more concentrated, as the division of labor became more specialized, and as tasks became organized and routinized, traditional values were distorted and discarded. The end result was a weakened social fabric characterized by alienating jobs, competitive values, and money-centered status norms.

Particularly in the area of work, irrationality abounds. For every responsible job created by new technology, many others are stripped of responsibility and creativity. For every job as a program analyst created by computerization, for instance, dozens of alienating keypunching and machine-tending jobs are created. Moreover, even responsible jobs are often stripped of their full human value by their end purposes. Over half of all research and development money, for example, is today military-related. Frivolous consumption items constitute another example.

The declining meaningfulness of jobs is part of the larger process of overeducation of the work force. Stabilized by the ideology of upward mobility and opportunity, the state finds it necessary to encourage faith in the efficacy of education and other government programs. But in fact, the greatest portion of upward mobility results from changing job structure, not education or manpower programming. Since World War II, American education has reached a point of crisis. Millions find themselves overeducated and unable to find responsible jobs suited to their specialized role training. They are de-classed.

Accompanying the crisis in occupational roles is the erosion of social values. Declining religion, weakening of traditional morality, and even the downgrading of patriotism result from the increase of critical rationality. At the same time, the economic system increasingly fails to meet culturally induced expectations. Socialization to dominant beliefs no longer suffices for social control. Other, more external forms of control therefore increase in importance: economic rewards and penalties, and the police and the courts. Playing a role to which they are inadequate, these institutions quickly become overburdened. Social malaise affects the country. The integration of social relations fails to keep pace with the integration of economic relations. The preceding discussion leads to the formulation of starting points in political economy 5, 6, and 7.

(5) The division of labor creates not only cooperation, but also diverging social role-sets. These roles and their associated interests cluster in classes, which are broader than can be understood by analyzing politics in terms of individual leadership personalities, or even in terms of the politics of organized interest groups.

(6) The prime functions of government affect different classes of interests differently. Opposing class interests are mobilized when socialization to unifying ideology breaks down.

(7) Stability decays when socialization is eroded. There is a limit to the efficacy of symbolic action in sustaining the legitimacy of state political economy when system performance falters.

Such breakdowns are often associated with wars and depressions, but in contemporary America the main factors undermining system performance are (1) the fiscal crisis of the state, based on social costs of capitalist production rising faster than can be financed without politically destabilizing levels of burden; and (2) the erosion of traditional social controls due to the contradiction of technology with the quality of work, and due to the diffuse effects of critical rationality on religion, the community, the schools, and the family.

INCREMENTALISM VERSUS PLANNING

Critics of group theories of politics often hold two seemingly contradictory opinions. On the one hand, they change American politics with being highly concentrated and elitist. On the other hand, they often charge that the American system so fragments power that comprehensive change is impossible. Baran and Sweezy, in addressing these views, noted that within the largest American enterprises planning is highly developed. Nonetheless, the contemporary, highly concentrated system is as unplanned overall as the more competitive economy of the past. The system is unplanned in the sense that neither business nor government exerts any systematic effort that would correct the abuses of noncompetitive production, or would reverse the inegalitarian distribution of benefits that results from capitalism.

Concentration of the economy and of power to maintain it in its present form is consistent with incrementalism and fragmentation. As others have observed, the fragmented federal system embodied in the Constitution was intended as a check upon democracy. It can be and was an instrument of an emergent elite. Incrementalism is not the opposite of elitism. Rather, incrementalism is a style of governing that favors preservation of the status quo, whether elitist or pluralist.

The failure to understand that concentration is consistent with absence of social planning, that elitism and pluralism are not opposites in this sense, has its origins early in the history of social science. Charles Beard noted that in the mid-nineteenth

century social philosophers became increasingly concerned
with the justification of the expanding economic system. "Political economy" was dropped in favor of the narrower focus
on "economics." That is, the economy came to be analyzed
separately from politics. "Of course it was absurd," Beard
wrote, "for men to write of the production and distribution
of wealth apart from the state which defines, upholds, taxes,
and regulates property, the very basis of economic operations;
but absurdity does not restrain the hand of the apologist" (Beard,
1922: 26). That is, the decline of political economy was a reflection of the sort of rosy justification of the American capitalist
system that critics often charge group theorists with espousing.
(See starting point in political economy no. 8.):

(8) Our political economic system is both "elitist" with respect to ends
   and "pluralist" with respect to means. Elitism and pluralism may be
   complementary rather than contradictory. Different degrees and
   kinds of property and differing relations to property form the primary
   basis for the formation of opposing interests. The principal task
   of government is the regulation of these various interests in a way
   compatible with the preservation and growth of the economic system.
   The ends of this process disproportionately favor an elite, but the
   means utilized by a liberal state need not be conspiratorial or even
   require central coordination.

PARAMETERS OF PLURALISM

Anthony Downs' *An Economic Theory of Democracy*
(1957) discussed the pluralist means characterizing American
politics. Using a free market competition model of politics,
Downs argued that voters vote on the basis of their perceived
utility or interest. To maximize votes, political parties shift
to the right or left as circumstances dictate. Thus, the Republican
Party shifted leftward during the New Deal, accepting, for
instance, the Social Security Act. Similarly, the Democratic
Party shifted to the right after its 1972 defeat under the leadership of a very liberal candidate. Downs' model predicted such
equilibrating shifts toward the center.

Downs' analysis also was contrary to the Marxist idea that the political framework of a nation (its system of courts, legislatures, and executive agencies) is "superstructure" of no fundamental importance. Downs argued that structure can matter a great deal: a system of single-party, majority-election districts, for example, makes voters feel that supporting a third party candidate is "throwing away one's vote." Such a system thwarts insurgent movements and favors the status quo.

Downs' model also emphasized the logic of voting and political participation. Because obtaining political information comes at a cost in time, effort, and expense, voters must weigh these costs against the supposed benefits of voting. Because expected payoffs is low, most voters are unwilling to incur more than minimal costs in time, effort, or money. More importantly, because the costs of involvement are proportionately greater for low-income, low-status groups, they are disproportionately less involved and influential in politics for this reason alone. In this way political structure reinforces the class nature of government.

Downs' analysis is limited in many respects. It neglects, for example, such nonrational considerations as the effect on politics of manipulative socialization, symbolic action, and what Bachrach called "nondecisions," to name a few. Downs likewise ignores Beard's injunction to integrate analysis of politics and economics, or to provide an explanation for the stratification of benefits in liberal democracies. But this analysis does suggest how pluralist means may coexist within a political-economic system that contains strong elitist traits. (See starting point in political economy no. 9.):

(9) Within the stability created by economic performance and socialization to dominant cultural values, opportunistic political parties may compete within a framework of representative democracy that is not inconsistent with either elitism or pluralism. The American political system perpetuates a two-party system discouraging insurgency.

Conclusions

If these nine starting points for political-economic analysis seem elementary, they are. If they seem plausible, they are not without controversy, for the perspective they contain is quite different from either the view of the group theorists and pluralists on the one hand, or of the stratification researchers and elite theorists on the other.

Elite theorists contrast elitism and pluralism, whereas the political-economic perspective outlined above emphasizes the systematic complementarity of the two. Elite theory emphasizes the self-conscious, if not overtly coordinated, elite effort to "dominate" politics and "manipulate" socialization. A political-economic perspective emphasizes instead the interdependence of political culture and economic systems. Elite theory focuses on an enduring elite that renders party conflict meaningless. Political economy emphasizes instead the conflicting political-economic programs of the competing parties (see Garson, 1977: Chs. 10 and 11). Elite theorists seek to show America to be elitist in both ends and means. Political economists emphasize the compatibility of pluralist means with elitist ends.

Pluralist theorists view business as one competing group among many. Political economists view business as the pre-eminent social group, reflecting the prime economic function of the state. Pluralist theorists focus on the competition of parties, the multiplicity of lobbies, the diversity of politics, and the fragmentation of government as proofs of the pluralism of American politics. But political economists view these phenomena as secondary to a broader system that perpetuates elite interests. Pluralist theorists emphasize popular elections and the correspondence of government action to public opinion to illustrate the democratic nature of American government. Political economists, on the other hand, prefer to emphasize the historic evolution of given opinions and their relation to the nature of the nation's political economy. Public opinion is not viewed as an autonomous and rational legitimator of state action.

American politics are neither the marketplace of group theory nor the conspiracy of simple elite theories. If America is elitist, it is elitist in a pluralistic way, or, if pluralist, then pluralist in a way that benefits an elite. Political scientists would benefit from shedding these terms entirely in favor of a concept of political economy as a system of power that integrates production, culture, and power. This concept has been latent in the writings of the more sophisticated authors in both camps for some time now. Perhaps some convergence can be derived from rendering this viewpoint explicit. It is misleading to speak of elite domination when governing policies are consensual in the main. Equally, pluralist theorists obscure the manner in which government policies systematically favor a business-based elite. America is neither a participatory democracy, nor is it dominated by a political-economic elite. It is, nonetheless, an elitist political economy. By emphasizing this point, political economy can be the basis of critical social theory that transcends the now-sterile debate between group theorists and their critics.

REFERENCES

BACHRACH, P. (1967) *The Theory of Democratic Elitism: A Critique.* Boston: Little, Brown.

BARAN, P. A. and P. M. SWEEZY (1966) *Monopoly Capital.* New York: Monthly Review Press.

BEARD, C. A. (1957) *The Economic Basis of Politics.* New York: Vintage.

BIRNBAUM, N. (1971) *Toward a Critical Sociology.* New York: Oxford Univ. Press.

DAHRENDORF, R. (1967) *Society and Democracy in Germany.* Garden City, N.Y.: Doubleday.

DOMHOFF, G. W. (1970) *The Higher Circles.* New York: Random House.

DOWNS, A. (1957) *An Economic Theory of Democracy.* New York: Harper and Row.

EDELMAN, M. (1967) *The Symbolic Uses of Politics.* Chicago: Univ. of Chicago Press.

GARSON, G. D. (1977) *Power and Politics in the United States: A Political Economic Approach.* Lexington, Mass.: D. C. Heath.

GIDDENS, A. (1973) *The Class Structure of the Advanced Societies.* New York: Harper and Row.

GREENBERG, E. S. (1974) *Serving the Few.* New York: John Wiley.

HARRINGTON, M. (1976) *The Twilight of Capitalism.* New York: Simon and Schuster.

KARIEL, H. S. (1961) *The Decline of American Pluralism.* Stanford: Stanford Univ. Press.

LOWI, T. (1969) *The End of Liberalism*. New York: W. W. Norton.
MADISON, J. (1966) "Federalist No. 10: The Source and Control of Factions," in R. Fairfield, ed., *The Federalist Papers*. Garden City, N.Y.: Doubleday.
MARX, K. and F. ENGELS (1954) "Communist Manifesto," in L. Fever, ed., *Marx and Engels: Basic Writings*. Garden City, N.Y.: Doubleday.
MILIBAND, R. (1969) *The State in Capitalist Society*. New York: Basic Books.
MILL, J. S. (1900) *Principles of Political Economy*. New York: Collier.
MONSEN, R. and M. W. CANNON (1965) *The Makers of Public Policy*. New York: McGraw-Hill.
O'CONNOR, J. (1973) *The Fiscal Crisis of the State*. New York: St. Martin's.
PARSONS, T. and N. SMELSER (1956) *Economy and Society*. New York: Free Press.

INDEX

ABOUT THE AUTHOR

G. DAVID GARSON is Professor of political science and department head at North Carolina State University. Dr. Garson has written extensively on interest groups, power structure research, political science methodology, and issues in democratic administration. Among his publications are *Power and Politics in the United States: A Political Economy Approach* (Lexington, Mass.: Heath, 1977); *Worker Self-Management in Industry: The West European Experience* (New York: Praeger, 1977; ed.); and *Political Science Methods* (Boston: Allyn and Bacon/Holbrook, 1976).